SOCIALIST MAYORS IN
THE UNITED STATES

STUDIES IN GOVERNMENT
AND PUBLIC POLICY

SOCIALIST MAYORS IN THE UNITED STATES

Governing in an Era of Municipal Reform, 1900–1920

David R. Berman

 University Press of Kansas

© 2022 by the University Press of Kansas
All rights reserved

Published by the University Press of Kansas (Lawrence, Kansas 66045), which was organized by the Kansas Board of Regents and is operated and funded by Emporia State University, Fort Hays State University, Kansas State University, Pittsburg State University, the University of Kansas, and Wichita State University

Library of Congress Cataloging-in-Publication Data

Names: Berman, David R., author.
Title: Socialist mayors in the United States : governing in an era of municipal reform, 1900–1920 / David R. Berman.
Description: Lawrence : University Press of Kansas, 2022. | Series: Studies in government and public policy | Includes bibliographical references and index.
Identifiers: LCCN 2021050542
 ISBN 9780700633371 (paperback)
 ISBN 9780700633388 (ebook)
Subjects: LCSH: Mayors—United States—History—20th century. | Municipal government—United States—History—20th century. | Socialism—United States—History—20th century. | Progressivism (United States politics)
Classification: LCC JS356 .B47 2022 | DDC 352.23/2160973—dc23/eng/20220118
LC record available at https://lccn.loc.gov/2021050542.

British Library Cataloguing-in-Publication Data is available.

Printed in the United States of America

10 9 8 7 6 5 4 3 2 1

The paper used in this publication is acid free and meets the minimum requirements of the American National Standard for Permanence of Paper for Printed Library Materials Z39.48-1992.

CONTENTS

Preface   vii

Introduction: Going from Outsider to Insider   1

1. The Party Framework   14
2. Municipal Reform: Where the Socialists Fitted In   29
3. The Socialist Municipal Program   43
4. Socialist Mayors: The Rising and Falling Tide   56
5. Getting There, Staying There   71
6. Coming in, Progress, and Problems   86
7. Being Mayor: Limitations, Opportunities, and Roles   101
8. Managing, Budgeting, Cleaning Up the Town   114
9. The Working Class, Labor, and Business   127

Conclusion   140

Appendix 1: Biographies of Featured Mayors   149

Appendix 2: Municipalities with Social Administrations, 1898–1920   154

Notes   165

Bibliography   205

Index   219

PREFACE

In the late 1890s Socialists in the United States urged that the Socialist Party move from the status of a doctrinal party functioning largely outside the political system to one actively involved inside that system by putting people in office. The focus of this book is on what happened when the Socialists followed up by turning to political action on the municipal level from the late 1890s to 1920 in the United States, a period that encompasses the Progressive Era from its beginning to its end.

I begin with how that involvement was conditioned by the nature of the party itself, how Socialists fitted in with an ongoing municipal reform movement as leaders in the cause of Municipal Socialism, and the essentials of the Socialist municipal program. This is followed by an analysis of when, where, and how Socialist candidates for mayor were elected, how they approached their job, and what they accomplished.

Much of the discussion focuses on the election and administrations of Socialist mayors in medium-sized and small towns—often very small towns—where Socialists enjoyed most of their successes, though relatively little attention has been given to Socialist activity in these places. If Socialist administrations did not do much or fell short of expectations it was not because they did not try but, in larger part, because of the condition of places where they won.

Like other mayors of the time, Socialist mayors were limited by lack of authority, financial resources, staff, and time. They had the additional handicap of being associated with a minority party, a status that reduced their ability to secure the support of city councils or state lawmakers. Being a Socialist also meant being associated with a party that the business community and powerful interests associated with it, perceived as a definite threat. Further difficulties stemmed from the conflict within the party between the right and left wings, and the constant interference of party members who insisted on exercising control over the mayor's actions.

I argue, contrary to the views of historians and contemporary observers, especially in the left wing of the party, that the move to political action did not generally produce Socialist parties that were like other political parties. The party continued to be far different from the major political parties in terms of membership control and ideology. I also have difficulty with the view that Socialist mayors were "Socialist politicians" without any fixed principles or beliefs or, alternatively, indistinguishable from Progressive mayors who were Republicans, Democrats, or independents. Socialist mayors were different. Compared to the ordinary mayor, they were more ideologically inclined, more innovative, more disruptive of the status quo, and more likely to take on the powers that be.

All in all, I see the Socialist mayors playing a distinctive role in pursuit of working-class objectives and the cause of municipal reform around the country and, while faced with a number of serious obstacles, holding their own in demonstrating their ability to govern. When it comes to accomplishments, one can reasonably argue that Socialist mayors equaled or excelled the performance of other mayors, achieving less of what they sought, but seeking much more than most of the others.

This book represents a continuation of a long line of published research I have done on political history in the Populist-Progressive Era in the United States, covering the years 1890 to 1920, and my life-long interest in local politics and administration. It delves into a time of considerable importance in the history of the Socialist movement and the municipal reform movement in the United States. It suggests much about the nature of the party system, municipal politics and administration, small-town government, and difficulties in bringing reform.

It also explores disputes over public policies and the role of government extending to such issues as inequality, corporate domination, workers' rights, and police control, of contemporary significance. My intent is that this book will contribute to the understanding of the Progressive Era, the nature of the municipal reform movement, and the problems and impact of third parties in the United States as well as provide a meaningful overall evaluation of Socialist activity on the municipal level during this period.

As with my other books, this study offers a perspective that integrates research by historians, political scientists, and experts in several other disciplines including public administration, urban and local governance, and various areas of public policy. It also draws upon a large number of newspapers and obscure publications of the period, including many published by the state or local Socialist parties or Socialists and labor activists around the country and various archival sources, including the Socialist Party of America collection, containing correspondence and various reports. I paid considerable attention to municipal platforms, the thoughts and behavior of the mayors as candidates and office holders, and the broader environment in which they operated.

In my quest for information on Socialist mayors I occasionally contacted city clerks in small towns. While few were actually able to help out much due to a scarcity of historical records, I appreciate the efforts made by Dani Taylor, of Coal Creek, Colorado; and Paula J. Durish, of Beaver Falls, Pennsylvania. Academics Katherine Benton-Cohen, Phil Vandermeer, John Hall, Marilyn Dantico, and John Sillito encouraged the undertaking of this work and took the time to help me out in one way or another. My wife, Susan, as always, contributed through her proofreading skills. A special word of thanks is extended to the outside reviewers, Greg Hall and Nigel Sellars, for their comments and suggestions.

Introduction: Going from Outsider to Insider

In the spring of 1910 newspapers around the country speculated about what was going to happen in Milwaukee, Wisconsin, as the result of the election of a Socialist mayor in that city. The mayor, Emil Seidel, tried to calm the fears of those who predicted that a dangerous revolution was about to take place. One writer noted: "Some people are a little surprised that Milwaukee's socialist mayor did not appear at his desk with a red flag in his teeth and a bomb under each arm."[1]

This book describes what generally happened when Socialists like Seidel turned to political action on the municipal level in the United States from the late 1890s to 1920. It shows practically minded Socialists with a strong working-class, pro-labor bias breaking away from a doctrine-based party of ideologues and outsiders and becoming involved in a drive to improve the operation, structure, and performance of municipal governments. Many of those Socialists hoped to become insiders as office holders at the municipal level, and, from that status, to facilitate the revolutionary cause as much as possible while, at the same time, bringing meaningful improvements in the quality of life for ordinary people in their communities.

BACKGROUND

During the last decade of the nineteenth century, there was growing sentiment within the Socialist movement in Europe and United States that Marxist theory had to be revised. To many Socialists it appeared that the pressures generated by industrialization were not bringing a revolution of the workers. The Socialist onlookers still felt that laissez-faire capitalism had serious ill effects and was doomed; but they recognized that in modern industrial societies, conditions for the workers had improved, class conflict was declining, and the political process seemed to be open to meaningful reform. Seeing these changes, Edward Bernstein, a leader of the German Socialist Party, and the Fabian Socialists in England called on Socialists to abandon class politics and revolutionary rhetoric and, instead, use the political process to bring necessary changes one step at a time by turning their attention to immediate practical problems in employment, education taxation, and a variety of other areas. They still felt Socialism—meaning the collective ownership of the means of production and distribution and the establishment of a cooperative commonwealth—would follow capitalism, but only gradually through the political process and without violence.[2]

In the late 1890s Victor Berger of Milwaukee, Wisconsin, emerged as a leader of the revisionist movement in the United States. Writing to Socialist Party leader Eugene Debs, another prominent Socialist spokesperson, William English Walling, described Berger as "a frank and outright opponent of everything revolutionary." He felt that Berger and others were conspiring to form a conservative labor party.[3] Indeed, Berger saw the Socialist Party's future closely linked to the growing labor movement and revisionist steps in Marxist theory as vital in establishing the linkage: "Milwaukee trade-unionists were practical people, and if Berger was to win them over, he had to lay much more stress on immediate things than on the revolution."[4] When it came to messaging, some Socialists had discovered that the American worker "did not recognize himself as a wage slave, nor did he pay much attention to orators who so described him."[5]

Berger and other more practically minded Socialists questioned the messaging value of the Marxian class struggle theme and the associated notion that the proletariat had a monopoly on virtue. The politically minded Socialists sought to reach out to the middle class as well as the lower working-class and to farmers and industrial workers, and, indeed, to whomever they could get to vote for them. As the revisionists saw it, the party had the choice of either becoming politically active in a practical sense or accepting the status of a limited doctrinal party of outsiders basing its appeal on principals and moral argumentation, being kept alive by a small cadre of true believers but having little, if any, effect in the political life of the country other than possibly in the realm of ideas.[6]

THE CONTROVERSY

During the first two decades of the twentieth century, members of the Socialist Party of America (SPA) were badly divided over the idea of engaging in political activity, especially on the municipal or local level. Socialists in the party's left wing, the orthodox Marxists or revolutionary Socialists, shunned political activity in favor of direct action on the industrial level.

Contrary to the views of those on the right, leftists contended the country's workers were suffering and were close to erupting in a revolutionary action. The goal, as they saw it, was to help usher in that rebellion as soon as possible rather than work for improvements in working conditions or do anything else what would temporarily get in the way of the natural and inevitable course of history. As a leftist Socialist leader in Utah put it in 1902: "Deductions from historic facts and observation of the trend of events tell us unmistakably that a great social change is at hand. It is inevitable, it is close. We do not need to truckle for votes. They will fall in line. What we do need is clean, clear, true Socialists, who will not be swerved from the straight path and who will know what to do when the hour strikes."[7]

To those on the left, Socialist political party organizations were useful only as a means of educating the public and furthering agitation toward the revolution. As Vincent St. John, a leader of the left-leaning Industrial Workers of the World (IWW), expressed it:

> The only value that political activity has to the working-class is from the standpoint of agitation and education—its educational merit consists solely in proving to the workers its utter inefficiency to curb the power of the ruling class and therefore forces the workers to rely on the organization of their class in the industries. It is impossible for anyone to be a part of the capitalist state and to use the machinery of the state in the interest of the workers.[8]

Those taking this position were commonly referred to as "impossibilists."

In sum, leftists depicted the proper role of Socialists as being outsiders trying to bring down the system. As outsiders they felt Socialists could maximize their ability to articulate the revolutionary message and raise hell. They criticized the right-wing types for trying to be insiders working in a system they could not control, compromising their principles to win votes, producing virtually meaningless measures or, even worse, ameliorative measures making things better for the worker and taking their minds off the revolution, and, in the end, perpetuating a basically unjust system.

Revisionist Socialists, also known as evolutionary or constructive Socialists, in the right wing of the party ignored these predictions. They dismissed violence and what they viewed as extremist left-wing labor organizations such as the IWW, which they feared would bring down the whole Socialist movement and continued to push for conventional political activity as the only hope for the attainment of Socialism. Championing the right's "let's change directions and get involved in politics" position, the Socialist Party of Colorado in 1910 declared:

> The Socialist Party is a political organization, and the time has come when it must take its place as such among the political parties of the world. It is no longer a mere propaganda club, as it was in the earlier stages of history.... As a political party it must meet the vital questions of the day as they arise. While it must never lose sight of the ultimate goal, the collective ownership of production and distribution, yet it must take a reasonable position on minor questions as they arise.[9]

Right-wingers were generally careful to let it be known that they had not forgotten the ultimate goal of collective ownership, hoping through this to reduce leftist opposition to political action and to bring in as many leftists as possible in support of the practical political cause. Their task was convincing those on the left that what was being done on the practical level was compatible with the revolutionary goal—that the argument of those on the left that one has to be either a revolutionary Socialist with his or her eyes on the future or a practical problem solver was based on a false dichotomy; instead, they could be both. In taking this position, right-wingers saw themselves as "political Socialists" who, while favoring political action, were still principled and committed to a revolutionary program. Critics, though, accused them of being or of encouraging the growth of "Socialist politicians" who did not have any fixed principles at all and who were willing to say or do whatever it took to get elected and were nonbelievers who would only use the party to further their personal pursuit of power.[10]

Controversy between the left and the right also extended to relations with organized labor. As an alternative to organizing labor unions on the basis of a shared craft, many Socialists favored the formation of industrial unions as a means of encouraging worker solidarity by bringing all workers, skilled and unskilled, regardless of their specific craft, together in one union. This, it was felt, would also help out the unskilled by bringing them into a union more powerful than they could establish on their own, and generally increase the bargaining power of workers in an industry. Establishing one industrial union after another was also view by some as the best way of putting together the building blocks for the revolutionary takeover of the means of production. Socialists on the left favored the industrial type and had little good to say about the craft unions (a.k.a. trade unions) and their spokespersons, especially Samuel Gompers of the American Federation of Labor. Many Socialists on the right spoke favorably of industrial unions but were more than willing to work with craft unions as well as industrial ones on political matters. Connecting with unions was to be a central preoccupation for politically active Socialists on the local level.

GOING LOCAL: PREDICTIONS AND OBSERVATIONS

During the early 1900s those who favored political action put considerable emphasis on securing victories on the local level. Berger and others argued that winning on the local level would give the party a chance to demonstrate that it could be trusted to govern, thus paving the way for success on the state and national levels. It also provided an opportunity to further educate the people in the principles of Socialism, generate support for broader and more fundamental changes, give Socialists experience in governing that would be drawn upon when the opportunity to do bigger things came along, and, on a more practical level, build the party by providing employment for party members. One Socialist editor argued that the prime benefit of capturing local office was that the public "will find that Socialists are merely people who are honestly seeking to promote the public good and the false things that have been told of them will cease to have effect."[11]

In response to right-wingers' call for local political activity, leftists supplemented their arguments against political activity in general by arguing that local activity was especially unlikely to accomplishing much of anything, even if by some miracle a Socialist slate of candidates captured a city or town. Making this point, a Montana Socialist editor argued: "If the Socialists elected every city official in Montana from Mayor to dog pelter, these officials could do very little in carrying out the Socialist program, except giving a good administration and municipalizing the water system, and the majority of Montana cities already own their own water system." The editor then declared that in order for Socialists in city councils do very much of value, state laws that deprived them of power would have to be changed. For this reason, if no other, it made greater sense to "concentrate our efforts to electing men to the legislature from a number of counties instead of attempting to capture a few cities."[12]

Beyond the legal and financial limitations on local action, questions were raised not only by Socialists on the left but by non-Socialist observers as to whether Socialists in office would want to, or dare to, do much to seriously promote the Socialist revolutionary cause. Socialist office holders, they argued, were likely to get mired down in trivia, dealing with day-to-day problems all local officials had to face and take their eye off the revolutionary goals. Such goals, moreover, were likely to take second place at best to the goal of doing what had to be done to win and keep winning office. All in all, they argued, power was going to shift from idealists to practical pragmatic people, bringing watered-down platforms and compromise with the party's principals in addressing issues.

Along with this came the prediction that simply winning an election would effectively sober up Socialist candidates, making them more conservative and cautious, fearful of taking chances, because they actually had to face reality, make hard decisions, and accept responsibility for what happened under their watch. These thoughts were expressed by an editor writing about what was likely to happen after the election in 1898 of Socialist John Chase in Haverhill, Massachusetts, the first Socialist elected in the United States:

> The Socialist is very much like other men. Give him the opportunity to speak freely, but to men who are not disposed to regard him as an oracle, and give him responsibility, and it is not long before he begins to weigh his words and to be careful of his actions. It is not at all unlikely that after a while he will develop into an extreme conservative. His elevation to public service will have made him a safer citizen, as it has opened his eyes to the fact that it is one thing to criticize and quite another to administer the affairs of government, and it tends to the discouragement of Socialism in the fact that it shows that when theories are put into practice they are sometimes apt to prove false.[13]

Some commentators predicted that in the end, Socialists in power would wind up losing much of their revolutionary zeal and their parties would be little different than the political parties they condemned.[14] Moreover, whatever meaningful reform, if any at all, that came out of a Socialist administration would likely be undone or used in the interest of the privileged few when the Socialists fell from power, as was bound to happen.

During the first decades of the twentieth century, observers saw the movement toward political action on the local level well on their way toward producing the predicted negative effects. Writing late in 1910, Eugene Debs, coming from the left, expressed concern that "some of the votes placed to our credit this year were obtained by methods not consistent with the principles of a revolutionary party, and in the long run will do more harm than good." As he saw it, "The truth is that we have not a few members who regard vote-getting as of supreme importance, no matter by what method the votes may be secured, and this leads them to hold out inducements and make representations which are not at all compatible with the stern and uncompromising principles of a revolutionary party." Debs contended that by bowing to the "pressure to modify the principles and program of the party for the sake of swelling the vote" the Socialist Party attracted "elements which it cannot assimilate" and risked becoming "corrupted with the spirit of bourgeois reform to an extent that will practically destroy its virility and efficiency as a revolutionary organization."[15]

Some observers noted the same kind of trends but were pleased to see the party and its candidates lose their revolutionary zeal. Non-Socialist municipal reformers of the more conservative "Good Government" school were happy to see this happening on the local level in the case of Socialists mayors, something the observers attributed to the fact that these Socialists had, in effect, grown up by becoming insiders. Writing in 1912, for example, one Good Government observer noted, "In municipal affairs the Socialists have been more directly brought face to face with current problems—and as all of us realize, responsibility tends to more somber judgment and to conservative as well as to constructive thinking."[16] He had less complimentary things to say about the revolutionary Socialist Party types on the outside who were trying to bring down the system. Three years later another observer concluded regarding the sobering effect on Socialists in power:

> Where the Socialist Party has won elections, as in Milwaukee and Schenectady, it has given further evidence of the impossibility of living up to its tenets in the face of practical problems. While it is of course true that little can be done by a Socialist mayor in a single city when the state and national officials belong to hostile parties, it is equally true that a Socialist administration dare not use the little power it has to put its reforms into effect. Responsibility brings sanity and judgment and the principles of an ideal system become greatly modified when put to the practical test.[17]

In 1913 reporter and political writer Walter Lippmann, at the time a Socialist who served for a brief period as the personnel secretary to Socialist mayor George Lunn in Schenectady, New York, offered a less than favorable assessment of what going practical meant. In a letter to a leader of the national party headquartered in Chicago, he argued that winning office had not meant much for true Socialists because Socialist winners owed much of their electoral success to the votes of non-Socialists and to issues and causes that had nothing to do with Socialism or were even incompatible with it. As a result, Socialists in office were tied to a constituency that did not support radical causes. When it came to reform, they were indistinguishable from Progressives on the left who won office, both pursuing moderate changes at best. He called on Socialists to distinguish themselves from the Progressives by moving left, even though this might cost them some elections, and work toward building up the number of genuine Socialists in the electorate to the point where they had a more radical clientele.[18]

The broader argument that the country at the local, state, or national level was not going to get Socialism until a majority of the people understood it and consciously voted for it also carried a warning to the right that Socialism "is not going to sneak in at the back door."[19] On this point those in the Socialist gradualist "one step at a time" right-wing camp begged to differ. They commonly acknowledged that winning a city or town was not going to fulfill many Socialist dreams, but they could take some slow steps in that direction. To the point, Daniel Hoan, later to become Socialist mayor of Milwaukee, in 1913 wrote to a Socialist alderman that if he became mayor of Milwaukee, "I may be able to give them some Socialism" but he'd "have to feed it to them in small doses."[20]

THIS STUDY

This book generally explores the history of political activity of Socialists at the local level as part of a municipal reform movement in the first two decades of the twentieth century in the United States. The central focus is on Socialist administrations: how they came about and what they accomplished.[21] In a broad perspective the book touches upon the history and nature of the Socialist Party of America, the municipal reform movement, small-town politics and government, and the office of mayor during this period. It does not focus on why or how Socialism failed in the United States as a political movement—the topic has been well addressed elsewhere—but does suggest the existence of problems in the movement itself, the governing system, and at the societal level that frustrated Socialist progress on the municipal level.[22]

When it comes to the Socialist Party, attention is given to party membership and activities, the relations between the party organization and the candidates it nominated and helped put into office, the reform message it sent out at the municipal level, and the difficult environment in which it functioned, not only because of its status as a third party but also because of the threat it posed to the status quo. The national party was organized in a fashion comparable to that of a national labor union, with state and local organizations having their own charters whose operations were built around dues-paying members with membership cards who had made various pledges. My focus is primarily on the local chapters. What impresses me is not how much the Socialist Party was like other political parties, but how much it was *unlike* other political parties. In addition, Socialist mayors were not like ordinary mayors.

Socialists who accepted the challenge of political action on the local level joined the battle for municipal reform by taking part in an ongoing crusade for what was commonly known as Municipal Socialism. In this cause, they shared space, not always in an amicable manner, with non-Socialist left-leaning

Progressives who belonged to other parties or no party all. Another wing of the municipal reform movement was a middle- and upper-class business-oriented group, known as the Good Government advocates, or "goo-goos," who had limited objectives of honesty and efficiency.

In the early 1900s municipalities were widely thought of as being corrupt and poorly managed—this is where the Good Government people stepped in—but there was also considerable sentiment not only to free them from corruption and make them more efficient but to make them responsible for more and more functions, and this is where the municipal Socialists stepped in. To the latter group, municipal ownership and operation of various public utility enterprises such as those providing transportation, communication, water, gas, and electric services constituted a major step in heading off municipal corruption. Though retaining some doubts and concerns about municipal ownership, Socialists made a campaign commitment to this goal along with several other reforms associated with Municipal Socialism. These, along with local issues, became the central focus of their campaign offerings. The more traditional Socialist themes of the class struggle and wage slavery were toned down in the public offerings, but the commitment to the working class and organized labor, a movement that grew along with Socialism, remained as strong as ever. I also see Socialists playing a much larger role in the movement for municipal reform than they have been customarily given.[23]

Contrary to the expectations of many Socialist leaders, the party did less well in the larger cities than it did in small towns and villages in terms of capturing offices, especially high offices such as mayor. While many of the generalizations that have been made about Socialist administrations have rested on what happened in Milwaukee, the only truly big city to have a Socialist mayor, and a few other medium-sized places like Butte, Montana, and Schenectady, New York, most of the work done by Socialist administrations took place in small, sometimes very small places. We do know something about the characteristics of some of the small places where the Socialists did well in terms of elections, most notably mining camps and industrial manufacturing centers with relatively large numbers of workers and considerable union activity, but we know relatively little about how Socialists did in other small towns and how they actually governed in these places.

As suggested above, Socialists had contending views over the distribution of political power on the community level and the significance of how power was distributed.[24] From the left came the view that power was so concentrated in a business/capitalist class pursuing its own interests that meaningful change toward the goal of the cooperative commonwealth was impossible. From the right came the view that power on the local level was more widely distributed among individuals and groups and was such that Socialists had an opportunity to join in and gradually bring changes that would further the revolutionary goal. I find that the system at the local level was generally far more open, at least in giving the Socialists a chance to govern, than the leftists predicted. Still, we cannot quickly dismiss the importance of class stratification in local communities—the existence of one class of people on top of other classes, enjoying a disproportionate share of influence (such a division, oddly enough, also existed within the Socialist movement). One can also sometimes find something like a tyranny of the majority in small towns, which made life difficult for those, like the Socialists, in the minority.

While far from definitive on the subject, this study provides a glimpse of what it was like to be a mayor, especially a Socialist mayor, in small cities, towns, and villages in the early years of the twentieth century. It suggests how conditions in these places conditioned the performance of Socialist mayors. The argument is made here that if Socialist administrations did not do much or fell short of expectations, it was not because they did not try but, in large part, because of the condition of the places where they won. These were often places with a strong working-class base but a government that lacked the capacity to do much; finances, power, and professional help were lacking, and mayors seldom had enough time in office to accomplish much of anything. More generally, governors and state legislators, most of whom were members of the two major parties, made life as difficult as possible for Socialists hoping to make gains on the municipal level. Socialists put considerable stress on the need for municipal home rule to increase their authority to act on their own and to prevent state interference with local operations, but the growing strength of Socialists on the municipal level made securing this reform even more difficult.

In the following pages the term *municipalities* refers to general-purpose local governments, designated as cities, towns, villages, boroughs, or another type of settlement. The title "mayor" is used here as shorthand for municipal chief executives who officially served under a variety of other titles such as village president, commission president, or burgess. The power and duties of municipal chief executives varied with population size. Generally, mayors in the larger cities had a broader range of power and responsibility. The amount of authority given the office varied with state laws and provisions in local government charters.

The dominant form of municipal government during the period under review was the mayor council variety in which there was a clear separation of powers: the mayor headed the executive branch, and the city council headed the legislative branch. Some cities, following the federal and state models, had two council chambers. The strength of the office of mayor was reduced somewhat by the adoption of commission and city manager plans, which put executive and legislative functions in one body, a small city council. Under the new plans the mayor was directly elected by the voters as one of the council members or chosen out of the council by the other members. During the period under review there was considerable controversy over structural arrangements. Socialists generally opposed many of the structural reforms, especially nonpartisan elections, commonly encompassed in the commission and council-manager plans promoted by the Good Government groups.

The commission and council-manager plans weakened mayors when it came to their ability to control administration. Still, under these plans, mayors were first among equals serving on city or town councils and, more importantly, like mayors serving under the mayor-council form, enjoyed the potential for political leadership because their position as mayor carried with it greater visibility, citizen expectation of executive leadership, and widespread assumptions that the holder of that office was responsible for what the municipality did or did not do. Socialist mayors, regardless of the form of government or the size of the population they served, commonly came into office on a platform calling for change—for example, for the purchase of privately owned utilities, better financial management, and improved law enforcement and making various promises by which their administrations could be judged.

In undertaking this study, I reviewed the relevant literature, including several studies on individual Socialist mayors, Socialist administrations in particular cities, and Socialist activity in particular states during the period under review. In building on this literature, information was drawn from traditional archival research, including the Socialist Party Papers (SPP) and other official party documents, including a large number of municipal platforms. The research relied heavily on the examination of a host of historical newspapers, including many largely unexamined ones from radical sources, which have more recently been made available online from various archives. The radical papers provided considerable insight into Socialist goals, strategies, and interparty conflicts. Considerable focus was also placed on how mainstream papers, especially in small towns, treated the Socialists in terms of the amount and type of coverage. I strove to fact-check accounts of events coming from the various sources.

Part of the research task was collecting information on Socialists who served as mayor, starting with the first one in 1898 and continuing through to 1920. Attention was directed to mayors who were tied to the Socialist Party of America, known in some states as the Social Democratic Party.[25] Information was collected on their backgrounds, election to office, and administrations. Lists of Socialist mayors were found in national party publications and various other sources.[26] To produce a final list I conducted an extensive check of online newspaper archives and various Socialist Party documents. Existing surveys were helpful, though they sometimes contain names that could not be verified by any other source and sometimes are incorrect as to the name of the office holder and/or the dates of election and service. Newspapers of the time also contained inconsistencies or errors, especially as to the spelling of names, but provided a considerable amount of new information.

The following pages touch upon the lives, views, and activities of many Socialist mayors. Central to the continuing discussion, though, are a few who were prominent in different phases of the period under review and whose views, as found in reports, interviews, speeches, letters, articles and books, and activities are commented upon in numerous chapters. Appendix 1 offers biographical information on several of these mayors. Appendix 2 provides a list of municipalities with Socialist administrations. I came up with a list of 237 mayors. They represented 216 municipalities in thirty-four states. This list, based on various sources, differs a bit from existing lists.[27] Details on what was found on the personal characteristics of the mayors (age, occupation) and their election (number of opponents and terms) are presented in various places in the text.

Although the time frame for this study is roughly 1900 to 1920, most of the Socialist administrations came to power after 1910, the peak year being 1911, and relatively few came to power in the 1917–1920 period. The fortunes of the party in municipal politics changed markedly over time. They started slowly, caught on, and began to decline. The 1917–1920 period was heavily influenced by the US entry into World War I. Several chapters refer to the particularly harsh conditions starting in 1917. As author/activist Eric Thomas Chester wrote: "After April 1917, and U.S. entry into the war, the Socialist Party went from being a mass-based party with a significant electoral base to a hunted pariah."[28] Yet, while there were far fewer Socialist mayors and public acceptance of the party had declined dramatically, those who served continued to be cast in the same basic ideological or philosophical mold as those who served earlier in the decade. The job became more difficult, but some were flexible enough to survive.

The following three chapters explore how the norms and practices of the Socialist Party and perceptions of the party generally affected those who ran for the office or won office, the nature of the municipal reform movement and how Socialists in general fitted in with others in the movement, and the basic nature of the municipal reform program Socialists offered. Chapters 4–6 focus on Socialist mayors, offering accounts of their election over the period, their coming to power, the conditions under which they served, areas of activity, and what they were able to achieve.

Overall, I differ with the views of many critics and commentators of the time as to the motives or pressures influencing the behavior of the mayors and the effects of their entry into politics, and I offer an essentially more positive view of what they accomplished. As predicted by many commentators, Socialist candidates for mayor watered down platforms and sometimes were, like other politicians, guilty of promising things they could not deliver in a search for votes, and Socialists in office played down their pursuit of revolutionary goals. At the same time, though, it seems to fair to conclude that Socialist candidates and office holders were usually far from conservative or cautious. They focused on immediate problems but also pursued policy goals that were highly disruptive in their communities. Being Socialists, they did as much as they could to promote the interests of the working class. Moreover, they saw their efforts as consistent with the long-term revolutionary goals of the party and the Socialist movement.

Socialist mayors were different from other mayors in important respects because of the doctrinal heritage they reflected, the conditions imposed by the party to which most of them belonged or which they identified, and the intensity of the political opposition this party often received. Compared to the ordinary mayor they were more likely to be ideologically inclined, more innovative, and more disruptive of the status quo. One can reasonably argue that looking at their overall performance in terms of improving the quality of life in their communities, they equaled or excelled the performance of mayors faced with the same limitations as to authority, finance, staff, and time or less constricting limitations when it came to political opposition.

1. The Party Framework

"You are nominated for mayor. You must accept. Great chance for propaganda. Need not neglect the state at large. Answer within two days."[1] J. Stitt Wilson, who had recently represented the Socialist Party of California as its candidate for governor, received this letter on the morning of February 23, 1911, informing him that his Socialist local had chosen him as their candidate for mayor of Berkeley. The Socialist Party to which he and other Socialists were tied differed a great deal from the major parties. This was particularly true when it came to membership and the relations between the party organizations and Socialists running for office and the Socialists they helped put in office. Here we look at these relationships, factions within the party, and the character of the party's platform building, nominating, and campaign activities. We are also concerned with the nature of the party press, party relations with organized labor, and problems incurred as a result of the third-party status of the party and, more importantly, of being a favorite target of the powers that be.

MEMBERSHIP, CONTROL, AND FACTIONS

The Socialist Party was distinctive from other parties when it came to membership and in the extent to which party organizations made demands on its candidates and office holders. One did not become a member of the Socialist Party by simply declaring themselves a member. Membership was restricted:

> You may declare yourself a Socialist, but you may not be one and the party with its organization reserves the right to allow you to be a Socialist or to read you out of its ranks. To be a Socialist depends upon your understanding and knowledge of the economic question; you must understand the political turmoil of the country and realize what is meant by the class-conscious revolutionary movement before you can become a Socialist.[2]

Another requirement was an oath of loyalty to the party, which prohibited working with or voting for the candidates of another party or taking a position under a non-Socialist office holder. In some places several years of membership were required to be eligible for a party nomination or to serve on important committees.[3]

Unlike the two major parties, members formally joined the Socialist Party and paid dues. At any given time, party leaders could supply complete counts of the number of members and of how many of them were behind in their payments. Leaders actively sought out members, especially from the working class. They considered the distribution of party literature in books, pamphlets, and, more importantly, eye-catching newspapers focusing on current events of prime importance in recruiting members as well as winning over voters.[4] They were, however, selective in whom they took in—looking for true believers and hoping to find future leaders. Membership was a special status.[5]

While what the Socialist locals did commonly reflected a decision of the members or a majority thereof, it is fair to say that a relatively few people, a "boss" or party elite, often had a large measure of control over nominations, the party platform, the conduct of campaigns, and, when the party was in power, appointments and matters of public policy. Socialists in Massachusetts readily admitted the existence of party elite.[6] And some bosses, such as Victor Berger in Milwaukee, stood out. Critics claimed that Berger and the other Socialist bosses were far worse than the bosses associated with the major parties they commonly condemned. Socialist mayor George Lunn of Schenectady, New York, who had his share of conflict with the leaders of his party, for example, contended that while Socialists "foam at the mouth as they denounce the injustices charged against the well-oiled machines" of the major parties, Socialist bosses and their small coterie of insiders were even more tyrannical.[7]

Socialists operated on the principle that dues-paying party members should have complete control over the decisions of Socialists holding office when it came to who should be appointed to public offices and matters of public policy. This was defended on the belief that "the Socialist Party is always wiser than its individual members." Member control also reflected the belief that while "few Socialists elected to office desire to betray the working-class," there was always a danger that they may "be deceived into acting against the interests of the workers." Because of this "the rank and file of the party must be awake to the need of INSTRUCTING their officials in all things these officials shall do, or attempt to do, as servants of the working-class."[8]

To enforce the will of the party members, candidates for office on the Socialist Party ticket were commonly required to leave with the local party an undated signed letter of resignation from the office for which they were running prior to the election. Should they win but fail to perform to the satisfaction of party members, the letter of resignation was dated and sent to the appropriate governing body, for example, the city council when the party member was holding the office of mayor. This advanced resignation practice, which originated in the United States within the Socialist Labor Party, was defended by Socialists "as a precaution against breaking party pledges by incompetent or dishonest officials and as a means of party control."[9] Socialists contended that having a recall provision in state or local law was a good idea, "but our way even beats the recall."[10] They commonly lauded their advanced registration system in campaigns as evidence that they took the need to fight corruption in office seriously and, more importantly, unlike other parties, had an effective deterrent or remedy for this problem.

Putting party members in control had some benefits. A big one was in encouraging members to pay their dues, because they had to do this to vote on important matters, including nominations for office, forced resignations, expulsions from the party, and who would get what government jobs if a Socialist won office. However, party control often became a campaign issue. Opponents frequently charged that the systems employed would subject Socialist offices holders to a "Red Hand" pulling the string behind the scenes, depriving them of their individualism and independence, forcing them to respond to the dictates of the small number of people in the Socialist Party rather than the people in general.[11] The recall system employed by the party was in fact far from perfect in implementation (see chapter 6), but it did subject Socialist office holders to considerable pressure, making it more difficult to govern, as did the threat of being formally expelled from party membership should the Socialist in office be found in conflict with party positions or rules.

Throughout the country there was considerable diversity in the left-right tendencies of Socialist locals. The moderate Berger types were in control in much of the Midwest.[12] The same can be generally said about much of California.[13] In contrast, more class-conscious Socialists, who focused on revolutionary goals, were especially active and influential in the mining areas of various states. As professor Robert F. Hoxie found in 1911, "there is something in the working environment of these miners which makes them think in different terms from those about them and gives them a different outlook on life and society."[14]

Divisions within the parties occurred along several lines. There were splits between ethnic groups, such as Finns versus native-born Americans, working-class revolutionaries versus bourgeois reformers, and pragmatists versus purists.[15] In some places, the state of Washington being a prime example, left-right conflicts became coupled with class differences between "Reds" and "Yellows"—with the revolutionary working-class Socialists being the Reds, and the moderate politically activist middle- and upper-class Berger-like Socialists being the Yellows.

The latter group, some charged, acted on the assumption that their superior social-economic status entitled them to have more than an equal say in the affairs of the party—that, indeed, it entitled them to a leadership role. The Yellows argued that their more respectful, go slow nonthreatening approach was the best way to build support for Socialism. The Reds, the real working wage slaves, wanted an equal share in running party affairs and immediate fundamental change through direct action on the industrial level. Observers saw much of the press as relatively friendly to the Yellows, presenting them as respectable and reasonable, whereas the Reds were viewed as un-American dangerous types.[16]

Members of the Industrial Workers of the World (a.k.a. IWWs or Wobblies) who belonged to the party settled in the Red, antipolitical, direct-action faction. Some of them had nothing but contempt for politicians in the political right wing. IWW leader Ralph Chaplin felt that way. Looking back at his career, he wrote, "I didn't think much of the politicians in the Socialist party. Too many of them looked like frustrated old businessmen or foxy young lawyers. Too many of them carried briefcases or bulged too comfortably at the waistline to suit me. I frequently asked myself bitterly, 'What are such petty-bourgeois characters doing in a revolutionary proletarian movement?' I have never been able to figure out the answer."[17] Radical Elizabeth Gurley Flynn had a comparable experience. Her parents were Socialists, but as a member of a younger generation she saw the party "as rather stodgy. Its leaders were . . . professors, lawyers, doctors, ministers, and middle-aged and older people, and we felt a desire to have something more militant, more progressive and more youthful and so we flocked into the new organization, the IWW."[18] Most Socialist mayoral candidates were unlikely to fit the Wobbly idea of what a revolutionary should look like or how one should act, though they confessed from time to time that having a Socialist mayor came in handy during labor disputes.

Socialists were apt to debate at length about nearly everything. In the Everett, Washington, local, for example, votes "were determined in lengthy private sessions at which a committee of ideologues debated the doctrinal dimensions of every issue. Each vote had to be measured rigorously by its implications for furthering the class struggle."[19] The factions were usually somehow able to pull together in preparing for campaign, but they often fell apart after the election if they won over questions of who should be appointed to office and questions of public policy. On the political action dispute, the right-wingers in the party often won out but the leftists did not go away—and they continued to make life as difficult as possible for the right-wingers who sought office or became mayor or holders of other public offices.

PLATFORMS, NOMINATIONS, AND CAMPAIGNS

Going beyond the debates over the value of political action at the local level, national conventions of the Socialist Party frequently featured debates over whether the national party should make suggestions as to what the state and local parties should adopt in their municipal programs and, if so, what suggestions should be made. Some said national action was necessary because local groups were having trouble putting together a program and going off in different and sometime ridiculous directions, often even following the programs of the old parties.[20]

Arguing for national action at the national convention in 1904, delegate Seymour Stedman from Illinois contended:

> Let us remember a few things; that this movement at the present time is a municipal movement; it will grow and develop within the states, and you will take possession of them long before you do of the national government. The municipalities are the natural homes of the proletariat. It will first assert its strength there. You will first be obliged to assume a constructive course and constructive propaganda there.[21]

Another Illinois delegate, Ernest Untermann said developing suggested local platforms was badly needed: "We already have elected quite a number to local administrations, and in various localities difficulties have arisen from the very fact that the comrades so elected did not have a program and did not know how to proceed along proletarian lines."[22] Coming from the left, delegate John Walsh from Montana declared that Socialist office holders who needed this kind of help had no business calling themselves Socialists and had no place in the movement. In his view, "There is no use in electing a class of 3 by 2 Socialists who, when they are in office, don't know what to do ... who can't pass laws in the interests of the laboring people, for God's sake let the old parties elect them; we don't want to elect them."[23] In 1912 the national party finally adopted a suggested municipal program, featuring recommended action regarding municipal ownership, worker protection, planning public health, recreation, education, and other issues.[24] The suggested guidelines reflected the platform that had helped Socialists capture Milwaukee in 1910. Some Socialists, though, were not very happy with the Milwaukee model, referring to it as "weak stuff."[25]

The national party, while offering guidelines and, on request, information, went out of its way to avoid interfering in state and local party affairs. The state and local parties had complete discretion when it came to making platforms, and they used their discretion to shape their platform demands to what was most appropriate in their areas. There was considerable similarity among the platforms on general principles, reflecting a great deal of borrowing on these matters, but also some differences. Left-wingers were a formidable force in some places. In Idaho they went so far as to eliminate all immediate demands for reform in the state platform in 1914.[26] In communities where the left was more influential than the right, the platforms and campaigns tended to put more emphasis on the eventual goals of Socialism and less on immediate demands. Most platforms wound up providing a blend of declarations showing the party's commitment to Socialism and detailed attacks on specific abuses. The platform of the Bennington, Vermont, Socialist Party in 1911, for example, contained language that combined a commitment to the goal of bringing an end to the exploitation of the producing class with an attack on the Bennington Gas Light Company for raising its rates.[27]

During much of the period under review, party members exercised complete control over the choice of nominees—though the growing popularity of direct primary systems presented a great challenge to parties to retain that control.[28] There were contested nominations, going several ballots, but often it was a case of party leaders courting potential nominees, trying to find someone to run, rather than potential nominees courting the party leaders or other members for the nomination. Proposed candidates often declined to accept a nomination. A report on a county convention in Missouri, for example, disclosed, "In some instances two or three men were tried before one could be found who would become a candidate at all."[29] In Butte, Montana, the inability of Socialists to find candidates—in one case they put a dead man on the ticket—was attributed by party leaders in large part to the threat of mining company executives, who dominated the town, to fire anyone who accepted a Socialist Party nomination.[30]

Many nominations had to be made if the party wished to present a full ticket. But the pool of candidates seemed limited—the same people ran and lost several times for the same office or different offices. Sometimes those who won a mayoral office would be immediately nominated for a higher statewide office. For example, in 1906, a year after his election as mayor of Oswego, Kansas, and while he was still mayor, Harry Gilham was nominated by the state Socialist Party for governor. Lewis Duncan of Butte, Montana, was also nominated for governor a year after being elected mayor and continued being mayor throughout the campaign. Setting the record straight in accordance with party practice, Duncan told a large crowd he was not running for governor, the party was running him for governor.[31]

Duncan's view of Socialist candidacy—that it was the party seeking office rather than the individual the party nominated—was tied to the more general doctrine of party supremacy. As a party leader in Florida described it, "We socialists are never candidates in the sense of being seekers after office. We will hold a city convention; someone will be selected to run for the office, and it will be the duty of the man so selected to obey. We socialists do what we are told to do by the organization."[32] In practice, strict obedience to the party often turned out to be elusive, especially when the candidate happened to win office.

Given the character of the Socialist Party, union members, especially from the skilled trades, were often prominent in the slate of candidates offered, though less so when it came to top-of-the-ticket offices such as mayor.[33] Sometimes all the nominees were union members. This is true, for example, of all fourteen nominees on the slate of Socialist nominees elected to office in the city of Barre, Vermont, in the spring of 1914. The number included eight from the granite cutters' association, three from the clerk's association, two from the tool sharpener's union, and one from the quarry workers' international association.[34] In 1915 Socialist mayor-elect John F. Higgins proudly reported to national headquarters that his town of Star City, West Virginia, was about to be governed by five glassblowers, a carpenter, and an ordinary laborer. The glassblowers, known to some as the "aristocrats of the labor world," accounted for 125 of the 167 employed workers in the city and were key to the success of the Socialists.[35] In Bicknell, Indiana, all of the Socialist officials elected to run the city in 1913 were miners or ex-miners.[36]

While working-class candidates often enjoyed a preference, party members were also inclined to consider other factors, including the likely general appeal of a candidate. For example, according to a newspaper account, George H. Millar was the front runner as the local's choice for mayor of Medford, Oregon, because he was thought to "be a candidate who will draw heavier outside of his party."[37] Socialist mayors who were not drawn from the working class, at least at the time they were elected to office, included several ministers, professionals, and successful businesspeople. Some were very wealthy. Among these was William Thum, a chemist who became a millionaire because of his role in the invention of sticky flypaper. He beat out two other candidates to become mayor of Pasadena, California, in 1911. Shortly after the election an article in the Socialist Party newspaper *Appeal to Reason* noted his wealth but was quick to point out, "He limits himself to the expenditure of $3,500 a year and keeps no servants because he says it is not democratic to do so. He spends most of his income in philanthropic educational work."[38] Another writer chipped in: "Wm. Thum doesn't believe in making a splurge, riding around in touring cars and surrounding himself with liveried flunkys. He doesn't care about being known as millionaire Thum, but prefers just plain Wm. Thum, citizen. He keeps no servants, his wife does her own housework. Thum dresses neatly, but without display. He wears no diamonds."[39] As mayor, he footed the bill for hiring experts to improve the city's operational efficiency.[40]

Tyler Lawton, who became mayor of Bicknell, Indiana, in 1913, was among the many Socialists with a personal story, quite unlike that of Thum, of a struggling outsider. He grew up in Kentucky in a shack rented out by a coal company and at age eleven joined his father in working in the coal mines. He went on to become a labor activist with the radical Knights of Labor, lost his job, and got blacklisted for being a "vicious agitator." Following this he became a tramp and Socialist, finally drifting into Bicknell, where his fortunes changed. Following his election as mayor, an article in the *Appeal to Reason* told his story and reported that he and his comrades running the government "are now showing the working people of his community and of the rest of the country that the workers have the power and the intelligence to be their own political and industrial masters."[41]

While the nomination process commonly produced candidates eager to plunge into the political fray, one still found candidates who saw their prime mission to be one of teaching about Socialism. One example was N. A. Richardson, a prominent Socialist leader in California who spent most of his time following his nomination for mayor of San Bernardino lecturing out of state about Socialism, thinking the education of the working class was of higher importance. He left the campaigning in San Bernardino to others. He lost the election by just seven votes, leading some to wonder what would have happened if he had gotten more involved on a personal level in his campaign.[42] Somewhat along the same lines, as historian Norman Clark related, at a public event in Everett, Washington, a Socialist candidate for the city council brushed aside questions about current issues of concern in the community, stating that if he could not talk about Socialism he was not going to talk at all. "After this singular statement, a burst of laughter and ridicule from the audience shattered (the speaker) and left him completely inarticulate."[43]

The everyday operations of the party and its political campaigns during the period under review appear to have been largely paid for out of membership dues collected monthly and distributed among local, state, and party organizations. Voluntary contributions, the sale of literature, tickets to meetings, and campaign novelties, along with sometimes "passing the hat" at meetings, were among the other revenue sources.[44] It might be added that starting to pass a hat around sometimes proved to be an effective way to immediately clear out a room.[45]

The general goal was to collect modest sums from as many people as possible in contrast to the practice of the major parties of collecting large sums from wealthy private donors connected to the business world.[46] Given their policy stands and goals, Socialists really had no choice but to find another way of raising campaign funds, as they were unlikely to draw from wealthy donors. Still, Socialists could take pride in shunning the old parties' practice of building up piles of money "by begging favors from the plutes."[47] Local Socialist parties were sometimes accused of taking funds offered by one of the major parties who were eager to build up a Socialist campaign so that the Socialist would draw votes away from candidates of another party. Socialists acknowledged such offers were made but denied charges they were accepted.[48]

Much of whatever work was done during the Socialist campaigns on the local level was generally financed and controlled by local party organizations. Party leaders organized speeches, rallies, and fundraising events and controlled or sought to control the general message being sent. One leader explained:

> Our party is, of course, intended to be radically different from all others. Standing as we do for a revolutionary program that is not quickly grasped by the average mind, we think it necessary to keep the control of its official propaganda in the hands of a body that can be disciplined. The republican, democratic progressive parties have no control over their members and do not even know who they are. But then who could imagine those parties caring what kind of spell-binding their candidates used just so long as they could deliver the votes. We do care what our candidates say.[49]

Another hard-liner added: "Our party pays our candidates' campaign expenses and $8.00 per day, this being something that no other party in this country does, and we claim the right to control them body and soul as far as political action is concerned."[50]

Socialist parties picked up most expenses such as those for renting halls and theaters for rallies, printing, and advertising, but they were not generally able or willing to spend a great deal on elections. In some cases, they tended to be parsimonious, with unfortunate results. As Marvin Wachman noted regarding the Milwaukee Socialists, "The entire campaign of 1909 had cost the Social-Democratic party only three hundred dollars, but they regretted having limited themselves to such a small sum. The feeling among party leaders was that they would have elected several more school board members, and two judges, if they had allowed themselves more money to work with. They vowed not to be penny-wise in their next political battle."[51]

With the party taking a dominant role, Socialist candidates generally spent little, if anything, out of their own pockets. In Ohio in 1911, Socialist Corbin

Shook did not spend anything to get elected mayor of Lima; Socialist Thomas Pape spent a grand total of $6.75 on his victorious campaign for mayor in Lorain; and Socialist Alfred Perrine put less than five dollars in his successful campaign for election as mayor of Mount Vernon.[52] In Schenectady, George Lunn spent thirty dollars out of his pocket to become mayor in 1911—he and other successful Socialist candidates spent virtually nothing compared to that spent by their opponents.[53] Millionaire William Thum in his expense statement filed with the county clerk reported he spent hardly any of his own money in his campaign to become mayor of Pasadena.[54] He and party leaders may well have considered it important to stress that only a minimal amount was spent to fend off charges that Thum had bought the election.

While the cost of the campaign to them personally may not have deterred many Socialists from running, there were other costs: some gave up jobs paying much more than they received as mayor, and some took the risk of losing their jobs. In Granite City, Illinois, Marshall Kirkpatrick resigned his job making four dollars a day to work for seventy-five dollars per month as mayor.[55] In St. Marys, Ohio, mayor Scott Wilkins went from a $1,100-a-year job to one as mayor that paid him only $400 a year.[56] John Menton also reported losing money, working for $100 a year as mayor of Flint, Michigan.[57] Mayor Wilkins and others elected along with him, including some council members and prominent supporters of the party, lost their jobs, were blacklisted, and had to leave town to find work.[58] The Santa Fe Railroad fired switchman John Schildknecht for simply accepting the Socialist Party nomination for mayor of Frontenac, Kansas.[59] He went on to win. Still out of work following his election, he proposed that the council approve his wife's appointment as superintendent of water works, a paying job, saying he would do the work, but the council would not go along with her appointment.[60]

LITERATURE AND THE PARTY PRESS

Socialists placed great importance on their literature in recruitment, campaigning, and generally communicating the party's message to the general public. When it came to recruitment, some Socialists operated on the assumption, supposedly supported by statistics, that "the quickest and surest way to convert a non-Socialist into a revolutionist is to get him to read Socialist literature."[61] From a leftist viewpoint there were few things more important to the revolutionary cause in spreading the word than a hell-raising newspaper continually focusing on the evils of capitalism. As an editorial in one such paper declared: "It is the high function of the Socialist press to expose the inherent brutality and viciousness of capitalist-class rule, to exhibit its essentially predatory nature and vulgar, degrading aims. . . . A strong Socialist paper in a community is of far more avail in the class struggle than even a whole city council composed of Socialists administering capitalist-class laws."[62] In addition, those in the party's right wing used newspapers to focus more squarely on current events or immediate problems that needed resolution and to encourage public support for Socialist candidates and office holders. Under the influence of the right, the mass distribution of party papers at election time, focusing on specific local issues like the need for bringing down utility rates and the virtues of Socialist candidates, became a common and highly valued campaign activity.

Socialists needed their own press both to circumvent what they called the mainstream newspaper's "trick of silence"—essentially ignoring any mention of the Socialists, forcing them to get their own publicity—and to defend themselves from attacks from the mainstream press.[63] To some extent, having a local Socialist paper deterred such attacks. In Toledo, Ohio, for example, attacks were said to have been relatively rare when the party had a newspaper but to have increased dramatically after the paper went out of business.[64] To circulate their message, local Socialist parties sometimes purchased space in mainstream newspapers under such headings as a "Socialist section" or "Socialist column" and sometimes raised just enough money to publish a small weekly newspaper for distribution during the election season. Privately owned Socialist papers and Socialist-friendly labor papers did what they could to further the message. Socialist party leaders generally preferred party-owned newspapers, under the control of the party organization, over privately owned or stock-company Socialist papers. As the editor of a party-owned paper in Arizona put it, "The party is in its childhood until it can control its own propaganda organs."[65] However, while having only a party-owned paper brought uniformity, it raised the possibility of ignoring the views of minority factions within the party.[66]

RELATIONS WITH LABOR: THE CRUCIAL TIES

The most important relationships of Socialist parties as they entered the political process were those with organized labor. Socialists on the right actively sought to win over labor unions, hoping to bring into them into politics through the Socialist gate, by getting them to endorse Socialism, the Socialist Party, and Socialist candidates. They contended that the labor unions could take the workers only so far—workers needed to join the cause of Socialism and line up behind Socialist candidates to get full relief, meaning emancipation from the present exploitive system. Many party activists were skilled workers who had joined a union on their way to the Socialist Party. Yet, while many Socialists were union members, relatively few union members were Socialists. Socialist infiltration of unions to bring them into political activity with Socialists leading the way often encountered the resentment and resistance of union members and a rejection of Socialist proposals.

Still, in many places party and union ties were strong.[67] This was especially true in Milwaukee. Writing in 1903, the state secretary of the Wisconsin Social Democratic Party was proud to report: "Perhaps in no other large city in the United States has the Socialist movement so well solved this difficult problem as in Milwaukee—the problem of working with and through the unions without dominating them or allowing them to dominate the party. The result of this happy solution of the question is that Milwaukee may boast of a thoroughly class-conscious movement."[68] Historian Sally Miller attributed rise of the Socialist movement in Milwaukee to its alliance with the Federated Trades Council in the city. As she noted, Socialists within the council directed its political activities "cautiously, to be sure, to avoid annoying rank-and-file unionists.... The planks of the Council's platform often matched those of the Social Democrats. After 1900, the close entente which had grown between the two organizations was cemented into a permanent alliance."[69] In Minneapolis, Thomas Van Lear and the International Association of Machinists virtually rebuilt the Socialist political organization, making it an effective force in city politics.[70]

Most Socialist mayors, being generally on the right wing of their party, had relatively good relations with unions, be they craft or industrial, that were inclined toward political activity. At election time Socialists around the country often received the support of at least some unions affiliated with the American Federation of Labor (AFL) or unaffiliated industrial unions such as those representing workers in the mining industry. Socialist administrations proceeded to give unions a seat at the table, support labor and working-class legislation, and protect and promote the goals of organized labor on the industrial level. Socialist mayors and other officials also showed their support of labor by protesting what they saw as violations of the rights of workers around the country. Mayors Lewis Duncan of Butte, Montana, and H. P. Houghton of Girard, Kansas, for example, were among those Socialists who protested the arrest and what they saw as the mistreatment of ironworkers involved in the dynamiting the of the Los Angeles Times building in 1911.[71]

When it came to building a strong relation with labor, politically active Socialists seemed to generally follow the advice offered by Guy Miller, Socialist and prominent labor leader: "It is not enough to tell the workers that you are their friend, that you are of them and that you are the only party that is fit to live at all. You must show them by the measures which you propose for their relief your ability to guide them and that you are fit to be trusted."[72]

DIFFERENCES AND CHALLENGES

Socialists throughout the period under review saw themselves and were seen by others as different. One observer, favorable to the cause, noted in 1900: "The Social Democratic party is so fundamentally different from the other parties that the old-time politicians are totally at a loss as to its meaning. They cannot even begin to comprehend that the Socialists are working, not for political jobs and party triumph, but for principles and ideals. There is in the Social Democratic movement an almost religious enthusiasm."[73]

Socialists were also somewhat distinctive regarding political techniques or practical political skills, frequently being accused of having virtually none of the latter. A common image was one of a group of politically naïve do-gooders or ideological zealots who were in over their heads when it came to fighting it out in the rough-and-tough political arena. Noting charges of this nature, the Socialists of Grants Pass, Oregon, responded:

> The Socialists here have been accused of having but little political acumen, from the fact that they are early in the campaign and are showing their hand to the other fellow. Our answer to this is, there is such a thing as clean politics. Truth has nothing to fear. We have nothing to conceal. Those who oppose us here had better get busy for they have a big job on their hands. We invite all voters of the city who favor these reforms we have proposed to join us in the fight.[74]

Coming from a different direction, Thomas Van Lear, at the time Socialist mayor-elect of Minneapolis, argued: "What the Socialist Party needs now is a school in practical politics. A great many persons object to the phrase 'practical politics.' However, if we don't find some way to meet the old-time politicians on their own battle ground and overcome them, the Socialist Party will never amount to very much." He went on to remark in reference to some recent losses in his home city, "We knew so little then that we thought all we had to do was to convince the people that they ought to vote for us, and then we could go home and go to bed."[75]

For much of the period under review, being a Socialist was not perceived as a bad thing. In much of the country, though, as time went on, increasing attention, largely unfavorable, was given to Socialists. By the middle of the second decade of the twentieth century, thanks in part to a campaign evidenced in mainstream newspapers (often corporate owned), the party and its candidates were increasingly "hampered by the unreasoning prejudice which large elements of the public attach to the word Socialism."[76] Socialist parties stood out in the extent to which they were discriminated against not only because they were third parties but because they were perceived as dangerous by business-related groups in their communities. Sometimes party members found it difficult because of political opposition to gather in commonly used public meeting places. One example was in Jasper, Tennessee, where, after being turned away at the local courthouse, fifteen to twenty Socialists wound up holding their county convention in a pool room.[77]

Socialists shared grievances with other third parties when it came to election laws and practices shaped by those lawmakers with the major parties trying to minimize competition. Rules and regulations regarding voting and election systems were rigged against them. They found reason to think, for example, that district or ward lines were shaped by those in power to limit the number of districts a Socialist could carry.[78] Many of the most-heated contests waged by Socialists were against structural changes like at-large city elections, which they felt were intentionally being proposed because it would hurt them. They usually lost these battles. They had to worry about state laws—some of which were aimed directly at Socialist parties—that restricted their ability to get their candidates on the ballot.[79]

They also had reason to feel the legal system was being used against them. One reason for this was that the successful elections of Socialist candidates were frequently challenged on the grounds of voter fraud or that, for one reason or another, the candidates were ineligible to serve. Challenges of this nature took place, for example, in Anaconda, Montana; Brookneal, Virginia; and Star City, West Virginia. In Butte, Montana, the administration of Socialist mayor Lewis Duncan came to an end when, Socialists charged, a judge tied to the Anaconda Copper Mining Company removed him from office ostensibly for failing to do his duty during labor disturbances. A Montana paper later noted that Duncan "was elected by some 5,000 people but it only took one man to unseat him when the A.C.M. gave the word."[80] The desire to prevent further Socialist gains at the local level was a factor in the decision to eliminate several Socialist-leaning small towns in West Virginia through annexation proceedings that put their citizens in a larger city.[81] Similarly, Socialists in St. Johns, Oregon, where they had a party member as mayor, did what they could but without success to avoid having their city absorbed by Portland.[82]

During World War I all hell broke out—the Socialist Party was targeted on suspicions of disloyalty, its offices were raided, its publications were banned, and many of its members were sent to prison. The party's negative image was to have a great deal to do with its inability to win office and govern. During much of the period under review, however, the party functioned largely in a more receptive atmosphere in a moderate reform-minded mode, offering a municipal program centering on labor rights, public ownership, and democracy.

2. Municipal Reform: Where the Socialists Fitted In

"The corruption of municipal government in America needs no describing here. The exposures of the past ten years have filled the magazines with facts and figures a little worse, to be sure, than was previously surmised."[1] Thus wrote Frank Bohn, a prominent Socialist and industrial labor advocate, in a November 1911 article. He went on to declare:

> But the American working people have always rightly despised the city governments. The water hose would not put out the fire. Epidemics of preventable diseases have raged. Public buildings have fallen to pieces before they were completed. The tribe of politicians, from those who rule the smallest towns up to the organized gangs in control of Chicago and New York, have probably been, during the past generation, the most contemptible class of social parasites on the face of the earth.[2]

The perception of conditions of this nature gave birth to a municipal reform movement in the late nineteenth and early twentieth centuries addressing problems in the operation of municipal government, especially focusing on corruption and inefficiency and a host of economic and social issues. The movement had two sets of groups pushing for change. One was the "Good Government" group—a middle- and upper-class movement of businesspeople and right-wing Progressives who put prime emphasis on rebuilding municipalities around the principles of honesty and efficiency. The second group, known here as the Municipal Socialists, also wanted honesty and efficiency—though efficiency was to be sacrificed if it conflicted with democracy or the provision of jobs or services benefiting the working class or people in general—but also to go beyond this by bringing a general enlargement of municipal activities in the social and economic realms and expanded public participation in governance. Right-wing Socialists joined left-wing Progressives in the Municipal Socialism camp. In this chapter we look at the different components of the movement and the relations or interactions among them.

GOOD GOVERNMENT AND MUNICIPAL SOCIALISM

The "Good Government" forces (commonly called "goo-goos") drew their strength from what was considered the "better elements" of the city—the middle and upper classes, business leaders, and professional people.[3] Commonly working along the same lines were civic uplifters, members of taxpayer's associations, newspaper editors, and college professors from various disciplines, especially political science.[4] Good Government proponents linked together in local organizations with a variety of names such as municipal leagues, civic federations, and Good Government clubs. Many of the local reform organizations were linked on the national level to the National Municipal League, which was founded in 1894.[5]

Initially, much of the protest coming from the Good Government advocates was channeled into election campaigns against corruption tied to political bosses and machines. These efforts often led to campaigns to "throw the rascals out" and replace them with reform administrations. The Good Government reformers, though, found that they could not rely on elections or on an assumption that the party out of power could be depended upon to seize upon the failures of the party in power when it came to honesty and efficiency, become the party of reform, ride into office, and bring better government. Politicians did indeed float into office on reform programs, but when the public sentiment that got them there died down, they often went back to the old ways. With the public no longer looking, the efforts of those genuinely interested in reform met considerable resistance and were often futile.[6] The targeted political bosses easily survived reform administrations—they came and went, in the words of boss George Washington Plunkitt of Tammany Hall in New York City, like "morning glories," without having much of an impact.[7] Citizens and academic reformers became frustrated with the failure of reform administrations to bring lasting change. This frustration contributed to a drive to find permanent solutions through structural changes in how cities were governed.[8]

Reformers set out to change local government structure so that it ran on a corruption-free, business-like basis, stressing efficiency in operations, keeping taxes and business regulations at a minimum, and doing what it could to encourage business growth and economic development. Local officials were to be honest but also business friendly. They were to sit back and defer to the leadership provided by the business community and to steer clear of getting involved in the running of the economy or the provision of extensive public services and imposing burdensome taxes. Their progressivism was limited in scope—honesty and efficiency were central concerns—and they were not out to enlarge the functions and financial costs of local government; for them, municipal ownership was a low priority, if a priority at all.[9]

As historian Melvin Holi once noted, the reformers had little faith in the ability of the "masses to rule themselves intelligently."[10] They called for literacy or understanding tests for voters, reducing the number of elective offices, smaller city councils elected at large, and greater centralized business-like management through a commission or city manager system. Hoping to take "politics as usual" out of the operation of government, they also called for civil service reforms to end patronage appointments, which brought incompetent party hacks into office and diverted a percentage of their inflated salaries to the party organizations. They also saw the need for nonpartisan elections to further discourage political machines from getting involved in local elections.

The central aim of the Good Government proponents was a smooth-running operation that filtered out lower-class grievances and demands. Main targets were political machines built on patronage and graft that drew much of their strength from immigrant voters. Goo-goos condemned these political machines because they were, in their view, tied to lower-class interests and were not business friendly, being opposed to their views on labor and development.[11] These Good Government advocates, reflecting business interests, left ample room for the Municipal Socialists to fill the gaps—that is, to play a prominent role in the cause of municipal ownership, reforms benefiting the representation and welfare of the working class, and the promotion and protection of workers attempting to organize and improve their conditions.

Municipal Socialism, inspired in part by developments in England and elsewhere in Europe, as well as in American cities in the late nineteenth and early twentieth centuries, initially focused on municipal ownership of what were commonly regarded public utilities, such as waterworks, electric power companies, and street railways. By the early 1900s, however, it had already become a much broader movement. In 1902, for example, a US consul reported from England, "Not content with municipal ownership of electric street railways, gaslights, water supply and telephones, in several cities the municipal corporations build dwellings for workingmen, run hotels and erect and operate magnificent baths. In Liverpool, the council has gone so far as to charge part of what should be the rent from municipal houses occupied by working men as homes, against the taxes of the community."[12] Municipal Socialism grew from there to become a more general reform movement intended to improve the lives of ordinary people. Right-wing members of the Socialist Party of America (a.k.a. the Socialist Democratic Party in some places) became part of the Municipal Socialism group along with left-wing Progressives belonging to other political parties or no political party at all.

In the United States, the cause of Municipal Socialism and the thinking of the Socialists and the left-wing Progressives involved in it were deeply influenced by domestic thinkers Henry George, Edward Bellamy, and others who lashed out at privilege and the unearned income of those having a monopoly, be it of land, natural resources, or the provision of essential services such as water, power, communications, or transportation. Both Socialists and Progressives were impressed by the work of George, a nineteenth-century political economist. He found that while the capitalistic unregulated free-market economy was efficient in producing wealth, most of it went to a relatively few, leaving many in poverty.[13] George's focus on the growing gap between the rich and poor; his rejection of monopoly, unearned wealth, and special privilege; and his argument that a single tax on the annual use value of land would effectively address many of the nation's economic and social problems had a profound influence on political and economic thought. George influenced a long line of reform politicians, be they Socialists, like Victor Berger, or non-Socialists.[14]

Edward Bellamy's most influential book, *Looking Backward*, was published in 1888, and the movement he inspired was evidenced in the creation of Nationalist clubs around the nation. These were directly involved in building the cause of Municipal Socialism by promoting the general goal of municipal ownership of utilities and expanded services on the municipal level and several specific reforms that were to appear in the platforms of Socialists, such as ending all franchises and contracts with private individuals or corporations in favor of giving the work to municipal employees—an idea aimed at both avoiding corruption and improving the pay and working conditions of people doing the work.[15]

Many in the cause of Municipal Socialism were also influenced by religious leaders on the left identified as Social Gospelers or Christian Socialists. These two movements had much in common though having different origins—the latter having its roots in utopian experiments in Europe as well as America, and the other being native to America. Both saw the need to make capitalism more compatible with Christianity, but while the Christian Socialists saw the need to replace capitalism, Social Gospelers simply wanted to improve the system.[16]

As George Hodges, an American Episcopal clergyman and Social Gospel exponent, saw it 1889, both movements were "nothing more or less than applied Christianity" heading toward "that Kingdom of God which Christ preached."[17] Both, he declared, understand that Christianity "does not concern the individual alone. Christ preached a social gospel."[18] In his view Christ's message was applicable to a wide variety of social problems, but the central core problem was simply that

> Business itself today is wrong. It rests upon a negation of the social law. Each man for himself, and company for itself. It is based on competitive strife for profit. But this is the exact opposite of Christianity.... We must change the system. We must found business upon social law. Combination must take the place of competition; we must have a system in which business shall be carried on not for private profits, but for the public good.[19]

The religious left called for a wide variety of measures to, among other things, improve industrial working conditions, eliminate slums, encourage education and nutrition, and fight alcoholism and crime. Proponents of the "Social Gospel" and Christian Socialism called for a new system of morality, where rugged individualism, selfishness, and greed gave way to cooperation and brotherly love, built around the Golden Rule ("Do unto others as you would have others do unto you").

The movement took hold largely in Protestant churches, especially the Congregationalists and Methodists.[20] George D. Herron, a Congregational minister, was a leading figure among the Social Gospelers. One of his most popular sermons was an attack on the privileged rich called "The Message of Jesus to Men of Wealth." Herron became an active member of the Social Democratic Party. Socialists were proud to announce: "There are hundreds of ministers who belong to the American Socialist movement and who are all militant Socialist propagandists."[21] Many had no problem being identified as Socialists but wanted to make sure their designation as such included the limiting prefix "Christian." They "wanted no association in the public mind with the godless Marxists."[22]

The list of ministers who identified as Socialists included some of the best-known Socialist mayors—George Lunn of Schenectady, J. Stitt Wilson of Berkeley, and Lewis Duncan of Butte—and several lesser-known ones such as Christian Socialists John S. McKay of Salem, Ohio; Robert Murray of Toronto, Ohio; and J. L Anderson of Hillsboro, North Dakota.[23] To these ministers and the many other members of the party, their status as Social Gospelers or Christian Socialists meant that they were truer to their religion than those Christians who opposed Socialism. Though Socialists had the strong opposition of the Catholic Church and the Mormon Church, members of these faiths could be found in the ranks of the Socialists.[24]

The push factor behind the thinking of one left-wing minister who felt compelled to abandon his position and get directly involved in the politics of the day and the cause of Municipal Socialism is found in the farewell sermon of Robert A. Bakeman, who resigned his church position to take a position with the administration of Socialist mayor George Lunn of Schenectady:

> The minister has about as much influence today as a man's grandmother. The church is paralyzed. The minister is in a castle; he stands unchallenged and says what he pleases so long as he keeps within his pledges. I am tired of being in castle unchallenged; I want to get out into the forum where a man can place his brains against mine and either find if I am right or show me if I am wrong. The minister's life is artificial and unreal. He has a code of morals all his own and a great majority of old ministers are bending over with the burden of trying to retain their influence.[25]

THE PROGRESSIVE PIONEERS

Municipal Socialism was manifested in the United States in the administrations of several Progressive mayors, some of whom took office prior to the election of the first Socialist mayor in 1898 and provided models of municipal reform administrations going well beyond the Good Government themes of honesty and efficiency. Chief among the pioneers in this respect were Hazen Pingree of Detroit, Sam Jones of Toledo, and Tom Johnson of Cleveland.[26]

Pingree, a Republican, was first elected Detroit mayor in 1889 and served three more terms to 1897. He was a rich man, making his money manufacturing boots and shoes, who initially did not appear to be very dangerous to the establishment. He started off as an honesty and efficiency structural-type reformer. His change in orientation toward Municipal Socialism began with a fight with the city's streetcar companies. He refused to give them franchises without securing guarantees of lower fares and improved service. In 1893 Bellamy's newspaper, the *New Nation* noted with pleasure that Pingree was "waging war against the local monopolies" and predicted that he "will succeed in breaking down the monopolies that have been drawing the life out of the municipality."[27] That same year the Detroit Socialist Party praised Pingree for his actions regarding the streetcar (a.k.a. traction) interests and later announced it would not put up a candidate against him in the upcoming election.[28]

While Pingree failed to bring public ownership of the transit system, through his efforts Detroit became the first city to get fares down to three cents. He was able to create a municipal light plant and through tough negotiations bring down the prices of gas, lighting, and water utilities. He also became known for the Potato Patch program he put together at the height of the 1893–1894 depression, which gave poor families the opportunity to grow food on unused land owned by the city. The depression stimulated his concern with the problems of poverty and the abuses of many of those who had become wealthy and brought him much closer to the foreign-born working class. Under him came public paths, better schools and new parks, and a war on corruption in city hall. Pingree continued his quest as mayor for municipal home rule, municipal ownership of utilities, an increase in corporate taxation, and other reforms as governor of Michigan, a position to which he was elected in 1896 and 1898.[29]

In Ohio, Municipal Socialism got off the ground in the administrations of Sam Jones, who served as mayor of Toledo from 1897 to 1904.[30] Jones was first elected mayor of this city with more than a 100,000 people as a Republican, but his reform policies brought a break with the Republican Party by the end of his term. However, he had no trouble winning reelection as an independent candidate in 1899 and again in 1901 and 1903. Like Pingree, Jones was a wealthy man (he made his money in the oil industry) who was deeply disturbed by pervasive poverty and unemployment. Becoming a Christian Socialist—he was closely associated with Christian Socialist Reverend Washington Gladden of Columbus—Jones built his good government ideas on the principle of the Golden Rule. Like Pingree, he sought to limit franchises and move toward municipal ownership. With him came improvements in kindergartens, more parks, and playgrounds. He also successfully fought against the renewal of the street railway franchise during his first administration.[31]

Many considered Jones to be a Socialist in all but party identification. Indeed, one contemporary observer thought he was as much of a Socialist (if not more than) as the first Socialist mayor, John Chase, of Haverhill, Massachusetts.[32] Jones had good things to say about Socialists but preferred not to join any political party. In a letter to Eugene Debs in December 1898 he declared that the "truth that you are standing and speaking for is taking hold upon the hearts of the people."[33] While he was supportive of the Socialist cause and may well have had reason to appreciate the support of Socialists in the electorate as far as his campaigns were concerned, by the late 1890s he had become on principle opposed to membership in any political party. In a letter addressed to Debs in 1900, he wrote, "As I see it, we must not only leave the 'old parties'; we must leave all parties and all party methods and learn the lesson of working together for the good of all."[34] Two years later he was quoted as saying at a meeting in Los Angeles, "There is room for but few thinking men inside political party lines. I want to be free to do my own thinking and

I want the same privilege equally accessible to every other creature on our planet."³⁵

Though popular with the people, Jones encountered strong opposition in the city council. He was a loner, having repudiated partisanship, and like many reform mayors he had little power under the city's charter, for example, to make appointments, or pursue his objectives regarding franchises and municipal ownership. Voters rejected his proposal for charter changes that strengthen his ability to pursue his objectives. Jones, however, secured a significant win in the state supreme court when it voided a state legislative move to shift his authority over the appointment of the police commission to a state commission.³⁶

Jones, described by historian Howard Quint as a practitioner of nonpartisan Socialism, made an unsuccessful bid for governor of Ohio as an independent candidate in 1899 with a platform calling for abolition of political parties, public ownership of utilities, the initiative and referendum, and a host of labor reforms.³⁷ The Social Democratic Party in Ohio did not put up a candidate for governor that year. Party leaders had no objection to their members voting for the candidate put up by the Socialist Labor Party but were cool to the idea of their members voting for Jones. This, they explained, was "partly because he ignored the existing Socialist parties, and partly because the interests of the movement demand that candidates be chosen by the Socialists themselves and be responsible to the party for the integrity of their principles when elected."³⁸ Brad Whitlock, Jones's successor as mayor of Toledo from 1906 to 1914, continued the city on a similar path.

Tom Johnson, mayor of Cleveland, 1901–1909, like Pingree and Jones had a highly successful business career. At one time he was a street railway monopolist who wheeled and dealed with Detroit's Mayor Pingree. "He was," as his biographer noted, "a rich man, made rich by special privilege."³⁹ His change of heart came after he came across the works of Henry George. "When Mr. George's writings opened his eyes to the truth about the established order, he went out to destroy the conditions which made his own class possible."⁴⁰ George, himself, encouraged Johnson to run for office, something Johnson first did by winning a seat in the US House of Representatives.⁴¹ Like Jones, he made an unsuccessful run for governor, though he ran as a Democrat.

Johnson had been a supporter of Democrat reformer William Jennings Bryan and had formed a friendship with Sam Jones while working with him on Bryan's campaign in 1900. Johnson won the first of four terms as mayor in 1901. Like Pingree and Sam Jones, he called for municipal ownership of public utilities. To Johnson, "The only good franchise is a dead franchise."⁴² He was able to take over several responsibilities from private businesses, including street cleaning and garbage collection. Though failing to get public ownership of the streetcar system, he was able to lower the fare to three cents.[43]

During Johnson's unsuccessful run for governor in 1903 on the Democratic ticket, US senator Republican Mark Hanna spoke up: "I charge that Tom L. Johnson is the national leader of the Socialist Party. I beg of you to rise and kill the attempt to float the flag of Socialism over Ohio. . . . A vote for Johnson is a vote for chaos in this country. . . . Socialists like thieves steal up behind to stab."[44] Following the election, a writer in a left-wing paper suggested that the problem for some papers who oppose Johnson is their feeling that he is a Socialist who "actually believes and preaches that the people have some rights which the great trusts and corporations are bound to respect."[45] Another newspaper during the period referred to Johnson as a "Socialist democrat," while another would not go so far: "Tom Johnson is not quite a Socialist, but he is looked upon as 'unsafe' by the capitalistic element."[46]

SOCIALISTS ON THE RIGHT AND PROGRESSIVES ON THE LEFT

During the period of reform, 1900–1920, some commentators contended that the only difference between the Socialists and Progressives was that the Progressives did not know they were Socialists. One could point to differences in overall objectives and worldviews. Socialists sought to replace the current economic system with a cooperative commonwealth and bring about the triumph of the laboring class over the capitalist class. Progressives, in contrast, sought to patch up and save the capitalistic system by making necessary reforms and to avoid class conflict by focusing attention on the public interest.[47] Yet, while these differences showed up in the rhetoric the two sides used, Progressives and Socialists resembled each other in terms of their platforms and policy outlooks. This is especially true of the right-wing Socialists and the left-wing Progressives who shared space in the cause of Municipal Socialism.

Given the common sources of inspiration and the commonality of the situations they faced, it comes as no surprise that it is difficult to distinguish the values and programs of Socialists on the right and Progressives on the left. Both sought to go beyond honesty and efficiency to make more fundamental changes toward improving the conditions of life for ordinary people. Both moved away from laissez-faire, individualism, and limited government. Both argued that no one came into this world to suffer and that poverty was not due to defects of character but to lack of education, opportunity, and environmental factors that individuals could not control. Both saw the evils of big business and were willing to take on private utility companies, especially the streetcar companies, and make the call for public ownership of these private enterprises.

Prominent Socialists and Progressives active on the municipal front were aware of each other and frequently made contact. Socialist mayor J. Stitt Wilson, for example, was familiar with Hazen Pingree's and Tom Johnson's records and knew Sam Jones personally, exchanging letters with him and working with him on various causes.[48] In California, right-wing Socialists, Wilson among them, and left-wing Progressives, often sharing middle-class and professional backgrounds, were closely tied together in the cause of moderate reform. Though unwilling to embrace notions of class conflict and revolt, the left-wing Progressives, including some very wealthy people, were more than willing to join the right-wing Socialists in the effort to improve the lives of those in the working class and the needy.[49]

With the similarities, however, came competition and conflict. Socialists and Progressives competed for the same voters and fought over which of them was a better choice when it came to municipal ownership and other issues. Sometimes Socialists won, sometimes they lost. For example, Socialist candidates had a spectacular success in Ohio in 1911, winning the mayor's office in several small towns—often defeating conservative run-of-the-mill candidates put up by the major parties—but failed to achieve victories in several larger Ohio cities, including not only Cleveland and Toledo but Columbus and Cincinnati, because of the popularity of the left-wing Progressive candidates they faced.[50]

To the Progressives, Socialists became a useful target of alarm. They frequently contended that the best way to fight off a dreaded Socialist takeover was by adopting various reforms Socialists were sponsoring, thus depriving Socialists of popular support. They, in effect, used the fear of Socialism to build support for reforms they as well as the Socialists were supporting. Left-wing Progressives in both major parties encouraged efforts to bring their parties together behind candidates who stood for measures that would steal the thunder of the Socialists. In return, Socialists frequently accused Progressives of stealing their ideas. Sometimes the charge was simple plagiarism. In 1908, for example, Socialists complained that the party platform of the Ohio Democratic Party said to be the product of Mayor Tom Johnson was lifted, sometimes word for word, out of the Socialist platform written some three years earlier.[51]

In Wisconsin, the strength of the Socialists in Milwaukee and other industrial areas cut deeply into the vote for the Robert La Follette Progressives. Seeing a common interest, at one point there was some talk about La Follette

Republicans and Milwaukee Socialists merging, but thanks in part to the antagonism between La Follette and Victor Berger this did not happen. They agreed to temporarily work together on some labor issues, but relations were unstable. For Socialists, a low point was reached in 1912 when Progressives in a statewide Republican organization backed the successful "nonpartisan" effort to defeat the reelection bid of the Socialist mayor of Milwaukee.[52] While Berger was willing on occasion to cooperate with Progressives, even his limited involvement with a non-Socialist drew sharp criticism from Socialists active at the national level.[53] Likewise, the involvement of prominent Socialists, including Berger, in the nonpartisan progressive Public Ownership League was condemned by the Socialist convention of Cook County, Illinois, as a violation of party rules.[54] In 1904 some Socialists even criticized J. Stitt Wilson for sending a telegram to Sam Jones of Toledo congratulating him on his election as mayor.[55]

For some Socialist leaders, a central problem was that many members of their own party thought a Progressive mayor was really a Socialist. Such was the case in Toledo, where left-wing Progressive Brad Whitlock was in charge. Writing in 1911, a Socialist leader in Toledo reported to a national journal:

> We live in Golden Rule Toledo, whose mayor is a philosophical anarchist and mistaken for a Socialist. It is strange, but true, that the workers have to be shown that their condition is not a whit better under the independent administration than it has been under former Republican and Democratic administrations. We are constantly asked, "Isn't Brad Whitlock a Socialist?" Then we are obliged to show the difference between a man who holds good private views but must be conservative in order to keep in office and an administration by, of and for the working-class.[56]

For his part, Whitlock may have been far from the revolutionary he was commonly thought to be, but he refused to renounce Socialism.[57] He wrote regarding the Socialists, "I hold with them in most things, in all essential points, indeed, and yet I cannot convey myself irretrievably to any system, or programme, or crystallized formula; for after all, the heart is everything."[58]

SOCIALISTS AND GOOD GOVERNMENT GROUPS

When it came to municipal reform programs, right-wing Socialists, as others in the cause of Municipal Socialism, commonly went out of their way to distance themselves from the Good Government types. As the Socialists saw it, the drive of the Good Government municipal reformers really did not call for much change at all. They were primarily asking for honesty and efficiency. Without other more fundamental changes, all this meant was that the people they put in office would "exploit the wage-earners more honestly and efficiently than before."[59]

Socialists had no objection to the Good Government goals of honesty and efficiency but argued much more was needed to improve the lives of the many. As a Socialist writer put it, "Socialism in the city is but an application of the Socialist program to the municipality. It accepts, yes, demands, honesty and efficiency but it puts these virtues to work for the mass of the city population."[60]

Socialists rejected the notion associated with the Good Government forces that political participation by immigrants and, more broadly, by the working-class led to corruption and inefficiency. Government could be democratic and open to all people regardless of class without inviting these evils. There was no need to restricted voting to the "better" people or any justification for so doing. Along these lines, in defending the right of those who could not read English to vote and otherwise participate in politics, a long-time Socialist who had recently changed parties but not viewpoints contended, "The danger to a state comes not from those that cannot read but from those who do nothing but read and scheme. . . . Never did that portion of the people of a country who could not read enslave the other portion; evils do not start at the bottom and work upward; evils have always started at the top and worked their way downward."[61]

Socialists were especially opposed to the structural reforms being pushed by the Good Government groups that centralized decision making and reduced representation. They generally disliked the commission or council manager plans, nonpartisan elections, elections at large, the abolishment of elective offices, and separating local elections from state and federal elections—moves they felt would be bad for democracy, the working class, and their party.

Socialists too were far more committed to home rule—giving municipalities greater ability to initiate action without having to secure permission from the state and greater protection against uninvited state action—than were the Good Government types, especially the business leaders within it. To the Socialists and left-wing Progressives, home rule opened the door to doing more things on the local level. For the goo-goos, in contrast, home rule was not necessarily linked to their primary demand for honesty and efficiency. They could get much of what they wanted by turning to the state, asking it, for example, to step in and take control of various functions, such as policing, that they felt had been mishandled on the local level. From their perspective home rule could be dangerous, giving more power to those who had already demonstrated their inability to govern and leading to a burdensome and costly enlargement of governmental regulations and programs.

Good Government proponents acknowledged that they and the Socialists operating on the local level shared many immediate objectives. They also felt that Socialist mayors, in contrast to many in the national party, had largely abandoned the revolutionary rhetoric and proven to be reasonable when it came to the exercise of power. Still, they objected to the Socialist emphasis on class differences. To them the divisive word *class* only created division, getting in the way of "that community spirit and lift which is essential to the development of the modern city."[62]

Good Government advocates also noted their differences with Socialists on structural matters, sometimes accusing Socialists of threatening the goal of efficiency by putting too much emphasis on democracy; were critical of the Socialist practice of making their elected officials responsible to party members and leaders; and objected to the frequently made Socialist argument that many of the reform goals they shared, such as clean government, could only be brought about if the Socialists were in control of the government.[63]

Good Government groups had considerable success especially in medium-sized and small-sized communities in sponsoring the adoption of structural changes embodied in the commission and city manager plans. These plans enhanced their ability to elect people who shared their beliefs and values. With the adoption of these changes, these middle- and upper-class business-minded groups supported like-minded candidates running as Democrats or Republicans or under different labels while, at the same time, continuing to work from the outside through research and watchdog activities to promote their goals.

Socialists entered the arena of municipal politics fully intending to be even more critical watchdogs than the Good Government proponents and perhaps even more fully committed to electoral activity. Socialists placed considerable importance on exposing conditions through their campaign and year-round publications. However, even with the help of their labor allies, Socialists generally had less going for them in terms of political influence than the many better-financed business and professional-based Good Government groups. Business groups, be they aligned with the Good Government forces or opposed to any reform at all, had exceptional political resources including money, control over jobs, control over information, social standing, a good public image, expertise, and organization.[64] The strength of goo-goos over the Socialists was often seen in the battles over adoption of structural changes (see chapter 3).

When it came to the operation of the two-party system, Socialists were convinced that the failure of both major parties, acting openly or under the cover of some other name, was guaranteed when it came to meaningful reform because they were hopelessly corrupt—the voters could only throw out one set of rascals and replace them with another set of rascals. Socialists were convinced that the only hope the voters had was in electing Socialists. For the Socialists, with relatively little impact as outsiders or through watchdog activity, becoming an insider in an elective office was a giant step.

3. The Socialist Municipal Program

What central messages, proposals, and promises did the Socialists feature in their municipal platforms and campaigns? Cynically, one might argue that they offered whatever they thought would get them the most votes—that, like other politicians, Socialists looked at a platform as something to get in on, not something they necessarily had to stand on once they got in. With the Socialists it is not so simple.

Socialists offered both permanent relief by correcting basic underlying problems sometime down the line through Socialism and immediate relief from existing problems through the adoption of reforms they outlined in their immediate demands for action. The promises of Socialism were something they sincerely believed in. The immediate demands in their platforms represented a mixture of the core messages with which the Socialist Party was historically associated, prescriptions and promises they shared with others in the cause of Municipal Socialism, and policy positions that more directly reflected the political objectives and interests of the party.

The core messages Socialists brought into the municipal reform movement centered on notions of class conflict and wage slavery and the idea that the Socialist Party was a working-class party devoted to the welfare of that class. As advocates of Municipal Socialism, Socialists advocated an array of causes going beyond honesty and efficiency, including public ownership, which became a prime feature of Socialist campaigns. Politically strategic concerns that emanated from the desire to win were also commonly at work. Such concerns led to toning down the emphasis on class conflict and revolutionary rhetoric, when and where these appeared likely to turn off voters, and to placing greater emphasis on Municipal Socialism and issues of importance to everyday workers and organized labor. Acting like a conventional political party, Socialist parties sought to take advantage of local discontent and failures of the major parties in power. In the practical mode, they shaped their stands with a particular audience in mind and touted issues that had little or nothing to do with the theoretical aims of the party or the broader cause of reform but were chosen for their anticipated value in winning office.

One policy area where these idealistic and practical concerns came together was that of local government reform. Here, right-wing Socialists put a strong general emphasis on democracy, expanded and unfettered voting rights, and effective working-class representation—stands that reflected their values and practical political concerns but also brought them into some conflict with the Good Government reformers.

THE WORKING-CLASS FOCUS

Socialists who entered the field of municipal politics made it clear that their party was distinctive from all others because it was a working-class party, indeed it was "the" working-class party. They commonly pledged that its office holders shall "always and everywhere, until the present system of wage slavery is utterly abolished, make the answer to this question its guiding rule of conduct: Will this legislation advance the interests of the working-class and aid the workers in the class struggle against capitalism? If it does, the Socialist Party is for it; if it does not the Socialist Party is absolutely opposed to it."[1] In one way or another nearly everything Socialists demanded in their lists of immediate demands or promised to do was or could be seen to be related to the interests of workers or the working class.

In the platforms shaped by those leaning more to the left we find strong emphasis on the urgent need for the proletariat or working class to become class conscious and fight back against the capitalist class that was exploiting them, a message customarily accompanied by a strong condemnation of capitalism. In its 1912 platform the Socialist Party in Perth Amboy, New Jersey, held the capitalist system "responsible for 69 precent [no explanation was given for such a precise percentage] of our diseases, moral and physical."[2] The platform went on to charge that the system

> is responsible for all the graft and corruption. It is destroying our homes. It deprives the children of an education, compelling them to leave school just when their education is beginning. It places the child in competition against the mother, the mother against the father and the machine against all. The Capitalist System is responsible for the thousands upon thousands of our daughters and sisters walking and selling their bodies for a miserable existence.[3]

The platform writers went on to make some demands for immediate action regarding existing conditions but wanted the voters to know that, by bringing down the capitalist system, it was offering permanent relief though Socialism as well as temporary or immediate relief from existing problems.

The dominant message in most Socialist platforms was that theirs was the party of the working class, and this class, being in the greatest need, would benefit the most should their party come to power. The platforms, however, also commonly attempted to broaden the appeal of the party beyond this class. An example of directly doing this is found in the platform of Socialists in Yuma, Arizona, which, after declaring it was appealing to the working class "upon the ground that Socialism is the only rational outcome for industrial evolution," went on to add: "To the intelligent and unselfish in all classes we appeal, upon the ground that Socialism is the only rational outcome for industrial evolution and the only equitable and permanent solution for the economic evils of the present."[4]

Eager to broaden the party's appeal, right-wing Victor Berger types who led the movement into political action put less emphasis on the class struggle, the failures of capitalism, or even on the differences between capitalism and Socialism.[5] In their platforms and campaigns, siding with the working class over the capitalist class was also frequently coupled with protecting the many from the few, the public interest from special interests, and the poor, common, or ordinary person from a privileged wealthy elite.

Socialists generally put strong emphasis on protecting and promoting the interest of people working for the municipality—people they could directly help as public employers should they win office—as well as those in the private sector. Socialist platforms commonly offered an array of benefits for municipal workers, including an eight-hour day at union scale and improved working conditions. The 1917 platform of the Socialist Party in Richmond, Indiana, included a list of reforms that would encourage city workers to form a union.[6]

Other promises made around the country during the period under review included an end to the employment of children, a free municipal labor bureau to help find jobs, a union label on all municipal printing, factory safety inspections, free water for widows making a living by doing laundry work, free legal advice from the city attorney to members of the working class, sidewalk and street improvements in working-class neighborhoods, and police protection for striking workers. In regard to the latter, the city platform of the Socialist Party of Richmond pledged: "A Socialist administration would guarantee that you would not meet a policeman's club when you went on strike."[7] Along the same lines, the Perth Amboy, New Jersey, Socialists promised their party in power would "direct the policeman's club, the militiaman's bayonet and the court's decision in protection instead of in opposition to the workers' interests."[8]

Most platforms also contained a list of immediate demands for an expansion of government services to improve the lives of ordinary people when it came to their health, education, housing, recreation, and their rights as consumers. With regard to education, the Socialists of Mt. Pleasant, Utah, for example, called for the "free education of all children up to the age of 18 years, and the furnishing of books, food and clothing by the municipality."[9] On health, Socialists in Daly City, California, promised, "To the end that the health of the community be safeguarded strict sanitary measures shall be enforced and a municipal dispensary with free medical attendance be established."[10] In Fitchburg, Massachusetts, the call was for "an efficient and economical hospital service, free to all. The equal enforcement of health laws among rich as well as poor. The establishment of a proper standard as to light, ventilation, over-crowding, and sanitary arrangements in tenements and other buildings, and the condemnation and destruction by the city of all buildings not conforming to the standard."[11] On matters of morality involving drinking, gambling, and prostitution, platforms commonly took a strong stand in favor of increased control, demonstrating a desire for moral uplift but also some strategic considerations (see chapter 8). As part of an effort to broaden its appeal we also find in Socialist Party platforms the Good Government advocates' pledge to bring honesty and efficiency to government, and sometimes even the promise of lower taxes for many other than the rich.

UTILITY REGULATION AND MUNICIPAL OWNERSHIP

When it came to the provision of electricity, gas, water, and street railway services, most cities initially chose to issue an exclusive franchise to a single private provider. As it turned out, however, securing a franchise from the city often involved bribing local officials and resulted in a highly lucrative agreement lasting several decades, sometimes even forever, that imposed few if any restrictions on the franchise holder. As many saw it, franchise holders were prime examples of a few securing special privileges worth untold millions at the expense of the many.

Socialist platforms commonly called for lower fares and better services from public utilities holding municipal franchises. Some Socialists argued that no franchise should be handed out without the consent of the voters and that election to decide the question be paid for by the company asking for the franchise.[12] Socialists preferred, however, to stop giving out franchises altogether and to turn to public ownership. In this they joined in an ongoing movement for which Progressive mayors like Sam Jones of Cleveland had provided leadership. A central driving force behind the movement was the perceived failure of the franchising system, especially the corruption associated with it.

Proponents of public or municipal ownership saw moving in this direction an effective means of eliminating a chief cause of municipal corruption. As a leftist editor concluded, "The advent of public ownership means not only greater privileges for the people, but it removes from the field of politics those influences which have ever contributed to the pollution of our local governments. Municipal ownership paves the way for honest governments."[13] While some commentators blamed the local politicians for the corruption, Socialists and Progressives singled out the greedy corporations as the real culprits.[14]

Basic public utility services were commonly viewed as best provided by a single provider—that this was necessary, for example, to avoid complicated service problems such as having several streetcar companies each with their separate tracks running through the city and telephone companies with their own set of polls and exclusive set of customers who could only connect with people using the same company. If, indeed, the provision of such services required a monopoly, reformers argued it was far better to have a public one than a private one—experience had demonstrated that governmental regulation of the private monopoly was not going to do the job. Along with ending or at least reducing corruption, municipal ownership, some agued, opened the door to better services at lower costs. Socialists commonly asked: Why pay more? The call for municipal ownership in the areas of communications, power, and transportation, however, encountered considerable resistance because this commonly meant shifting control from privately owned enterprises to publicly owned ones.

While Socialists made municipal ownership a prime issue in their campaigns, they did have some reservations. Many, no doubt, agreed with the views of Joseph Medill Patterson, a millionaire who had recently converted to Socialism, that "municipal ownership is only skin deep Socialism. I'm for the real brand, public ownership of all the sources of wealth."[15] Some critics within the party contended that in calling for this limited reform, Socialist were simply copying what many Progressive candidates were doing rather than calling for substantive change. As in the case of other reforms, some Socialists warned that public ownership could only be carried on in an honest and efficient manner if the Socialists were in control of the government. Otherwise, it was likely to be a tool of capitalistic exploitation, working in the interest of the capitalists rather than the working class.[16] Some Socialists cautioned that the government ownership movement had as its true objective inducing the government to purchase worthless corporate properties at fictitiously high prices.[17] Indeed, a study released in 1907 found that "an advanced school of Socialists" had declared municipal ownership "a bourgeois scheme for community money-getting and an obstacle to the development of their ideal social state, wherein acquisitive zeal is repressed, if not extinguished."[18]

Countering the first argument, many Socialists proffered that while municipal ownership was only skin deep, it was a meaningful first step toward the goal of governmental ownership of the means of production. They also conceded that it was true that the Socialists were promoting a cause embraced by left-wing and sometimes right-wing Progressives, but "while municipal ownership was an end in itself for the Progressives, it was only the beginning for the Socialists."[19] Some Socialists were quick to concede that they were not likely to accomplish much in the short run, but they were going to try to get as much as they could. The city platform of Socialists in Bennington, Vermont, for example, included this statement: "We realize that this primary aim of the Socialist movement can only be accomplished in a very small degree through the medium of our village government, but whenever possible, our candidates, if elected, will at all times favor the principle of collective ownership, as against capitalist ownership, which is based upon the principle of profit for the few, at the expense of the many."[20] Some party members argued that municipal ownership would be valuable even under capitalism in making conditions better for the working class. One proponent added, "I believe capitalists realize this as they are unalterably opposed to public ownership as every industry taken away from them and operated successfully by the people will be an object lesson on the uselessness and folly of maintaining a horde of parasitic tyrants who virtually live on the life blood of the useful classes."[21]

During the 1890–1920 period no cause being promoted on the local level by Socialists was more salient to the party than municipal ownership. The issue surfaced in two different situations. One, already discussed, involved the municipal purchase of private companies that had been providing water, electricity, gas, transportation, and other services deemed to be public utilities under franchise agreements with a municipality. The issue also surfaced over proposals that a municipality enter the marketplace and directly provide goods or services that were or could be provided by private firms.

Socialists frequently called for new municipally owned and operated enterprises that would compete with private firms in the provision of goods such as coal and ice and various services. They drew no clear lines between what should be provided publicly and what should be provided by private firms and promoted an almost unending list of what should be offered publicly. In addition to coal and ice, Socialists called for municipal rock quarries, slaughterhouses, loan offices, hospitals, dance halls, employment offices, and a variety of other products and services.[22] In Schenectady, New York, Socialists called for a municipal paving plant to "bust" the paving trust that was said to be ripping off the city.[23]

Socialists valued the creation of various municipal enterprises for a variety of reasons—as a way of lowering the cost of living, coming, in particular, to the aid of those with limited incomes; providing a better product or service than was being provided in the private sector; improving the pay and working conditions of those involved in the provision of certain goods or services; and simply taking a step, no matter how small, toward the broader goal of public ownership of the means of production. Such enterprises were also valued for providing "yard stick regulation"—a way of conditioning the prices and services of private businesses with which the municipal agencies competed.

As to helping to lower the cost of living, Socialist mayor Emil Seidel of Milwaukee declared upon coming into office: "The government of any city is a business proposition and all of the people are stockholders.... Public officials are employed to run the enterprise and it goes without saying that if a city can furnish its stockholders with cheap commodities that enter into the cost of living then it is the duty of its servants to see that measures are adopted to bring about this much desired result." He pointed to the special need for city-owned ice-making plants—cold storage having become especially important in the matter of food supply—and city-owned slaughterhouses.[24] Some Socialist platforms pledged to work for the establishment of cooperative stores, owned by residents, to bring down costs. Such was the case, for example, in the small town of Star City, West Virginia.[25]

Opponents of municipal enterprises argued that government could not do the job of providing a service as well as a privately owned company. Proponents countered that municipally operated enterprises were as efficient if not more efficient than privately owned ones. In his defense of his proposal for a municipal ice plant, Socialist mayor Thomas M. Todd of Grand Junction, Colorado, declared, "To contend that the people are not capable of managing a plant of this character or any other public utility would be to deny that the collective knowledge of the people was equal to the collective knowledge of one or more who might represent corporate ownership."[26]

A related reform commonly advocated by Socialists was to end the practice of contracting out with private companies to undertake public works and turning over the task to municipal employees. This too was felt necessary to avoid graft in the awarding of contracts but also to avoid the abuses of the contractors when it came to skimping on the work—for example, using cheap materials—and to eliminate contractor mistreatment of workers in regard to pay, hours of employment, and working conditions. In the view of a leading Socialist: "The contractor, driven by his desire to make profit, works in every direction to keep down his expenses. When possible, he puts in cheap material: he drives labor long hours, forces the work and keeps down wages by every possible means."[27] In Socialist mayor John Chase's view, requiring a city to contract with the lowest bidder made the situation even worse: "Low bids mean cheap work; cheap work means cheap money and low wages, and low wages lower the standard of citizenship." Chase concluded that "the city should perform its own work and furnish its own materials, giving employment to its citizens."[28] Putting it succinctly, Socialists in Fond Du Lac, Wisconsin, declared that work done by private contractors "can be done better and more economically by direct employment of the workers by the city at an eight hour day and at the prevailing union wage."[29] All in all, with public employment "wages can be raised to the trade union standard, hours of labor and other conditions made good, the profits of the middlemen saved to the public and good work guaranteed."[30]

STRUCTURING LOCAL GOVERNMENT: IDEALISM AND PRACTICAL CONCERNS

As Socialists began to make inroads on the local level, especially in Milwaukee, more party leaders subscribed to the view already held by many Socialists that the future of the party rested in the cities. Acknowledging this, the Socialist author of one study conceded, "We should therefore do our best to make the cities as democratic as possible and while we may not be able to get control of them for some time to come, we should fight tooth and nail every move that is made to take the affairs of government out of the hands of the public."[31]

When it came to questions of municipal structure, Socialists, considering both principle and strategic concerns, took a stand in favor of making them as democratic or as open to citizen control as possible. The emphasis on democracy put Socialists in favor of electing a wide range of officials, rather than having them appointed, and of empowering the voters through the initiative, the referendum, and the recall—which, respectively, allowed them to directly make laws or amend city charters, pass judgment on the laws made by the local government, and remove local officials from office prior to the expiration of their terms should they care to do so. These reforms were also valued for their utility. As a Missouri Socialist put it, "We are going to use the Initiative and Referendum to bring about the things we want."[32]

Socialists also stood against voter restrictions such as those imposed by the poll tax.[33] Socialists in Biloxi, Mississippi, and Grafton, Illinois, even went to jail rather than pay the tax. In Grafton the jailed Socialist, after serving three months for nonpayment of the tax, used the publicity to run for mayor and came close to winning.[34] Socialists on the local level as on the national and state levels commonly called for woman suffrage. In 1908, for example, Socialists meeting at the Miners' Union Hall in Globe, Arizona, resolved: "We demand the universal and equal suffrage for both men and women."[35] Putting the call within a broader framework, Socialists in Fitchburg, Massachusetts, called for "equal civil and political rights for men and women."[36]

Socialists commonly opposed the Good Government people on questions regarding local structure. Good Government proponents accused Socialists of placing too much emphasis on democracy at the expense of efficiency, whereas Socialists argued that the goo-goos placed too much emphasis on efficiency at the expense of democracy. Some Socialists also saw the drive for efficiency as sometimes being a cover to justify taking away or deny working-class benefits.[37] Much of the effort of Socialists regarding local structure consisted of opposing reforms made by Good Government groups that, they argued, would reduce the potential for working-class control. Many Socialists had trouble with what was known as the commission plan, especially when it was combined with other reforms such as nonpartisan elections. The basic plan as developed in Galveston, Texas, in 1901 vested municipal authority in an elected five-member board that had both legislative and administrative functions. Along with serving on the commission, each board member headed one of the city's departments. As implemented around the country, the mayor was elected out of the commission by the other commissioners or was one of the commissioners who had been directly elected by the voters as mayor.

The commission idea quickly caught on, becoming increasingly popular especially after its adoption in Des Moines, Iowa, in 1907, where it was coupled with a variety of other reform ideas.[38] Popular opposition to the commission plan was greatly reduced by its inclusion of the initiative and referendum.[39] Socialists supported these instruments of direct democracy but continued to be very critical of the other aspects of the plan as it was proposed in various cities. For example, they objected to provisions calling for holding elections at large rather than by districts or wards. This, they feared, would reduce working-class representation because this segment of the population was typically concentrated in specific areas rather than widely dispersed in a city or town. Moving to at-large elections was also objected to on the grounds that Socialists and working-class candidates would find it much more difficult to finance their campaigns. Socialists saw plans reducing the number of elected officials as a step backward in terms of democracy and as a move to reduce the possibility that Socialist candidates would win office. Socialists also had trouble with the direct primary. Even though it was a popular vote reform,

Socialists generally opposed it, arguing that it violated the right of their dues-paying members to control who gets their party's nomination. Like those in other third parties, they were concerned about how such laws would affect their ability to put candidates on the ballot because of stringent requirements as to how many votes the party had to receive in previous elections in order to qualify and because of high entrance fees for candidates.

Some Socialists saw the commission form as established in Des Moines—one that concentrated power in a small city council and eliminated party designations on the ballot—as essentially a tool of the capitalist class They also contended that contrary to what its supporters said, it did not offer any advantages over noncommission structures when it came to efficiency or bring better people into office, unless you believed that those in the merchant and capitalist class were better people than workers.[40] From 1911 to 1913, Socialists actively condemned the commission plans in Sheboygan, Wisconsin; Everett, Washington; Bridgeport, Connecticut; Pocatello, Idaho; Eureka, California; Beatrice, Nebraska; and other places.[41] They won in Pocatello and a few other towns but usually lost even in places where they enjoyed some success in running for office.

During the 1912 Socialist National Convention some delegates expressed their support for the basic commission plan on the grounds that it provided greater efficiency and "more ready action" in getting things done in the interest of the working class. Most speakers, however, were against it. Many argued that it concentrated power in a few hands, was packed with provisions that were undemocratic, and discriminated against the working class.[42] Socialist delegates to the party's national conventions in 1908, 1910, and 1912 were largely cool to the commission plan but, in 1912, finally decided to leave the question of whether to support or oppose the plan up to individual state parties or locals.[43]

The provision sponsored by the Good Government advocates that was generally incorporated into the commission plan that generated the strongest Socialist opposition was the one calling for nonpartisan elections. At the 1912 national convention of the Socialist Party one delegate declared, "Nonpartisanship? Why, we are the very essence of partisanship. We have got to be; we must; we can't help it. Necessities of the class of which we are a part demand it, and we cannot do otherwise."[44] At the same convention, a committee appointed to study the commission plan reported:

> Whether it be the mere stupidity of our so-called reformers or the clever design of politicians who seek to manipulate municipal government to their advantage or a little of both, we can see no logical reason whatever

for the nonpartisan idea.... Such a proposition would take out of civic life the responsibility of fighting together for principles. By eliminating all designations by which people would work together for some principle or idea, municipal campaigns would be thrown back again upon the worst elements in our political life.[45]

To many Socialists, partisanship was important because the political parties represented important differences when it came to class interests: the Socialists were partisans working for the laboring class, and the major parties were partisans working for the owners and upper classes. Nonpartisanship was wrong because it disguised this fundamental difference that should be recognized and acted upon. Nonpartisan elections, they felt, were also part of a broader scheme to confuse the voters, especially the workers, depriving them of an important cue at a time when it was especially important for them to make more informed decisions.[46]

Another argument against the nonpartisan ballot was that it, like another commonly proposed reform that scheduled municipal elections at different times than state and federal elections, often in the spring, would, as the proponents hoped, separate local politics from state and national politics. Socialists argued that the separation would weaken the ability of local governments to secure needed help in dealing with problems it could not handle on its own.[47] Separation also conflicted with an idea that helped draw Socialist attention to local politics in the first place—that victory on the local level would be a stepping-stone to victory on the other levels. Socialists felt they could do well on the local level, but the idea being fostered that local government was something different from state and national government, that it was properly nonpartisan and needed protection from the influences of state and national politics, made moving up from the local level more difficult.

Many Socialists felt that the party would do better if party labels were known to the voters—that this worked against Democrats and Republicans but worked for the Socialists. Indeed, many of their successes on the local level had come in contests where Republicans, Democrats, and Socialists had each nominated a candidate with the party labels on the ballot, and the Socialists picked up the most votes though seldom a majority of the votes cast. Socialists were far more likely to lose contests when Republicans and Democrats disguised their involvement by getting together to nominate candidates under some nonpartisan label such as the Citizen's ticket to run against Socialist candidates. Going one step further and forcing the Socialist Party name off the ballot would, Socialists felt, create a situation where it was not only difficult for voters to identify the bad guys but also make it more difficult for voters to identify the good guys.

Such considerations appear, for example, to help explain the joy expressed by Pennsylvania Socialists to the decision of the state legislature to repeal legislation requiring third-class cities in the state to hold nonpartisan elections, thus allowing elections along party lines. The nonpartisan system, a Socialist paper declared, had been adopted to diminish the chances of Socialists winning elections and had been somewhat successful in this regard.[48] In Wisconsin, Socialists also opposed nonpartisan elections for cities. In 1909 they were able to bat down a measure aimed at cities in the first class, meaning Milwaukee, because it was the only city in that class. Socialists pointed out that even their enemies admitted that measure was intended to defeat the Socialists in the 1910 Milwaukee election.[49] Socialists took control of the city in 1910, but a similar measure imposing nonpartisan elections later became law in an apparent effort do something to prevent future Socialist victories in the city.

The bulk of Socialists appeared wary of, if not outright hostile to, nonpartisan elections. Some Socialists, however, argued that nonpartisan elections worked to the Socialists' advantage because they eroded the strength of regular parties and strengthened the input of tightly bound ideological groups such as the Socialists.[50] For example, speaking at the 1912 national convention of the Socialist Party, delegate Arthur Le Sueur from Minot, North Dakota, noted that "it has been our experience in our town that the Socialist Party organization is the only party organization that can maintain its efficiency and its integrity and hold its party together without the party name on the ballot. We have demonstrated that at least in North Dakota the Socialists can do that and can survive and flourish in the face of a nonpartisan ballot."[51] In a different way, nonpartisanship also had some benefits in Milwaukee. Although Socialist mayor Daniel Hoan was frustrated by the decision of the Wisconsin legislature to eliminate partisan elections in cities, done, in part with the aim of hurting the Socialists, he found it may have helped more than it hurt because it weakened boss control of the Democrats and Republicans on the city council with which he had to deal.[52]

Sometimes the "nonpartisan" character of the contests disappeared at least as far as the Socialist candidates were concerned because their opponents were more than willing to call attention to the fact that they were running against Socialists. According to a Socialist report on the mayoral election in Traverse City, Michigan, in 1916, for example, nonpartisan contests "made it a difficult proposition for the Socialists at first to designate their candidates. The parties in power, consisting of Democrats and Republicans, made this easier, however, by using the slogan 'Down With the Socialists,' as their battle cry."

The Socialist candidate, Edward Lautner, won this contest by twenty-seven votes.[53]

While Socialists debated the actual effects of nonpartisan elections on their chances of winning an election, there was little disagreement among them starting in the early 1900s, when they began steadily gaining favor with the electorate that being known as a Socialist was not a bad thing. As the party came under attack during World War I, however, Socialists all around the country chose to run under different labels to avoid the stigma of un-Americanism associated with the party. Sometimes this worked out well. In Star City, West Virginia, for example, the Socialists continued to enjoy considerable success as the "Independent Citizens" party.[54]

Socialist concern about the loss of partisan elections that characterized much of the period seems to have been unmerited. While many Socialists felt they did better in partisan elections, at least in peacetime conditions, it is perhaps more accurate to say that when they did well in these elections it was usually only because both major parties put up candidates, splitting the anti-Socialist vote. The number of competitors, rather than the existence of party labels, was the key.

The Socialist attempt to continue playing the partisanship game on the local level also butted up against two central arguments: it was not needed, and it was not appropriate. Partisan tags were felt not to be needed, especially in the smaller local jurisdictions, because, compared to elections on the national or state levels, voters were far more familiar with the candidates, better able to interact with them and judge them on an individual basis according to their merits. Partisanship was felt to be inappropriate because it conflicted with what appeared to be a widely accepted norm, adopted and disseminated by the Good Government types with considerable success, that municipal government is the government closest to the people, an extension of the family, a community government, and the chief focus in guiding municipal affairs should be on what is in the best interest of the community rather than the interest of a political party. Too, the basic work to be done on that level was not partisan: there was no Democratic or Republican way to pave a road.

Even in the early 1900s many observers, including some Socialists, saw partisanship at the local level as largely irrelevant or out of place. Thus, as the masthead of a Socialist journal in Topeka, Kansas, put it in 1902: "In national politics, a Socialist, in local politics, an independent."[55] Some Socialist mayors were among those who felt that partisanship really did not matter when it came to city officials; that they were judged by performance, not party.[56]

4. Socialist Mayors: The Rising and Falling Tide

In 1898 a Kansas editor wrote, "Let the east no longer point the finger of scorn at Kansas. Staid old Haverhill, Mass. . . . has elected a Socialist mayor. Kansans may be Populists but they are not Socialists; no, they are not that bad—not yet."[1] Kansas avoided "going from bad to worst" only until 1900, when it joined a few other states in having a Socialist mayor. It added eleven more by 1920. Research conducted for this book indicates that from 1898 through 1920, there were an estimated 216 municipalities in thirty-four states headed by a Socialist chief executive, commonly known as mayor. There were as many as 237 Socialist mayors in all, some jurisdictions having more than one Socialist mayor, and a few having several. The election of Socialist mayors over the period built up slowly, enjoyed a major surge early in the second decade of the twentieth century, and went into a gradual decline. This chapter traces the chronology, pausing to reflect upon the major elections, but deferring a more detailed discussion of factors affecting election outcomes to the following chapter.

THE EARLY YEARS

Massachusetts was the first state to elect a Socialist mayor. This came with the election of John C. Chase in December 1898, who ran as a Social Democrat and came out ahead of four other candidates to become mayor of Haverhill, a manufacturing city, principally of boots and shoes, with some forty thousand people, which had long been considered safely Republican. At the time he was elected mayor, Chase was a twenty-eight-year-old clerk in a cooperative grocery store. He was also the founder and president of the Haverhill Cooperative Society and a seasoned activist in Socialist agitation and politics.[2] Labor unrest due to recent wage cuts in the dominant shoe industry helped the Socialist surge, which also resulted in the election of three Socialist aldermen and three Socialist council people. Chase and his fellow Socialists, steeped in the revisionist, Berger-like mold, had set out to court labor. Most of the Socialists in the city were in unions, but Chase hoped to appeal to the many more unionists who were not Socialists and more middle-class voters. They received considerable support from shoe workers.[3]

The right-wing Municipal Socialist platform Chase ran on included calls for municipal ownership of public utilities, the initiative and referendum, programs to provide jobs for the unemployed, and educational aid for poor children.[4] He greatly benefited by having a pair of Socialist representatives from his party in the legislature who "drew favorable public attention to the party," giving it "an aura of success and respectability."[5] Chase won again in 1899, this time more impressively, with a majority vote victory over a single candidate who had the backing of the Republican, Democratic, and Prohibition parties. Chase, however, lost to a Republican candidate in 1900 who was aided by the decision of a popular Democratic candidate to resign shortly before the election in favor of a virtually unknown Democrat—"an action that created a more harmonious coalition than the formal effort to fuse the two parties in 1899."[6] Thought to be more important in explaining the defeat was a local depression due to the refusal of wholesalers to purchase shoes produced in a Socialist city. Republicans used the scare of further business loss should the Socialists remain in power.[7] The Socialist Party, however, continued to show strength, and, following a court decision that threw out some contested votes, Socialist Parkman B. Flanders took office as Haverhill mayor in 1903, serving one term; he came back to take office again in 1920.

On the same night in 1889 that Chase was reelected, Social Democrats enjoyed a victory in Brockton, Massachusetts, with the election of Charles H. Coulter, a journeyman plumber, who, running on a platform similar to Chase's, won the office of mayor by defeating a Republican and a Democrat running for the office.[8] He managed to narrowly win reelection in 1900 by getting thirty-three votes over his closest competitor in a three-way race.[9] He lost by a relatively large margin to a Republican in 1901 but made a strong comeback in 1902, winning a one-on-one battle with a Republican candidate.[10]

The victories in Haverhill and Brockton stimulated Socialist Party activity around the country and produced several mayoral victories for the Socialists. In 1900 a Socialist mayoral victory was reported in Hoxie, Kansas. The following year a win came in the mining camp of Northport, Washington, and in 1903 voters chose Socialist mayors in Anaconda, Montana; Rich Hill, Missouri; and Sheboygan, Manitowoc, and Kiel in Wisconsin. In 1904 came a victory for a Socialist running for mayor in Coalgate, Oklahoma, and the following year similar victories took place in Bingham, Utah; Manitowoc, Wisconsin (again); and Oswego, Kansas. In 1906 the list included Ishpeming, Michigan; Two Harbors, Minnesota; Red Lodge, Montana; and Cedar City, Utah. In 1907 there were Socialist mayors in Mystic, Iowa; and again in Northport, Washington. In 1909 they won the office of mayor in Colville, Washington;

Grand Junction, Colorado; Boone, Iowa; Minot, North Dakota; Stillwater, Oklahoma; and Brainerd, Minnesota.

With his 1903 victory in Sheboygan, Wisconsin, over Republican and Democratic candidates, Social Democrat Charles A. Born became the first Socialist mayor in the state. The platform of this former Republican called for what by this time had become standard reforms: municipal ownership, elimination of the contracting system, and free textbooks, along with the demand for local improvements. Socialists credited the victory to years of literature distribution and increased prestige and goodwill for the party built up by sending Socialists to the city council.[11] The election of Socialist Henry Stolze in Manitowoc two years later brought to power a Berger-like Socialist and successful businessman who placed an emphasis on the public ownership of utilities but otherwise pursued only a mild reform program. He went on to serve several more terms.[12] The right wing of the party was also aptly represented by Arthur Le Sueur, who became president of the city commission of Minot, North Dakota, in 1909.

Elsewhere during this period we find Socialist Harry Gilham, a butcher by trade, running on a municipal ownership platform and defeating a Republican incumbent seeking reelection to become mayor of Oswego, Kansas, and the first Socialist mayor in the state; a Socialist candidate for mayor in Two Harbors, Minnesota, coming out on top with a boost from railway brotherhoods; a Socialist barber who had lost two years earlier, winning in Red Lodge, Montana, drawing upon a base of Finlanders; and, in Eureka, Utah, a silver and mining town, Socialists riding to power with the election of a nonpracticing Mormon carpenter as mayor. In Grand Junction, Colorado, Socialists attributed their victory in a nonpartisan contest to the ability of party workers to flood the town with so much literature that it "made every parasite" in town "sit up and rub his eyes."[13] An item in the *Appeal to Reason* noted the victory and how the Socialists were strongly supported by union labor. Seemingly eager to dispel the notion that the appeal of the party was limited to a certain type of settlement, the item also noted that Grand Junction "is not a mining town."[14]

VICTORY IN MILWAUKEE

In March 1910, Madrid, Iowa, which had been transformed from a farming village to a coal-mining town, a Berger-like Socialist, businessman George W. Crank, won in a three-way contest for mayor with a mixture of miners, farmers, and professionals behind him.[15] A month later came the big news:

Socialists had captured the city of Milwaukee, home to some 374,000 people, giving them their first victory in a major American city. Socialist Emil Seidel became mayor with around 47 percent of the votes cast in a three-way contest and carried with him enough aldermen to give the Socialists control of the council, holding twenty-one of the thirty-five seats.[16] Seidel was a longtime Socialist who waged a losing battle on the Socialist ticket for governor in 1902 but won three elections to the Milwaukee city council, including an at-large seat. On the council he, among other things, waged a war against the lighting company.[17] Seidel developed his skills as a wood carver and pattern maker as a child and at the time of his election was a secretary-treasurer with the Milwaukee Pattern Manufacturing Company.[18]

The Social Democratic Party Seidel represented had taken root in Milwaukee in 1897 under the leadership of Victor Berger, who became known as the dictatorial "boss" of the party.[19] By focusing on the practical immediate problems and soft-pedaling revolutionary ideals, Berger was able to build strong relations with the trade unions of the city, represented by the Federated Trades Council, a central body affiliated with the American Federation of Labor. Socialists were well represented in the Trades Council and especially in the unions representing cigar makers and brewery workers.[20] The party first became involved with city elections in 1898, offering a highly detailed revisionist platform in which the objective of municipal ownership of utilities was coupled with a list of other demands such as free medical services and slum removal projects. In 1906 Berger and others hoped to both broaden party appeal and facilitate the ability of Socialists to govern should the time come by dropping its long-standing opposition to franchising any public utility and demanding instead a course of public ownership. The problem was that improvements in transportation services were badly needed and franchising was the only alternative because the city lacked the authority and funds to take over provision of the services. The always-practical Berger pointed out to his fellow Socialists, "If we carry Milwaukee next spring, we cannot tell the citizens that they must wait for additional streetcar or railroad facilities until the Co-operative Commonwealth is established."[21] Berger successfully pushed for a change in the 1906 platform that allowed franchises to be given under various conditions.[22]

A dozen years of campaigning and educational activities brought a steady increase in votes for Socialist candidates for mayor from 2,430 in 1898 to, with Seidel's victory in 1910, 27,622.[23] Seidel's campaign benefited from the fact that the party had over the years been able to elect its members to the state legislature and, including Seidel, to the city council. Socialists in the state legislature demonstrated their commitment to organized labor. More importantly: "Union men who had no enthusiasm for Socialism had observed that the Socialist legislators worked for their interests, and the result was a tendency on the part of organized labor to support Seidel in preference to either of the old parties."[24] Seidel also benefited from a well-organized political machine. Of note was the "Bundle Brigade," composed of party members and Socialist sympathizers, through which party literature could be distributed to virtually every house in the city, in a language understood by the recipients, within forty-eight hours. This operation could be done economically because the party owned its own printing presses.[25] In the spring of 1910 the Bundle Brigade "distributed three quarters of a million pieces of literature denouncing crime and corruption in the city. For five weeks preceding the election the party claimed to have put its literature in every home on every Sunday."[26]

Also going for the Socialists was the fact that since the early 1900s, "Milwaukee had joined the ranks of corrupt municipalities."[27] As historian Melvin Holi wrote, Seidel's victory was due to "'a kind of civic nausea' over the corruption infecting Democrats and the passive complicity of the Republican opposition."[28] Socialists worked hard to make the case that they were the only party that could clean up corruption. The issue of corruption had the additional benefit of opening a temporary alliance with Good Government advocates. Seidel also had the support of organized labor and the disposition of many of those in the city's German population going for him.[29] During the campaign Seidel offered pretty much what the other candidates offered, but, to his advantage, he was far more likely than his opponents to be believed.[30]

THE SURGE: 1911

The Milwaukee breakthrough helped foster the belief among Socialists and non-Socialists that momentum was on the Socialists' side—that there was a general rising tide of Socialism. It helped produced a rash of victories, especially in the Middle West and Far West. In 1910, though, a year in which there were relatively few municipal elections, there was not much evidence of a tide. That spring, Socialists enjoyed some other mayoral victories that seemed to turn on local issues. In Coquille, Oregon, for example, the victory of the Socialist candidate for mayor in May 1910 appears to have largely rested on the incumbent mayor's support of an ordinance prohibiting cows to run at large on city streets.[31] Later in the year, a Socialist candidate won reelection in Colville, Washington, and another Socialist took office in the small town of Edmonds, Washington.

In 1911, however, the dam burst open with at least eighty mayoral victories.

The highest number before then was eight in 1909, and the highest number after 1911 was thirty-four in 1913.[32] In 1911 we find a Socialist millionaire interested in public ownership getting a majority vote in a two-person contest in Pasadena, California; a Socialist teamster who drove a street sprinkler and oil wagon owned by the Standard Oil Company defeating an incumbent in Beatrice, Nebraska; a Socialist winning in the mining town of Victor, Colorado, where not too many years earlier the radical Western Federation of Miners had engaged in a fierce struggle with mine owners; a Socialist medical doctor in Coeur d'Alene, Idaho, edging out two competitors; a Socialist candidate with the support of railroad shop workers and ore dock employees winning the office of mayor in Two Harbors, Minnesota; a Socialist, a carpenter by trade, winning the top executive position with the backing of the labor council in Girard, Kansas, the home of the newspaper *Appeal to Reason*; a Socialist in a West Virginia village of three hundred people taking advantage of discontent over a sluggish economy and with the support of workers in local glass companies becoming mayor; a railroad brakeman running as a Socialist in New Castle, Pennsylvania, becoming mayor by edging out a Republican in a three-person race; and a cigar maker, labor leader, and former pugilist running as a Socialist for mayor and coming out on top in a three-cornered race in Flint, Michigan, an automobile manufacturing city with close to forty thousand people.

Much attention was given to Socialist mayoral victories in Ohio in 1911 in various places, mostly small and medium-sized industrial centers. Socialists in these places had the backing of labor organizations and a message that appealed to working people. Platforms of the Ohio Socialists were similar, calling for municipal ownership of various enterprises such as ice and coal plants, devices of direct democracy, better pay and hours for municipal employees, and more educational, health, and recreational programs.[33] Among those Socialists elected mayor in Ohio were a thirty-year-old letter carrier in St. Marys, who outdid candidates of the two major parties by circulating literature, campaigning from door to door, and drawing support from some nationally known radicals, like "Big Bill" Haywood of the IWW, who came in to speak on his behalf; a thirty-nine-year-old printer, union member, and worker on a Socialist newspaper in Canton who was aided by the distribution of five thousand copies of a party paper each week in this city of fifty thousand during the campaign, which was supplemented by nightly meetings in various parts of the city, noon-hour talks at factories, and constant street speeches; a forty-five-old printer and former Republican who had served on the city council, running in Lorain as a Socialist and coming in first in a five-person race with working-class support; a Socialist linotype operator who benefited from an economic downturn, abuses of the local gas company, and a spillover from a strike against US Steel, becoming mayor of Martins Ferry with a 41 percent plurality; a thirty-six-year-old railroad machinist in Mount Vernon who had recently become a Socialist, running a low-key campaign, relying primarily on a visit by Eugene Debs to rally support, and came in first in a three-person race; and a forty-five-year-old owner of a printing shop in Lima.

THREE ELECTIONS: BUTTE, BERKELEY, SCHENECTADY

Three elections outside of Ohio that captured an unusual amount of public attention in 1911 were in Butte, Montana; Berkeley, California; and Schenectady, New York. The election of Lewis Duncan, a preacher who listed his occupation as "agitator," as mayor of Butte in April 1911 was interpreted by the mainstream press as a protest of how the major parties had governed the city government, rather than a vote for Duncan or Socialism. The city, they pointed out, was financially bankrupt and facing major health and sanitation problems at election time and simply had not been well run by Republican and Democratic administrations, who had been plagued by graft and corruption. Reviewing conditions in Butte, the non-Socialist *Montana Lookout* offered the observation that the Socialist victory "signified Butte's return to civic consciousness, rather than Butte's conversion to Socialist principles."[34] As the paper saw it, the respectable people of the city had simply risen in rebellion and were willing to give the Socialists a try.

The Socialist press, as might be expected, joined in offering a more positive view of Duncan's victory:

> The Socialist victory last spring was by no means the result of the sudden rising of public indignation in revolt against rotten politics that the capitalistic newspapers would like to have it appear. It was the legitimate outcome of a long, hard, forceful, never-ceasing campaign to bring the working-class of Butte to a class consciousness that would make them see that their interests are the interests and purposes of the Socialist Party.[35]

Chief among the factors cited by Duncan that influenced both the victory and unanticipated large vote not only for him but for other Socialists on the ballot was recent state legislative action that "opened the eyes of even the most conservative trade unionists to old party perfidy and to the necessity of united political action on the part of organized labor for its own class interests." Because of this, he felt, he "received the almost unanimous support of organized labor." Ranked second in importance by the mayor was the campaign effort of party workers, particularly their distribution of a party newspaper, the *Butte Socialist*, which was "distributed freely to every house in the city at bi-monthly intervals throughout the campaign."[36]

Another of the most noted Socialist victories during the period came in April 1911 with the election of J. Still Wilson as mayor of Berkeley, California, the home of the University of California, with forty-five thousand residents and the reputation of a "staid old republican town."[37] Wilson was a well-known Socialist lecturer who had been the Socialist Party's nominee for governor in 1910, speaking all over the state and picking up 12 percent of the vote. In the mayoral primary contest in Berkeley he won a close election over the incumbent mayor, edging him out with 2,750 votes to his competitor's 2,466 votes.[38] Under the city's charter provisions, Wilson's victory in the two-person contest eliminated the need for any further election. During the campaign Wilson placed emphasis on the need for public ownership of all public utilities and the corruption of the local governing political machine. He had the support of the editor of the local newspaper, who, it was reported, felt slighted by the local machine.[39] The incumbent mayor, Beverly Hodghead, a Republican, had the endorsement of Theodore Roosevelt, who happened to be lecturing at the university in Berkeley while the mayoral campaign was in progress. An observer from the Good Government reform element attributed Wilson's victory to the fact that he was an exceptional candidate with a "magnetic personality" and "compelling" oratorical skills who conducted a vigorous campaign against the incumbent, who he successfully, but falsely, labeled "a machine man." The observer went on to note that Wilson and other Socialist candidates did as well in rich districts as in working-class districts, if not better (something he said the Socialists were proud of) and went on to conclude, "Certainly the Socialist Party of Berkeley is not a very revolutionary organization, to be feared by business or the good government forces."[40]

The major single prize coming in November 1911 was winning both the office of mayor and the city council in Schenectady, New York, a rapidly growing city of more than seventy thousand people, where one found most of the work force employed in the local plants owned by two powerful corporations: General Electric (GE) and the American Locomotive Company. Leading the Socialist victory was mayoral candidate George Lunn, a Christian Socialist and longtime crusading minister, who had recently joined the Socialist Party.[41] Given his popularity with the public as a municipal reformer, Lunn probably could have won the office no matter what ticket he ran on. He could not, however, turn to the major parties, having condemned them over the years, and naturally gravitated toward the Socialists, who were looking for a winning candidate. In June 1911 the Socialist organization in Milwaukee warmly received him when he visited the city to gather information on governing techniques. In September he accepted the mayoral nomination of the Schenectady local.[42] After joining the party his language became more Marxian in championing the cause of the working class.[43] However, he never developed anything like a deep attachment to the Socialist Party.

Running on the Socialist ticket in November 1911, Lunn defeated a "workingman's" candidate put up by GE and the Republicans. Socialists also won control of the common council, which had been Republican for several years. Lunn's platform called for the reduction of the city payrolls, cheaper gas and trolley rates, and the establishment of a municipal paving plant to break the so-called paving trust or paving gang that had been, in his view, ripping off the city and the taxpayers.[44] During the campaign Democrats made a mistake by not letting him into the hall to participate in a scheduled debate. Lunn went to the streets and dramatically made his case during a rainstorm. A leading Republican remarked in an interview three months after the election, "If you could have seen him bareheaded in the pouring rain haranguing thousands on the street corners! Schenectady never saw a campaign just like that. And people haven't stopped talking about it yet."[45]

HOLDING ON AND DECLINING: 1912–1920

Studies on the number of Socialist mayors or comparable chief executives holding office conducted in 1911 prior to the elections in November and December that year produced estimates ranging from twenty-eight to thirty-three.[46] At the end of 1911 the Socialist Party was proud to report there were fifty-six Socialist mayors or their equivalent (those elected late in 1911 did not take office until 1912).[47] Following this high point, however, the count gradually declined to thirty-four in 1913 and twenty-two in 1915 to a handful in later years.[48]

An organizer traveling through the state of Washington in the fall of 1912 stopped off at a place called Concrete, which owed its existence to the cement industry. This community of 945 people had recently elected a Socialist mayor and marshal. The organizer was pleased to report that the Socialists there "are proving that socialists can take hold and run a town." He asked, "If a town, why not a county, a state and a nation?"[49] As far as the national situation was concerned, Eugene Debs dramatically increased his vote total but was left with but 6 percent of the vote in his bid for the presidency in 1912. Still, many viewed the Socialist Party as a threat. In the fall of 1913 the national party warned, "Apparently there is some kind of concerted action on the part of the capitalist class to make sure that, in every city where the Socialists have previously won a victory, this year our party must be wiped out completely. All over the states of Ohio and New York where municipal elections take place, Progressives, Republicans and Democrats have joined hands, in fusion tickets for the express purpose of beating the Socialists."[50]

The years 1912–1913 brought some setbacks for Socialists in terms of holding on to the mayoral offices they had won. Socialists in Milwaukee were taken out of power when Seidel lost a bid for reelection to Gerhard Bading, a candidate supported by the Democratic and Republican parties on a fusion ticket, by a vote of 43,174 to 30,272. Bading was a former health commissioner whom Seidel had refused to reappoint. Seidel later wrote about this loss, "The opposing politicians saw clearly that they could not risk another three-corner fight. Among themselves they agreed to fuse and call themselves, non-partisan. And the seven dailies were as one in their support of hybrid non-partisans. It was a cleaver ruse and caught the unwary."[51] In 1912 Socialist mayor John Menton also lost a bid for reelection in Flint, losing to a "nonpartisan" candidate backed by both major parties—Charles Mott, one of General Motors' founders, who ran on a platform closely resembling Menton's. The Socialists, though, did well in other contests and gained control of the city council.[52] The following year, Schenectady's Mayor Lunn lost in a bid for reelection, going down to a candidate backed by a coalition of Republicans, Democrats, and Progressives.[53] He would, however, come back. In 1912 Socialist George Crank lost his bid for reelection as mayor in Madrid, Iowa—he too would return to office. On the plus side, a Socialist mayor was reelected in Gulfport, Florida. In 1913 only a few of the Socialist mayors who won in Ohio in 1911 were able to make it to a second term, though the losses were partially offset by Socialist mayors coming out on top in other races.[54]

In 1912 new Socialist mayors emerged in Adamston, West Virginia, an industrial town of some 1,200 where a Socialist candidate, a carpenter by profession, won with the strong support of glass factory workers in a two-way contest; in Bear Lake, Michigan, where a Socialist defeated an incumbent to become village president; in Daly City, California, a working-class suburb of San Francisco with some three thousand people where a Socialist charged incumbents with machine politics, graft, and inefficiency and reportedly benefited from popular opposition to the adoption of an anti–free speech ordinance; in Eau Clair, Wisconsin, where the Socialist candidate was backed by a Social Democratic Committee in a nonpartisan election; in Girard, Alabama, where a nationally known Socialist speaker and editor of a radical newspaper squeaked through by ten votes; and in Haledon, New Jersey, where the Socialist received more votes in his city than did Eugene Debs running for president. In Fairhope, Alabama, a resort area of some one thousand permanent residents, the Socialist candidate, a carpenter and cabinet maker, defeated the incumbent mayor and a single-tax candidate for the position—he won with twenty-three votes, the candidate coming in second got twenty-two votes, and the third-place finisher received twenty-one votes.[55] In Hartford, Arkansas, Socialist Peter Stewart, president of the United Mine Workers' District 21, won a three-corner contest to become the mayor of that coal town. His victory was followed by a dramatic increase in the number of Socialists filing for office in that state.[56] Other victories for local chief executives that year came in Oak Creek, Minturn, Ophir, and Paonia, Colorado; and Naugatuck, Connecticut, with the election of A. Barton Cross Jr. as warden in an annual borough election. Cross won again in 1913.

Socialist mayors in Butte, Montana (Duncan again); Granite City, Illinois; Murray, Utah; Curransville, Kentucky; Martins Ferry, Ohio; and Toronto, Ohio, were also reelected in 1913. Duncan's reelection over a fusion ticket came with a bonus thanks to those who opposed him. His opponent was approached by corporate leaders but initially refused to run because he said the office offered too little in compensation, only $2,000 a year. The executives got the legislature to increase the pay to $4,000 a year. Their candidate ran. He lost. Duncan returned to the office at twice the salary he had been making.[57] New faces in 1913 included Socialist mayors in Two Harbors, Minnesota, where the Socialists had won in the past; West Brownsville, Pennsylvania, where the Socialist candidate took the top office by gathering seventy-eight votes, compared to seventeen for his Republican opponent and fifteen for his Democrat opponent; and in Bicknell, Indiana, a mining camp with some six thousand people, where Socialists elected nearly their entire ticket "against a citizens combination and free booze for all who would accept it."[58]

In Ohio newcomers were elected in Canal Dover, Conneaut, Coshocton, Hamilton, Kenmae, Shelby, and Warsaw. In Warsaw, the victory margin was just two votes. In Shelby, the Socialist candidate defeated a fusion candidate, and in Conneaut the Socialist candidate for mayor made up for his loss in 1911 to a fusion ticket by defeating such a ticket. The victor in Conneaut, Duff Brace, a thirty-one-year-old railroad worker and union man, won by 150 votes, with the backing of ship and dock workers, many of whom were Finns. Many of these workers were driven into political action by a bitter three-year strike against the Carriers' Association, aligned with US Steel, that had recently concluded. They were joined in support of Brace by railroad workers and just enough middle-class voters beyond the party's normal constituency to make the difference.[59]

In Hamilton, a town with some thirty-two thousand people, a twenty-six-year-old college graduate running as a Socialist won a three-way race.

From 1914 to 1916 the number of successful reelections and the emergence of new faces declined somewhat, though the party continued to have a significant presence in several places. In 1914 William Brueckmann was reelected in Haledon, New Jersey, and the following year George Lunn in Schenectady came back to win another term in a three-cornered race, defeating the fusionist candidate who had defeated him two years earlier. A Socialist mayor was also reelected in the Socialist stronghold of Two Harbors, Minnesota, that year. Going down in 1915 were Socialist incumbents in Martins Ferry, Ohio, in a one-on-one match, and in Granite City, Illinois, where a fusion candidate came out on top. Brace in Conneaut, Ohio, won again in 1915, defeating a Republican and a Democrat.

Newcomers surfaced in 1914–1915 in St. Johns, Oregon; Eskdale, West Virginia; Canton, Illinois; Adamston, West Virginia; and Euclid, California. In St. Johns, a doctor running as a Socialist defeated a fusion candidate who was running for reelection and another candidate, also a doctor. In 1914 voters in the coal town of Eskdale threw out a set of officials backed by the mining companies, replacing them with a mayor and other officials running on the Socialist ticket. Noting that the owner's ticket got but seven of the over two hundred votes cast, a left-wing paper observed, "The coal miners have evidently seen enough of capitalistic politics during the past two years to last them for some time to come."[60] Voters in Canton, Illinois, another coal town, with just over ten thousand people, in 1915 chose a prosperous Socialist contractor who was also a former carpenter and long-time union activist who drew upon the support of miners and the backing of the United Mine Workers Union. In Adamson, the mayoral contest wound up in a tie in 1915 and the Socialist won a coin toss to decide the winner. The victory in Euclid, California, that year resulted from a four-person race, where the Socialists had diluted their platform to the point where it was almost indistinguishable from the other parties, and their mayoral candidate, associated with the lumber industry, was strong enough to gather 41 percent of the vote.[61]

The year 1916 bought reelection victories in Haledon, New Jersey; and Madrid, Iowa; and new faces including the election of a Socialist mayor in Brookfield, Virginia, thought to be the first Socialist mayor in the state; in Camas, Washington, with the election of a worker at a local plant who was in charge of the fire-fighting apparatus defeating a prominent merchant; and in Barre, Vermont, with the election of Robert Gordon, a forty-five-year-old lathe operator and granite cutter working for a local company who had lost in several other runs for the office.

The more publicized victories that year were in Milwaukee and Minneapolis. Socialists bounced back in Milwaukee with the election of Daniel Hoan, who moved up from city attorney and defeated the incumbent by some 1,600 votes. The nonpartisan coalition that had defeated Seidel in 1912 had fallen apart. In Minneapolis victory went to Socialist Thomas Van Lear, who had lost in two previous attempts to win the office. This time he ran in a system that banned the use of traditional party labels as a candidate on the Public Ownership ticket. He defeated a fusion candidate by drawing upon workers who had been brought together by a violent strike in the summer, public concern about the renewal of the street railway franchise, and what appeared to be a working agreement between Van Lear's supporters and local supporters of President Woodrow Wilson's bid for reelection.[62]

Meeting in St. Louis in April of 1917, the national Socialist Party went on record in opposition to the United States entry into World War I. Socialists around the country soon joined the opposition, taking an antiwar campaign into elections including those on the local level. In Ohio, for example, state leaders urged locals to take such action in the following party paper editorial: "WE'VE GOT TO TELL EVERYBODY HOW TO END THE WAR. The very best way to tell is to enter municipal elections: hold campaign meetings; explain our position upon war; make thousands of Socialists and sympathizers by doing so, and as a result receive the largest vote ever cast for our party in municipal elections."[63] The stand of the national party and Socialist organizations on the state and local levels did not immediately work to the disadvantage of the party—indeed, drawing on antiwar sentiment, it did relatively well in the 1917 municipal elections.[64] There were, though, relatively few mayoral elections that year, and few Socialist mayors were elected—three or four in Ohio and one in Eureka, Utah.

As time went by, public support for the war effort grew, and though the party softened its stand somewhat, public support for its candidates greatly declined. Some mayors publicly resigned from the party over the war issue.[65] Hoan of Milwaukee had difficulty handling the issue, finally breaking with the party by backing the war effort and, with this, was barely able to win reelection in 1918. As historian Melvin G. Holli noted, "His close relations with the German dominated Socialist Party, and his well-known lack of enthusiasm for the war, cost him votes in 1918."[66] In that year, being a Socialist, especially a German Socialist, worked against Brueckmann in Haledon, New Jersey, and he lost his bid for reelection.[67] In 1918 George Crank in Madrid, Iowa, easily won another term even though super patriotism was as strongly felt there as elsewhere. The simple answer for his ability to hang on may have been that no one considered this long-standing public servant and conservative right-winger a dangerous revolutionary.[68]

However, things went badly for Minneapolis mayor Thomas Van Lear, who was also up for reelection in 1918. He initially took a strong antiwar position. In February 1917 he presided over an antiwar rally, reportedly attended by thousands, at which he declared that "the majority of the people do not want war" and protested President Wilson's decision to sever diplomatic ties with Germany. All this prompted the organization of the Minneapolis Liberty Society, which proceeded to organize a patriotic demonstration in support of Wilson.[69] In August 1917, Van Lear was reported to have declared at a meeting, "It has been said that this is a war for democracy, but I tell you that it is a war for Wall street and munitions manufacturers. If our boys are sent across to France and give up their lives in this war, they will have sacrificed them on the altar of Wall street and the munitions trust."[70]

Van Lear continued to make antiwar speeches even after announcing his reelection effort but backed down a bit in his opposition to US involvement in the conflict as the election drew closer, even aligning himself with a national group known as the American Alliance for Labor and Democracy, which favored US involvement. Samuel Gompers, the AFL leader detested by many Socialists, headed the organization. Although Van Lear changed his position, he refused to explicitly repudiate the Socialist Party's policy opposing US involvement. He declined to comment on the topic on the grounds that it had nothing to do with local politics.[71] His stand or stands on the war likely worked against him and contributed to his loss—alienating both those who supported the war—who felt, as his opponents charged, that he was a traitor to the country—and those who opposed the war, including many Socialists, who felt he was not strong enough on the issue.[72] Socialist Party members in a statewide referendum in 1919 expelled Van Lear from the party for his prowar activities, which conflicted with the stand taken by the national party at the St. Louis convention and for joining up with the Gompers organization.[73]

While the party had declined in its appeal during the war, on occasion it was still able to produce some victories on the mayoral level, though some of these came under a different label. In 1919 Socialists won in Massillon, Ohio, putting Henry H. Vogt, a tinner (tinsmith) and former city councilman, in office. He defeated two other candidates representing the major parties. Socialists also took comfort in November of that year in the upset victory of Socialist John H. Gibbons as mayor of Lackawanna, New York, over the incumbent mayor, John A. Toomey, a Democrat, whose reelection was backed by both the Democratic and Republican parties and the steel firm after which this company town was named. The results were generally attributed to Toomey's handling or mishandling of a steelworkers' strike, known as the "Great Steel Strike," that had broken out a few weeks earlier.[74] Because of this Gibbons received the backing of a temporary coalition of native-born and Eastern European immigrant steelworkers.[75] In 1920 victory came in Davenport, Iowa, with the election of Dr. Charles Barewald, who ran as a Socialist on a relatively conservative platform featuring promises such as the reduction of taxation and no bond issues without public approval through a direct vote, along with some reforms such as lower streetcar fares. Socialists also elected five of the eight aldermen.[76] The party, though, had fallen far from its 1911 peak.

5. Getting There, Staying There

New Jersey governor Woodrow Wilson, on a train that pulled into Wymore, Nebraska, in the spring of 1911, expressed his surprise to the Socialist mayor of the city who came up to great him that the Socialists were strong enough in this part of the country to elect a mayor. The mayor responded, "It isn't so much that, but the people out here are not satisfied with the way thing[s] are going. The vote that elected me was only about 20 per cent Socialist and 80 per cent protest."[1] The mayor's observation about support was commonly echoed. In 1912, for example, a Good Government leader wrote, "Socialist mayors, village heads and officials have been elected in a long list of communities within the past two years. Some of these are out and out Socialist victories, but the great number of them have been made possible by the votes of non-Socialists disgusted with local conditions."[2]

Socialist candidates and party officials who took elections seriously (not all of them did) adjusted their campaigns to capture the votes of the protesters or discontented. In pursing the vote, they also commonly offered a long list of immediate demands aimed at pressing local problems and fought off charges that they were dangerous radicals, even to the point of describing their campaign as reformist rather than Socialist. An example of a campaign put together along these lines is one conducted by Socialists in Grants Pass, Oregon, in the fall of 1911 that promised: "If elected, we do not expect to start the co-operative commonwealth now. You won't wake up and find Bellamy's principles in operation. What we intend is a strict honest and business-like administration and eliminate all suspicion of graft. We would audit the city books to date and publish a report in future from time to time. We are not in this campaign as Socialists, but as a reform ticket."[3]

In this chapter we are concerned with further exploration of where Socialists won, and how and why Socialists became mayors. We touch upon several factors involving the ability of Socialists to reach the office of mayor and their tenure and reelection as mayor. We also note some instances where elections were not enough to get into office or stay in office.

WHERE, HOW, AND WHY THEY WON

Information collected for this study indicates that during the period under review, voters elected 237 mayors. Midwestern and Western states stood out. Ohio topped the list with thirty-four, and Illinois came in second with eighteen. Minnesota and Wisconsin were also among the leaders, with fourteen and thirteen respectfully. With the addition of Indiana, Iowa, and Michigan, the Midwest accounted for 43 percent of the Socialist mayors. In the West we find Washington and Colorado with sixteen each and Utah with eleven. The numbers were relatively low in the East, where only Pennsylvania stands out, with seventeen, and in the South, where only West Virginia stands out, with ten. Most victories came in small towns and villages. The average population of the 167 places where Socialist mayors won at the heart of the period under review, from 1905 to 1915, was 8,337 (raw numbers using 1910 census figures are in appendix 2). If Milwaukee, whose population of 373,867, is excluded, the average drops to 6,135. The population of forty-one of the 167 places, around 25 percent, was under one thousand.

Success often came in places, though small in overall population, that were industrial centers filled with mine, smelter, railroad, glass, steel, and other workers, many of whom were highly skilled, and places with considerable union activity. In these locations workers were caught up in conditions Socialists had long pledged to address—their success likely had less to do with the honesty and efficiency remedies they commonly offered than with their image of being a friend of labor, an image they tried hard to live up to. Socialists sometimes benefited from corporate anti-union activity. Labor strikes resulting from US Steel's decision in 1909 to wipe out unions in its industry, all by itself, may well have laid the groundwork for the election of eleven Socialist mayors, seven of these in Ohio, in the subsequent two to three years. As historian Arnold Kaltinick has noted, "It is possible that the directors of United States Steel, through their open-shop decision of 1909, did more to put Socialists in office than did Eugene V. Debs."[4]

In the early 1900s the growth of Socialism among steel, iron, and tin workers in the large mills in the Wheeling, West Virginia, area and across the Ohio River in Ohio was noticeably underway. Here we find several general factors evidenced not only in this region but around the country causing labor unrest and fueling Socialist growth and electoral success: economic decline accompanied by an increase in the cost of living and a scarcity of affordable housing; the tendency of state legislatures to not only reject labor demands but act against labor interests; and anti-union policies by large corporations, in this case, the US Steel trust.[5] In Ohio in 1904, workers belonging to a leading unionized mill owned by the US Steel trust attributed the lack of work to the desire of the trust to punish them for belonging to a union. They noted that the nonunion mills tended to be the first to start up and the last to close.[6]

Socialist gains at the polls were demonstrated for a short period following the anthracite coal strike in Pennsylvania in 1902. Company abuses contributed to this "coal vote." In some places, railroad companies also helped induce at least a short-term Socialist spurt. In Florida, for example, the state secretary of the Socialist Party reported in 1904, "The railroads have proved to be our best allies in this state. They have oppressed and plundered the truckers and fruit growers until they are nearly frantic. This has made them ready to listen to us and to read our literature with avidity, until in some counties our propaganda take like wild-fire."[7] John Chase in Haverhill, Massachusetts, credited depressed industrial conditions in the shoe industry as the chief cause of both his success and failure. As he saw it, during "the depression of business for two years prior to the Socialists' first victory, the shoemakers were idle, which gave them plenty of time, and therefore they were more willing to listen to the arguments of socialism and it was much easier to propagate the principles." However, industrial conditions did not improve while he was in office, and people blamed the existence of a Socialist administration in the city for this failure.[8]

While Socialist mayoral candidates often did well in towns with a strong working-class base, they sometimes also did well in relatively well-off middle-class or upper-class locations such as Pasadena, California, where some were astonished to find that "so much Socialism should flourish in such gracious surroundings," and Grand Junction, Colorado, described in a Socialist paper as "one of the richest little cities on the Western Slope, with a population of some 12,000 people of which a great number were well-to-do business or professional men now engaged in horticulture."[9] The Grand Junction community had long demonstrated left-leaning tendencies, being supportive of candidates of the Socialist Labor Party, single taxers, and Populists.[10]

Overall, what we see in mayoral elections is consistent with Robert Hoxie's study of various elections in forty-two localities in 1910–1911 in which he concluded that there is no single reason for Socialist success; the existence of corruption, a large foreign-born population, severe labor management disputes, and other factors sometimes mattered and sometimes did not matter.[11] Campaigns, be they winning or losing ones, were commonly built around calls for public ownership, appeals to labor, and specific local issues. The party, no matter what the outcome, generally enjoyed labor support. In some places Socialists pointed to the corruption of both major parties and told voters, "If you really want good government, you're going to have to turn to us." Utah Socialists, for example, commonly argued that it was in fact impossible for other parties to provide good government.[12] Still, even charges of corruption and mismanagement did not always work.

Running for office in a small town can be said to have offered Socialists some advantages. In an environment in which everyone knew everyone else, they were likely to be evaluated by their personal qualities rather than by their party affiliation. This stood to help Socialists in places where the party label was unpopular. The fact that only a small number of voters were involved (election results often resembled those of a low-scoring basketball game) also helped by making it relatively easy for Socialist organizers to round up the support they needed to sway an election; sometimes only a handful of votes was necessary to make a difference. Workers controlled some communities and when spurred into united action could put whoever they wanted in office be they Socialists or nonsocialists—the task for the Socialists was to convince workers they were the best if not the only alternative or to somehow draw enough labor support to win by a plurality.

Workers could at times bypass the need to concentrate on the need for political support in the first place by taking advantage of the small town's social structure, which narrowed the gap between employer and employed, often putting them in contact on a one-on-one basis and enabling them to work things out should there be difficulties.[13] Absentee ownership heightened the possibility of conflict and presented a greater opportunity for Socialists and others to build a following among workers, local businesspeople, and the community in general. As noted labor historian Herman Gutman concluded, "There is a certain irony in realizing that small-town America, supposedly alien and antagonistic toward city ways, remained a stronghold of freedom for the worker seeking economic and social rights."[14]

Yet, whatever advantages the small town had to offer Socialist candidates, smallness itself was not enough to guarantee Socialist success. Even at the height of Socialist popularity, politics in many, if not most, small or medium-size communities was dominated by the business class, leaving very little room for Socialists, union organizers, or even progressively inclined ministers.[15] Socialists regularly encountered small towns where commonality in the social-economic characteristics, backgrounds, and beliefs of the people produced majority backing for a relatively stable conservative regime, leaving little opportunity for those in favor of change and encouraging them to withdraw from political involvement or leave the locality.[16] In smaller towns where campaigning customarily had much more to do with personalities than with substantive issues or "raising a ruckus," Socialist candidates ran the risk of simply being out of place. Putting emphasis on class conflict may have been particularly unwise. While welcomed by Socialists on the left, this stood to offend many in the electorate. In many places, large or small, the theme of class conflict had its use to candidates in securing the party nomination but had little if any utility in the general election campaign.

In explaining their victories, Socialists leaders were more likely than their opponents in the press to give much of the credit to the long-term work of Socialist organizers in building up class consciousness, hoping, no doubt, to encourage more of the same. Conservatives also saw Socialist organizers doing well in this respect, though viewing this with alarm, and coming down hard on who they viewed as uneducated riffraff who had been taken in by Socialist propaganda.[17]

The ability of Socialist organizers to build up the party to the point where they won council seats and state legislative seats sometimes helped the Socialist Party make a breakthrough in winning the mayor's office. By having already put Socialists in elective offices, electing a Socialist as mayor was not seen as out of the ordinary, and the performance of those who served helped pave the way by drawing favorable attention to the party, helping Socialists establish a solid standing with labor and a worker consistency, and increased the disclosure of the shortcomings of members of the other parties in power.[18] In Massachusetts two Socialist legislators "gave the party an aura of success and respectability" and were an "invaluable campaign asset" in the mayoral campaign in Haverhill.[19] In Sheboygan, Wisconsin, Socialist members of the legislature "not only showed strength but unmasked the pretentions of the party politicians and showed the workers capitalism's naked and forbidding visage."[20]

When it came to campaigning, Socialist efforts frequently benefited from the help of state and national parties and visits by high-profile Socialists like Eugene Debs and labor leaders like Bill Haywood of the IWW.[21] Some local organizers built their campaigns around holding a few large rousing meetings rather than many small ones.[22] The distribution of campaign literature was also a highly valued activity by Socialists, be it handed out on street corners to anyone coming by, to workers as they left their place of employment, or left on doorsteps. The distribution of literature was particularly effective in small towns, where nearly the entire population could be reached door to door in virtually no time at all. The same could be done in a large city like Milwaukee, but this required a usually well-organized political machine and many party members and volunteers. Still, simply distributing literature had its limitations. As a Socialist leader in Alliance, Ohio, reported to national headquarters in 1913, the local party had handed out around forty thousand pieces of literature since 1910 and was not any better off than it was in 1910 in terms of support: "If we keep educating the mutts as fast as we have in the past, we will get there in about a thousand centuries."[23]

One sometimes finds highly spirited multifaceted locally originated campaigns. In the fall of 1913, for example, the national party was delighted to pass along information on what was happening in Hamilton, Ohio:

> The Socialist campaign in Hamilton, Ohio, goes along from week to week with ever increasing enthusiasm. The young people have organized a fife and drum corps. The women have organized a "Willing Workers Socialist" club patterned after the ladies' aid societies of the churches. They recently held an all-day sewing circle to help raise campaign funds. Frederick Strickland is pouring a broadside into the voters every Sunday. William Schumacher and Ferdinand Aker are speaking in German. The candidate for mayor, Fred Hinkle, is addressing street meetings in the wards nearly every night. Great quantities of free literature are being distributed. Surely something will happen in Hamilton.[24]

Less spectacular in appearance or comprehensive in scope, but by no means ineffective, were the types of activities undertaken by Socialists in Eastern cities in 1916:

> Every night their speakers, often illiterate and untutored, but terribly in earnest and speaking with a sort of rude eloquence enhanced by their zeal could be found addressing small groups at street corners and in out-of-the-way parts of town. They did not rent halls, had no bands nor processions, but mounting a store box or a stoop, or old chair, would soon have their audience listening to what was more frequently only a harangue, but casting lavishly the seeds of Socialism, some of which must have found lodgment and nutriment, from the election returns.[25]

Campaigning as a reform party, virtually pulling out all the stops, likely helped bring in more votes and more victories for the Socialists. At the same time, the determination, enthusiasm, and zeal in campaigns brought the danger of promising too much, of setting winning candidates up for failure because they could not do what was promised. Frank Bohn, a prominent left-wing Socialist and labor activist, was among those who saw this happening. Following the flood of Socialist victories in November 1911, he wrote:

> Almost everywhere, our comrades are in the habit of making large pre-election promises, which, their officials having been elected, they are

absolutely incapable of fulfilling. If the working-class is not to lose the faith of our movement which they are so rapidly developing we must call a halt and take stock of our political possibilities. A very common error is to promise that "as soon as the Socialist candidates are in office we shall have public ownership of public utilities."[26]

Often the crucial move toward success was one of putting together a temporary, or what turned out to be stable, coalition of various groups behind the Socialist candidates. On the explosive prohibition issue, which could dominate an election, Socialists came out on top by sometimes aligning themselves with the wets and sometimes with the drys. In some cases, Socialists such as Lewis Duncan in Butte and, as noted later, Daniel Hoan in Milwaukee were even able to draw upon the Catholic vote, which usually went against Socialists.[27] A mild reform program, strong working class and ethic support, and divided opposition seemed to help explained the success of Socialist candidates in small Midwestern towns like Manitowoc, Wisconsin.[28]

OBSTACLES: FUSION, CO-OPTION, AND BRANDING

In looking for obstacles to election, one has to start with the problem that the Socialist Party, being a minority, often had to depend on dividing the vote among three or more candidates so that it could win with just a plurality. When it did win this way, the opposing parties commonly fought back during the next election by agreeing among themselves on a single candidate to oppose a Socialist candidate. These joint or fusion tickets were a major obstacle to Socialist candidates. Several incumbent Socialist mayors, including Emil Seidel in Milwaukee, George Lunn in Schenectady, and John Menton in Flint were turned out of office by candidates backed by both major parties.[29] Fusion arrangements came after a Socialist victory or even a strong Socialist challenge. In Edgewater, Colorado, successive strong showings by Socialists even brought an invitation from other parties to join them in 1913 in backing a Union ticket. The Socialists promptly refused the offer and proceeded to win the mayor's office and just about everything else.[30]

Along with forming fusion tickets, Democrats and Republicans commonly adopted policies or champion issues that appeared to have helped contribute to the success of Socialist candidates. The idea of co-opting surfaced immediately following the election of the first Socialists mayors in Massachusetts. Writing in 1900, a reporter noted, "The Socialist victories at Haverhill and Brockton have aroused comment from Maine to California. The editors of our daily papers are still busy trying to explain away such a remarkable phenomenon, and both Republican and Democratic leaders in Massachusetts are discussing how many of the Socialist demands they can safely incorporate in their respective platforms."[31] Indeed, the victories of John Chase and Charles Coulter had already led one Republican leader to openly declare, "The only thing for us to do now will be for us to adopt some of the best of the Socialist ideas, just as we have been ready to ' lift' Democratic ideas that the voters were ready to accept."[32] Looking at the election results, leaders of both major parties in Haverhill saw the wisdom of making the Socialist call for public ownership part of their offering.[33]

Beyond pressuring the major parties to take appropriate action, business leaders took direct steps to minimize Socialist votes. For example, owners of large enterprises shut down operations prior to elections, forcing workers out of the electorate because they had to leave town to find work, or warned workers and the broader community that they would have to shut down if Socialists were elected. Reports of voting turnout problems because of the blacklisting and wholesale deportation of Socialists or Socialist-inclined workers were common in Colorado, Montana, and other mining locations.[34] On the more positive side, some enterprises hoped to offset Socialist advancements by engaging in varying degrees of "business Socialism" and giving into some labor demands.

On a year-round basis Socialists were targeted with charges that they were anti-church, anti-family, anti-union, and anti-American. Socialist opponents made good use of what historian Richard Hofstadter referred to as "the figure of the renegade from the enemy cause" to make their case against Socialism.[35] Former Socialists wrote and toured the country under the sponsorship of the Knights of Columbus and various right-wing groups exposing the sins of Socialism. Late in April 1912, for example, close to three thousand people made their way to hear a debate in Minot, North Dakota, between David Goldstein, one of the best-known renegade Socialists, and the former Socialist mayor of the city, Arthur Le Sueur. The former mayor held nothing back: "When you say, Mr. Goldstein, that the Socialists are against religion and the Christian family you lie." He declared the party had never been against these things and never would. As for another charge: "If we had free love in our platform you couldn't keep our people in the Socialist Party with a club." As for Goldstein's charge regarding the disintegration of the family, Le Sueur countered: "Under capitalism the father works in one factory, the mother in another, the boy in another and a girl in another. . . . Capitalism and not socialism is destroying the family."[36]

Among the more common attacks on Socialist candidates that seemed especially effective were charges that the election of a Socialist would bring economic disaster, government control by a hidden elite, and officials who were out of touch with American values if not disloyal to the country. Voters were warned a Socialist victory would bring plant closings, worker layoffs, higher taxes, and the label of a "Socialist city," which would, in turn, scare off businesses looking to relocate, thus retarding economic development. In Coeur d'Alene, Idaho, Socialist John Wood was a highly regarded candidate, even by the editor of a local paper, who nevertheless opposed him. The editor explained, "It is not the harm that Dr. Wood as a mayor might do if elected, as he would doubtless make a capable executive; it is not the ideas advanced in his platform, as they are for the most part excellent. But the danger consists in the inference that will certainly be drawn by the prospective citizens at a distance."[37] The editor dreaded "the unenviable advertising the city will get throughout the country as a Socialist stronghold. Property owners and business-men cannot afford the notoriety."[38]

Another common line of attack was on Socialist Party control over elected officials it helped put into office. In 1912, for example, a West Virginia newspaper passed along the word that in Adamston, where Socialists controlled the town administration, "a few men constituting the inner circle of the Socialist organization are absolute dictators so far as the town council is concerned. These few men hold secret meetings, at which they map out programs for the town council and then they see to it that the council carries out those programs."[39] In Canton, Illinois, in 1912, opponents used a paid opinion piece in a local paper to charge that if the Socialist candidate were to be elected mayor, a "little inner circle" of 201 dues-paying members in the party would have more to say about public policy than the more than 2,500 voters in the city and that the candidate, while widely respected, was destined to be subservient to the Socialist "dream machine." He would be simply a figurehead and the tool of the inner circle.[40]

In the same year a pamphlet circulated by the Milwaukee Voters' League and directed against Seidel's reelection effort claimed that his administration was "controlled by a secret ring which is the real governing body—a condition intolerable and subversive of the true principles of popular government."[41] During the same election season one of Seidel's newspaper opponents declared that the Social-Democratic brand of government in that city had not only been "a government by secret ring" but "a government for class, a government for spoils, a government hostile to American principles."[42] Following his victory over Seidel in the mayoral contest, Gerhard Bading issued the following statement: "Once more Milwaukee stands in the eyes of the world redeemed as an American city, believing in the American constitution and the American government. We have thrown off the disgrace under which we have suffered for the last two years and have made it apparent to the world that Milwaukee people are loyal Americans and not Socialists or anarchists."[43]

Even before US entry into the European war in April 1917, Socialist mayors found it was dangerous to say the wrong thing about the military. For example, in 1913 W. M. Lawson, Socialist mayor of Des Plaines, Illinois, provoked outrage from some of his constituents for writing an article in a local paper in which he declared, "No man can fall lower than a soldier."[44] A mob of local citizens, seeing him as encouraging young men to avoid service, talked about not only impeachment, but riding him out of town on a rail tarred and feathered. At a council meeting, several spat on him and demanded his resignation. Calling him a "riot-threatened Socialist mayor," a reporter related that the mayor took a train to work two hours earlier than he customarily did—good thing too, because "a menacing crowd gathered" at the station at his usual departure time.[45] Lawson saw the liquor interests behind the attack and initially refused to back down, but he later explained he had borrowed these words from Socialist author Jack London not to attack the army but merely to oppose "the false inducements held out by the recruiting officers to entice young men into the army."[46]

Difficulties such as those experienced by Lawson did not deter Socialists from expressing antiwar sentiment when war broke out in Europe in 1914. Socialist-sponsored war protest meetings and antiwar resolutions were common. In 1914 a large rally took place in New York with George Lunn, then out of office, the principal speaker.[47] Perhaps an even larger one took place in Minneapolis in February 1917 with Socialist mayor Thomas Van Lear leading the way, declaring, "Now is the time to raise your voice for peace."[48]

Charges of disloyalty to the country and traitorous collusion with the enemy fed into a paranoiac red scare directed at Socialists around the county, including those who happened to be mayor. In June 1917, protest over the party's stand on the war prompted Socialist mayor Tyler Lawton in Bicknell, Indiana, to take down a red flag hanging in city hall and call off a Socialist parade.[49] A few months later Socialist mayor Marshall E. Kirkpatrick in Granite City, Illinois, was widely condemned for refusing to participate in a demonstration in honor of those who were drafted into the service and for statements he was said to have made against conscription.[50] In 1918 the Socialist mayor of Piqua, Ohio, was indicted for violating the espionage law.[51] The same year, a newspaper in Frontenac, Kansas, felt compelled to come to the defense of its Socialist mayor, pointing out, "Mayor [John] Schildknecht may have a name that is Teutonic in spelling and sound but there is nothing in his official actions that would indicate that he has any sympathy with the central powers."[52] In 1919 Socialist mayor John Lewis in Elwood, Indiana, got in trouble with a citizens group for refusing to call off a talk in a local school by the author of a Socialist antiwar publication, "War, For What." While confronting him in his city office on this, some in the group tore down a picture of Eugene Debs that hung over his desk.[53]

TENURE AND REELECTION

Though, as indicated in the following chapter, there was considerable concern in the Socialist movement and among some leading Socialist mayors about doing good and being rewarded for this by being reelected, relatively few Socialist mayors attempted to serve more than one term. For one reason or another, many did not run for reelection, including some very successful ones like J. Stitt Wilson and William Thum in California, who stood a decent chance of winning. In many cases the refusal to run had much to do with simply not liking the job and little to do with fear of facing the electorate. Also affecting reelection bids was that some mayors who were elected as Socialists left the party while serving, resigned, or were expelled, and if they ran for reelection they did so as candidates of another party or as independents.

Election returns examined for this book show that in fifty-three contests in which a Socialist ran for reelection as mayor from 1899 to 1920, the Socialist came out ahead in only twenty-three of the contests, around 43 percent of the total. Incumbency is usually associated with a higher reelection rate.[54] In the case of the Socialists, one factor that appears to have contributed to the relatively low success rate is the unity of the opposition behind a single candidate. About half (fourteen out of thirty) of those who lost were defeated by a fusion or "nonpartisan" candidate supported by two or more other parties. Going through the list of 237 Socialist mayors, I can say with certainty that just sixteen of them were reelected to another term. Five of the sixteen were reelected two or three times. Eight of them were turned down in a reelection bid at one point or another in their careers.

After assessing what it took to get the Socialist mayor of Martins Ferry, Ohio, reelected in 1913, a study done in the late 1960s concluded that his victory was "not because he was a Socialist and professed to be for workers but because during his administration certain benefits were provided for the working-class," such as higher pay and lower hours for city employees, lower utility rates, and a cleaned-up milk supply.[55] One can reasonably argue that the ability to give a significant number of voters something that materially improved their economic or social well-being contributed to the reelection prospects of Socialist incumbents and in some cases made the difference between winning and losing. Many Socialist mayors found it difficult to deliver on reforms or the types of reforms that would engender even short-term support. At times Socialist candidates and parties made the failure to deliver even more damaging by overpromising on what they would do.[56] At times too, the fault was with supporters who demanded the impossible. As one veteran Socialist noted in tongue-in-cheek fashion regarding Mayor Lunn, "There were many cranks in Schenectady who wanted Lunn to do the impossible, and he wasn't capable or desirous of doing even the possible."[57]

The epitome of electoral success must be Daniel Hoan, who came late in the period under review, getting elected in 1916 and 1918, but, in all, serving continuously twenty-four years, to 1940 as mayor of Milwaukee. In accounting for his success, a study by Todd Fulda concluded, "Hoan's long tenure as mayor came in spite of, not because of, his Socialism. Indeed, Hogan's popularity was due in part to his willingness to break from the Socialist Party platform when it was politically necessary.... Ultimately, the people of Milwaukee embraced a popular reformer rather than the ideology he represented."[58] To Fulda, Hoan's success also had much to do with his being a pragmatic moderate, who, realizing he needed more than Socialist support, built a following reaching out to a broader constituency, including a sizeable number of Catholic voters.[59] A contemporary observer saw Hoan's success tied to the quality of the political organization he led.[60]

The qualities associated with Hoan are also found in studies of other Socialists who enjoyed long-term electoral support. Henry Stolze, who won four terms as mayor in Manitowoc, Wisconsin, is aptly described as a constructive Socialist and a practical politician who used the popular municipal ownership issue in campaigning and, in office, offered a mild reform program while focusing on efficiency and economy in city operations.[61] The ability of George Crank in Madrid, Iowa, to get reelected even in wartime has been attributed to his avoiding revolutionary rhetoric and confining himself to everyday problems. Though an active member of the Socialist Party, he "did not call directly for emancipation of the working-class, the nationalization of the coal mines, or condemn the bourgeoisie to which he belonged. Instead, he fought passionately to have hitching posts removed from downtown streets while other business leaders called for more to be added."[62] A study of the frequently elected William Brueckmann of Haledon, New Jersey, suggests, "He was reelected not so much because he was a Socialist but because people generally felt that he was honest and worked hard as mayor. Most of all, they knew he spent the taxpayers' money as grudgingly as he spent his own."[63]

Brueckmann's strong support for striking workers, if not helping, did not get in the way of his getting reelected—his only loss in 1918, from which he recovered, came as the result of wartime hysteria, which worked against Socialist candidates generally.

Another success story in terms of getting reelected, also accompanied by one loss, was that of Socialist Marshall E. Kirkpatrick, mayor of Granite City, Illinois. This was a manufacturing town in the southern part of the state where labor played an important role. Kirkpatrick was first elected in the spring of 1911 along with a couple of Socialist aldermen. An editor of a left-wing newspaper visited the town in the summer of 1911 and passed along the following observations to his readers: "Mayor Kirkpatrick is a young man, 29 years old, and I heard him spoken of only in the highest terms. 'He is on the job,' is the way they put it. The city was exceptionally clean and orderly."[64] Being "on the job" in Kirkpatrick's case meant pursuing an aggressive agenda that included going to war with the local transit company over the renewal of its franchise, coming to the defense of workers in their disputes with their industrial employers, and, to the dismay of some, being soft on drinking or punishing those who drank too much. At the time of the editor's visit, he noted that the Socialists were having some problems with the council controlled by the opposition in their attempt to municipalize the gas plant.[65] Kirkpatrick's performance, though, was good enough to get him reelected in 1913. He hit a snag in 1915, going down to defeat at a time when concern was being raised over high taxes, to a ticket backed by both major parties.[66] He was, however, reelected in 1917, defeating an independent candidate by a clear majority, 1,986 to 1,911.[67] Here we find an "on the job" persistence, though undoubtedly much more was involved, helping to carry him into several terms.

WHEN ELECTIONS WERE NOT ENOUGH

In December 1901, during a labor strike in Northport, Washington, a slate of candidates put together by Socialists and the Mill and Smelter Union won the mayor's office and made significant gains in the city council.[68] Not long after, the victors reported to the radical *Appeal to Reason*: "The labor strike is still on and we will win it as we have won the election, although the democrat-republican press of this place tells us we have not got enough brains to run the affairs of Northport and that we should stay out of politics. But we are in them to stay, so turn the bull dog loose."[69] The opposition was up to the challenge. The victorious Socialists tried to take office in January 1902 only to find they were locked out of city hall.[70] The council was unable to do any business because it was equally divided between anti-Socialists who controlled access to city hall and the Socialists. The Socialists were able to overcome the problem by seizing an anti-Socialist councilman as he left the city hall building. With his addition they had a quorum and began conducting business on the street.[71] Here as elsewhere, Socialists discovered that just winning an election was not enough.

In Star City, West Virginia, two of the Socialists voters chose as mayor were ruled ineligible to serve by outgoing city councils who found they had not complied with laws regarding the payment of property taxes.[72] A challenge to the eligibility of a Socialist mayor-elect in Virginia because he had not been a registered voter at the time of election apparently had the same outcome. In Anaconda, Montana, in 1903 the right of the Socialist mayor John Frinke to hold office was contested because opponents charged he had not met the legal requirement of filing the oath office within ten days. Frinke testified that his letter of notification had arrived late, and a judge accepted this explanation.

Perhaps no Socialist candidate had more trouble getting into the office of mayor and staying in office than Harry S. Schilling of Canton, Ohio. In July of 1911 the thirty-nine-year-old printer who had been a member of the Typographical Union for sixteen years and a Socialist for nine years began his campaign "speaking from store boxes."[73] In a contest with four other candidates he wound up in November in a tie with Democrat Arthur Trumbull, the incumbent.[74] The tie was resolved by a contest between the two candidates over whether the number of kernels of corn in a bowl were of an even or odd number.[75] Turnbull turned out to be the better guesser, winning with the even number (there were 100 kernels). Schilling, however, went to court and secured a ruling that he had in fact won the general election because illegal votes had been cast for his opponent. The court also ruled that the tie-breaking law employed was unconstitutional. Following the decision, some "3,000 citizens flocked into the city council chamber and saw to it that the hostile council approve Schilling's bond and let him take office."[76] By this time, though, Schilling had already been expelled from the local Socialist Party, many party members being upset that he had indicated that he was going to act independently of the party when it came to making appointments.[77]

After his expulsion, Schilling "softly, rising to the height of his five feet five and doing a Colossus of Rhodes pose," told a reporter, "I am still a Socialist."[78] He carried on as if nothing had happened into a series of adventures (noted elsewhere) and continued his alliance with the reform and labor constituency that put him in office.[79] However, his tenure was shortened in the spring of 1913, when two judges, following a recount, declared Turnbull the winner of the 1911 election by two votes. According to one press report, "Schilling immediately barricaded himself in his office in the city hall, locked all the windows and stationed a policeman on guard at the door to prevent being ousted should Turnbull make the attempt to take office. Turnbull, however, said he would not act until his right to the office had been fully confirmed."[80] Schilling wound up serving a few months, from November 1912 to May 1913.[81]

6. Coming in, Progress, and Problems

Following his election as mayor of the borough of Rockaway, New Jersey, in 1911, the Socialist victor, William H. Matthews, was quick to publicly announce: "I did not expect to be elected."

Matthews, coming into office at the age of sixty-eight, said he had run several times in the "last ten years for offices ranging from constable to congressman" only because his party wanted him to do so. He never won, and never expected to win. He added, with a mixture of bitterness and triumph, that he had had a life of hard work, limited education, and one in which "I have been ridiculed, hooted and persecuted for my beliefs, but I'm here yet." As for what he was going do as mayor, he said, "I will try to do what I think is right, just and for the best interests of all" and would produce detailed plans after talking things over with other people.[1]

Once they were able to get through the election process, which commonly surprised everyone including themselves, and whatever legal challenges were thrown their way, Socialist mayors moved into the often-unexpected governing phase. Coming into office, they commonly tried to assure their citizens that contrary to what their political opponents had warned or were warning, they were not going to be all that dangerous—that they realized that they could only do so much to reach Socialist objectives and were going to focus not on that, but on addressing a wide range of pressing problems. As they moved ahead, there were mixed reports as to progress being made and often evidence of considerable friction between the mayors and their city councils, as well as between the mayors and members of their own party. Here we look at these conflicts and a broader set of constraints on the ability of the mayors to govern. The following chapters look more closely into what they were able to do within this framework.

SETTING THE TONE

The first Socialist mayor, John Chase, was perhaps more optimistic than others to come as to what a Socialist mayor could accomplish. Being the first, it was difficult to predict how far the forces that brought him into office would take him. He began his inaugural address in January 1899 by stating, "While it is not possible for any municipality to guarantee to its citizens all their economic rights, I believe that much can be accomplished in this direction, and that every power the municipality possesses should be placed at the disposal of the people in the interest of civilization, that mankind may progress to a grander and nobler life." He followed up by offering a program comparable in many respects to those of contemporary Progressive mayors such as Hazen Pingree and to that later offered by Socialists in Milwaukee. He proposed a long list of measures featuring, as he had in his campaign, municipal ownership of all public utilities (street railroads, gas and electric-light plants, and other businesses requiring a franchise) but also including higher wages for various municipal workers, increased public works, more public jobs, a version of Pingree's Potato Patch idea to help the unemployed, the elimination of contract labor for city work, home rule, the initiative and referendum and recall, and money for park improvements.[2]

In his 1910 inaugural address Emil Seidel of Milwaukee also presented a long list of reforms but, overall, placed considerable emphasis on the theme that the people of the city had nothing to fear. He told the audience:

> The first step of the Socialist Democratic party will be to reassure the people and relieve their minds of apparent fear that our victory means the entire overturning of business in this city.... There will be no Utopia, no millennium, none of the wild antics that our opponents have charged to us. ... We will do nothing revolutionary, nothing that would turn the tide of sentiment against us. If any question arises which the administration cannot handle, we will refer it to the electorate as a whole. After all, they are the only bosses.... The Socialist has been given a chance to show his merit. We can do this by insistent and consistent conservatism. In a way, we are on trial, and will show the people of what metal we are made.... We have not promised the workingmen or the city at large an immediate panacea for ills. We have promised the best government that we can give and we are going to live up to that promise.[3]

Several other incoming mayors set a similar conservative tone. J. Stitt Wilson announced, "There will be nothing dramatic or spectacular in my work as mayor of Berkeley. We are now face to face with the practical problems and in that respect expect to follow Milwaukee." He "did not expect to usher in Socialism."[4] In Canton, Ohio, a public statement from recently elected mayor Harry Schilling read, "Don't be alarmed. I am not going to turn things upside down. I will give the city a clean and careful administration and will put into effect Socialists-principles only where prudent and legal."[5] Socialist Homer Whalen in another Canton, this time in Illinois, came into office declaring he was going to adhere to the following motto: "Be as careful and as conservative as possible on all questions." He added reassuringly, "You might say for me, I am not going to move any of the big smokestacks."[6] Coming into office as mayor of Liberal, Kansas, in 1912 Socialist M. M. Jones told a reporter he was not going to undertake any Socialist innovations as it was impossible to do so at this time, but would spend what money the city had on improvements that would give men work, including building a new city hall.[7] The incoming Socialist mayor of Edmonds, Washington, W. H. Cook, a fifty-year-old carpenter and engineer, declared in an interview in his home (which he built by himself) that he was a true believing Socialist, but not a fanatic. All he wanted to do "was to make some things easier for the man who works [and] to make Edmonds a better town to live in." He impressed the interviewer as someone who "had learned sanity and had leavened his philosophy with common sense."[8]

In a statement immediately following his election as mayor of Butte, Montana, Lewis Duncan acknowledged that his election was largely due to the votes of many Democrats and Republicans. He wanted the public to know: "I am not mayor of the Socialist Party, and I shall try to do my duty as the servant of the people. . . . It shall be my purpose and I shall exert every effort to give as good service as possible and to do all that can be done to restore the credit of the city."[9] Later, when listing what he intended to push for during his administration, he gave special attention to the need for a moral crusade to clean up his city. Much of his concern had to do with conditions in the city's restricted red-light district.[10] Around this time he wrote to a supporter, "I think you must realize that at the present time the eyes of the comrades throughout Montana and indeed throughout the United States are centered upon this administration. We simply got to make good."[11] Making good as a practical politician meant convincing enough voters that he, a Socialist, was up to the job and merited reelection. He viewed conducting a successful moral crusade and setting the city's finances on a sound basis as central to achieving this goal.

A couple of other Socialist victors initially took a much more publicly aggressive tone, though being more conciliatory to business leaders in private. Socialist John Menton, at one time a pugilist, announced shortly after his election as mayor of Flint, Michigan, in the spring of 1911, "I will give Flint a clean, business administration. . . . I am still a fighter; a fighter for good government, a fighter for Socialism, for universal brotherhood of man. When I fought in the prize ring it was for . . . a purse. Now I am fighting for principle."¹² Still, as Richard Judd noted, the Socialists were "a minority of political novices in a potentially hostile situation" and for this reason they reached out to the business community to assure them that the election was not going to be followed by a stampede into Socialism.¹³

George Lunn was another exception to the common practice of toning down the public rhetoric immediately following a successful election. Following his victory in November 1911, those who saw him as a revolutionary radical likely had their worst fears confirmed by his instruction to reporters: "Tell the people that a Socialist minister, elected mayor of Schenectady, a city of 80,000 inhabitants, is no dilettante, milk and water parlor Socialist. He is not a rosewater revolutionist. Say that I am a Socialist of the revolutionary order. I am just as radical as Eugene V. Debs, just as much opposed to the existing industrial order."¹⁴ He was all the more threatening because the election had left the Socialists in control of the council with eight of the thirteen aldermanic positions.

Lunn, however, toned down considerably in his inaugural address the following January, stating he would apply the principles of Socialism "insofar as possible."¹⁵ In an interview a month later Lunn stated, "We are going to try our best to give an example of clean, efficient, honest municipal government. We shall be more concerned with giving a good administration than with giving a Socialist administration, although we hope to make them one and the same thing."¹⁶ He went on, as Duncan had, to acknowledge the pressure to make good, telling the interviewer, "Enough of the voters of Schenectady believed us to vote practically the entire Socialist ticket into office. Now we must make good. We've got to make good. We're on trial before the State and the country. And by our achievements we must stand or fall." According to the interviewer, "Dr. Lunn paced up and down the floor as he declared over and over again: 'We have got to make good.'"¹⁷

Interviewed as part of the same story, a General Electric official in the city did not appear fearful of a run-in with Lunn. He said that shortly after the election Lunn had told him that the Socialists had no intention of being unreasonable. He was satisfied with Lunn's emphasis on efficiency. The executive went on to point out that the amount of damage Lunn could do should he try to go off in a radical direction was severely limited by legal restrictions on his authority. He also noted, "Both the General Electric and Locomotive Companies have large plants in other cities, and it would be suicidal for the Socialists to drive them away from Schenectady by excessive taxation."¹⁸ For his part Lunn was anxious to assure industrial leaders that they had no desire to drive them away: "The last thing a Socialist administration would do would be to injure factories or do anything to close them. We indeed have always preached the gospel of more factories, as the more they produce the better it will be for the workers provided they receive their share of the production." He also pointed out that industry had not been driven away in Milwaukee.[19]

For various reasons predictions found in mainstream newspapers as to what Socialist mayors coming into office for the first time were likely to accomplish often also tended to downplay the gravity of the event or the extent of likely change This sometimes reflected the belief that the Socialists were not really going to ask for much. As one paper put it regarding the election of a Socialist mayor in Crookston, Minnesota, "Socialism there means public ownership of public utilities and protest against gang rule. There is nothing to be afraid of in that sort or Socialism."[20] Another editorial writer hedged a bit in regard to the performance of Socialist John Knapp, who had just been elected mayor of Sisseton, South Dakota: "Mr. Knapp is a level headed citizen of general principles, and just how much of Socialism he will be able to put into his city administration remains to be seen, but perhaps he may be able to take out some of the wrinkles that are plainly evident in municipal life, even in our smaller towns."[21]

Along with the notion that incoming Socialist mayors would not be disposed to do anything radical or unwelcomed by most people, editorial writers stressed that those who were inclined to do something radical would be constrained by legal limitations and political opposition, especially in the council, from taking such action. Newspaper critics, for example, argued that the proposals made by incoming mayor John Chase in Haverhill meant a dramatic increase in spending and taxes and that some of them also tended "to smack too strongly of a tendency to provide for the lame and the lazy to find much favor in this thriving New England city." Given the unpopularity of his recommendations and the resistance of Republicans who controlled the council, they predicted Chase would enjoy only limited accomplishments: "With the exception of a ripple here and there upon the surface of municipal life, things will move along in the same old way."[22]

Several years later a similar prediction came from a Montana newspaper: "It will be impossible for the Socialists of Butte to put into operation any of their platform; except to give a good administration, no Socialist ideas can be put in operation at present," largely because the city lacked home rule and Socialists, being a minority in the council, could not do much with what power the city had.[23] Another Montana editor chipped in, "The Socialists now have an opportunity to make good, and the future standing of their party in Montana will greatly depend on how they acquit themselves. It is understood that no radical measures will be introduced by the new mayor of Butte, but that he will give the city a strictly business administration.[24]

Following J. Stitt Wilson's victory in the spring of 1911, a writer for one paper predicted, "Doctor Wilson's magnificent promises and vaulting ambitions will be hampered in the execution by his sober minded colleagues, so that there need not be any expectation either of bread riots or municipal bankruptcy in Berkeley."[25] Another observer added that he was likely to be limited in accomplishment by the council, the lack of legal authority, and by the fact that in several areas little really had to be done: the city "has no saloons, gambling dens or houses of prostitution. It has always had a very clean and efficient administration of city affairs."[26]

A newspaper editor in Red Cloud, Nebraska, responded to the election of Socialist Sam Foe as mayor by remarking:

> If we understand that [party] rightly it professes to more real reform than any other party. Its principles stand for a square deal, for efficient service to mankind, for the betterment of humanity. If Mayor-elect Foe is true to the principles of his party (and we have no reason to believe otherwise) he will enforce all the laws and ordinances, give the man of ten dollars the same treatment as the man of one dollar, make no discrimination as to which violator of the law shall be punished and which set free. If socialism is all that its adherents represent it to be, we ought to be the best governed city in the state of Nebraska.[27]

The editor was anxious to see if Foe would carry out his party's principles; if so, he would support Foe, though he noted that the mayor had plenty to do. A few months later the editor warned that unless the Socialist Party in power shows that "it is more efficient, more capable, possesses a higher degree of honesty and uprightness than the other parties, its life is limited. There is no middle ground; if it is not better it must cease to exist."[28]

Socialist Party leaders and journalists often went out of their way to point out the political and legal challenges to incoming Socialist mayors, likely hoping to lower expectations.[29] Many of the incoming Socialist mayors who took the position that they were going to be cautious probably felt they really had no choice and that it was better to lower expectations than set out to do what they could not do. For the more action-minded, initially reaching out in a conciliatory manner bought time to experiment and to see how far they could go. In predicting that the Socialists were not likely to do much, newspapers editorials aligned with local business interests sought to calm fears and reduce anxieties and, while willing to wait to see what was going to happen before lowering the boom, they subtly suggested that it would be unwise for those coming into power to try to be radical or revolutionary.

Despite this overall tone of caution and restraint when coming to office, Socialist mayors often called for a long list of things they wanted to accomplish. While falling short of being full-fledged revolutionaries, they planned to be change agents, innovators, and disruptors of the status quo in a wide variety of areas. Many Socialist mayors turned out to be more assertive than their opening comments or initial efforts of accommodation with business interests suggested. They proved willing to stick their necks out on a variety of causes, especially those dealing with rights of workers caught up in disputes with employers.

The overriding objective for many Socialists, though, appears to be one of demonstrating that Socialists could govern effectively. This they felt was extremely important to the future of the party and the ultimate ideological goals they shared with the left. The tactical road map outlined by the Berger-type moderates coming into office was to do as much as they could to implement Socialist principles at the local level, but to govern wisely and pave the way for doing far more for the cause at the state and federal levels than they could do locally. They felt if the party did well with the municipal electorate, this success would build up support for the party on the state and federal levels, where Socialists could use their power to bring about Socialism in a big way. Success on the local level meant being practical and opportunistic when it came to policy choices. At the same time, those moderates in power could reassure party leftists and idealists that the ultimate revolutionary goals were still the ultimate objective to be reached sometime down the road.

The thought that Socialists in power were being watched and had to make good found expression not only in the words of Duncan and Lunn and other mayors but in the words of national party spokesman Carl Thompson, who wrote in 1913, "When the Socialist Party is entrusted with official position, it is, in a sense, on trial—being put to the test. And unless we can make good, our movement will suffer, not only locally, but nationally."[30] In addition to or perhaps even more important than making their party look good, some Socialist mayors expressed a strong desire to make people in their class or station in life look good. An example is found in the remarks of Socialist Robert Murray, a working-class preacher and clay miner. As mayor-elect of Toronto, Ohio, dressed in "grimy clay-miner clothes," he told a reporter that he hoped to "prove that a clay miner can administer [community] affairs better than could those heretofore chosen from other walks of life."[31] Around the same time, a report came in from Martins Ferry, Ohio, with a Socialist mayor and a supportive council dominated by steel workers, that the new regime set out to prove that "the workers can take hold of the affairs of a municipality and administer them more efficiently than had been done by old-party officials."[32]

PROBLEMS WITH THE COUNCIL

In 1912–1913, the Information Department of the national Socialist Party, headed by Carl Thompson, surveyed officials and party workers around the country to find out how well Socialists in power at the local level were doing. The responses provided a mixed picture. Many of the returns from Socialist officials elected in small towns reported they had made some progress but not as much as they would like. The mayor of the town of O'Fallon, Illinois, with a population of just over two thousand, for example, reported that officials in towns as small as his just "don't go up against big problems like a large city," but he had "accomplished some little things" like improving the wages of city employees, cutting back on contracting for city work with private companies, and forcing railroad officials to put a flagman or watchman on street crossings. He would have done more but had aroused the opposition of the streetcar company, Business Men's Association, the saloon men, and the churches.[33] From the village of Davis, Illinois, came the message, "Since the scope of administrative affairs is necessarily small in any village we have nothing ... to offer as yet. Our object has been mostly to encourage the growth of Socialistic sentiment which I think we are doing."[34]

Officials in several reports declared their biggest problem was the lack of support in their city or town councils, sometimes even having trouble with council members belonging to their own party. In 1913 the Socialist mayor of Fostoria, Ohio, W. M. Ralston, reported to Thompson that thus far the story of his administration had been "a tale of trials and privation." His election had been challenged on a technicality, and when it came to getting things done, he had to work with a seven-person city council, only one of which was a Socialist. He related, "Everything we have tried to do has been opposed by the old party members on the Council and what we have accomplished has been done in SPITE of them."[35] In another letter from Ohio, Socialist mayor E. E. Robinson of Mineral Ridge related he was told by the non-Socialist council that they would never help make any improvements in the city while a Socialist was mayor.[36]

Other mayoral accounts of a similar nature showed up in various publications. Socialist Fred Swain, elected mayor of Minden, Missouri, in 1911, reported early in 1912 that the greatest obstacle he was facing "is an old party council who do not believe in anything Socialistic." Still, he was proud to report:

> I have given the city a good administration. The town used to have no Sunday: today it is as peaceful as any town on that day. We had an empty treasury to replenish and the street work had been left undone for a long

time which has all been repaired. As to what we expect to do in the future, it is simply to try to capture the council at the spring election and we have several things Socialistic to do.[37]

Swain's remarks showed up in the same issue of the *Appeal to Reason* that contains a report from Socialist mayor W. E. Griffin, in Beatrice, Nebraska. Griffin related that at the start of his administration he had some trouble getting his appointments confirmed. He had made some progress on this but was having trouble getting ordinances and resolutions adopted. He noted that the council tabled consideration of his proposal to raise the hourly wages of unskilled workers and turned down the appointment of a Socialist to fill a vacant council seat.[38] In Flint, Michigan, nine non-Socialist councilmen who regularly turned down the Socialist mayor's proposals became known in Socialist circles as the "automatic nine."[39] In Manitowoc, Wisconsin, the Socialist mayor was frequently frustrated by an obstructionist group of three, the "rule or ruin" element, who were often able to win over one other member on the seven-membered council to vote down the mayor's recommendations.[40]

Mayor William Brueckmann, of Haledon, New Jersey, had a royal battle with a council dominated by Republicans over his attempt to appoint a Socialist as city clerk. The struggle finally broke in his direction after many citizens (reportedly four hundred of the borough's five hundred eligible voters) showed up at a council meeting to protest the deadlock, which was holding up all council business. Faced with this demonstration, the councilmen backed down.[41] Lively disputes of this nature also took place in Eureka, Utah, where the Republican majority on the council turned down every appointment made by Socialist mayor Andrew Mitchell. The press reported, "The whole town is in an uproar and there promises to be more excitement if some sort of an agreement is not reached."[42]

A similar, if not more emotional, outbreak occurred in New Castle, Pennsylvania, where Socialist mayor Walter V. Tyler's recommended appointments, most of whom were Socialists, were regularly turned down by the council. Tyler was eventually able to get some of these through, but others were more difficult. To break the deadlock, Socialists organized protest rallies and at one point encouraged their followers to pack the chambers at an upcoming council meeting. As Arnold Kaltinick described the following events:

> A pack of high-spirited Socialists, many of them young, marched on City
> Hall, banners of protest aflutter, accompanied by a Finnish brass band blaring
> the "Marseillaise" for all to hear. After a brief rally they moved inside where

they packed the chambers wall to wall. Then came the vote on the mayor's appointments. When the motion lost on a strictly partisan vote bedlam broke out; taunts, hisses, boos, cries of "liars," "cowards," and "crooks" broke forth from the crowd.[43]

Tyler reported to Thompson in September 1913 that "the stand pat members" of the council "handicap us by cutting appropriations or failing to appropriate [and] failing to confirm appointments; in fact, we have had no Food Inspector for four months."[44] His frustration was also demonstrated in a Socialist newspaper article where he reported that under a reorganization prompted by a change in state law calling for a modified commission plan, he was still mayor but had lost much of his authority and was the only Socialist on a five-member commission. Being outvoted four to one, Tyler was unable to do much for the working class and was unable to stop the other commissioners, who, working together, were "doing everything that could be expected of capitalistic politicians from (the) giving away of franchises to preparing to club strikers. . . . When we go into session everything is 'cooked' in fact it is simply a question of introducing and voting. They refuse to publicly discuss even questions of the most vital importance." About the only thing he could do was call attention to their rottenness.[45] In December 1913 the other commissioners fired everyone who had been appointed by the Socialist mayor.[46]

In remarking on his accomplishments as mayor, J. Stitt Wilson began by saying, "As a matter of fact Berkeley has never had a 'Socialist Administration.' There have been a Socialist mayor and one councilman in a board of five. The anti-Socialist majority worked harmoniously with us on general municipal matters, but stood pat for capitalism each time we presented a genuine Socialist proposition."[47] Wilson cited council opposition to his proposals for municipal ownership and adoption of the single tax as his chief reasons for not seeking reelection. Difficulty in getting along with other council members also prompted Arthur Le Sueur to resign as president of the Minot, North Dakota, city commission in 1911. His action was in accord with a recommendation of the local party, which did not disapprove of what he had been doing but felt that under present conditions, he could not effectively govern, because of the unpopularity of his policies and his minority status on the council.[48]

Although Socialist mayors commonly had problems with their councils, they did have some resources—using their formal powers to veto measures or make appointments, though these, as indicated earlier, were not likely to do much good if the council was solidly against them, which was often the case. More important was taking their case to the public and appealing for public support. Some drew upon the assistance of union members and rank-and-file Socialists in exerting pressure on the council. As the editor of a left-wing newspaper reported with considerable admiration in 1909: "In Milwaukee, with seventeen of them on the council, whenever the Socialists have an important measure that they wish to push, they send word to the unions, pack the galleries, and when the question comes up the trembling representatives of great corporation interests look upon the voters crowding the galleries, watching their moves of profit-grabbing legislation, and are impressed with the fact that it behooves them to be cautious."[49] Socialist Party members too were known to show up in the galleries. This appears to have been the case in Sisseton, South Dakota, which had a Socialist mayor in 1913 and 1914. Here a party organizer noted that while there were only twenty-three Socialist members in the town of around 1,400 people, they "think we are many because we holler so loud."[50]

To be sure, most Socialist mayors had serious trouble with their city councils regarding appointments and policy recommendations because they were dominated by non-Socialists; but in addition they also sometimes found it difficult to get along with fellow Socialists on the council. Socialist council members sometimes were less radical or serious about their commitment to Socialism and more willing to compromise on Socialist principles when it came to policy than the Socialist mayor. At other times, the opposite was true. In Iowa, for example, Socialist mayor Charles Barewald resigned from the party late in 1920, charging that several of his fellow party members on the council were too radical, too unwilling to consider anything that savored of conservatism. Speaking to reporters, the mayor declared, "My leaving the Socialist party is the best thing I have ever done. I've been trying to get along with the radical aldermen in the council but it is no longer possible. I have no cooperation from Socialist aldermen in the council and they have permitted their radical ideas to interfere with the welfare of the city."[51]

AT WAR WITH THE PARTY

In April 1911, shortly after voters chose Socialist John Wood mayor of Coeur d'Alene, Idaho—a victory that surprised everyone, including the Socialist candidates—national organizer Anna Maley arrived in town. She told a gathering of party members that the Socialist city administration could accomplish much in terms of reform, just as the Socialist administration had done in Milwaukee, but that there were likely to be "misunderstandings" between the local Socialist organization and the newly elected Socialist officials:

"The Socialist organization may not always promptly perceive the practical difficulties with which the elected candidates must cope. These officials, on the other hand, will not appreciate the anxiety of those who have given years of bitter struggle to the building of our organization even to its present imperfect stage."[52]

Not long after this, the local party declared it was going to take a position on all matters coming before the council by majority vote and if the mayor and council people refused to be bound by these decisions they would face removal from office.[53] Wood, however, rejected efforts of party members to dictate policy, saying he was a servant of the people, not a particular party, and that the party was no more than one source of advice. Following a dispute over the selection of the police chief, the local party voted to submit Wood's resignation through one of the Socialist city council members, but Socialists on the council split two to two over accepting the resignation and non-Socialists on the council uniformly supported Wood's retention. Wood declared he was "proud of being a Socialist" but would not resign from office. The local party responded by expelling Wood. He went on, however, to complete his two-year term, pushing for reform measures along with the four Socialist city council members.[54]

Intraparty conflict usually came early on in a new mayor's administration, when appointments had to be made and when Socialists were trying to map out an issue agenda. In the spring of 1911, for example, Mayor Griffin of Beatrice, Nebraska, was in deep trouble with party leaders less than a month in office.[55] The local Socialist Party got around to asking the mayor to resign from office in December because he had, against their wishes, appointed non-Socialists to the police department and had signed an ordinance that increased the price of gas to consumers. Griffin shrugged off the request, saying he had already withdrawn from the party.[56] One can cite other examples of mayors brushing aside resignation demands coming from the local parties. In July 1911, members of the Socialist local party in Berkeley became angry with Wilson over his appointment of a city attorney and asked him for a letter of resignation that they could present to the city council. He had not, in violation of party norms, provided the party with such a letter. Wilson simply refused to provide such a letter, noting he was responsible to the people of the city, not the party.[57]

In Missoula, Montana, we also see attempts at forcing a resignation easily averted. In 1915 party members from the more radical wing of the party took control of the local party and demanded that Socialist mayor Andrew Getchell and Socialist commissioner Dale Hodson take various courses of action. Their demands were ignored. The local party then voted to submit the resignations Getchell and Hodson had filed with the party to a commissioner named Houston, the only remaining member of the city council. Houston refused to participate in the vote on whether to accept the resignations. At a special session of the council, Getchell moved that Hodson's resignation not be accepted and both of them vote in favor the motion. This was followed by a motion by Hodson that the resignation of Getchell not be accepted and both of them voted in favor of the motion.[58]

In Ohio, there were a series of attempted ousters of Socialist mayors by Socialist Party locals. In January 1912 Lima, Ohio, Socialists, unhappy about an appointment made by Socialist mayor Corbin N. Shook, presented to the city council the written letter of resignation the party had secured from Shook prior to his election. Shook repudiated the resignation and asked the council to ignore it. The council, except for two members who were Socialists, went along with the mayor and refused to recognize the right of the party to force the resignation. Socialists in the gallery reportedly responded with a chorus of hisses and cat calls.[59] Shook was later expelled from the party for refusing to cooperate with it.[60] In March 1912 Mayor Thomas Pape in Lorain, Ohio, asserted his independence from the local party in making appointments, prompting angry Socialists to call on the city council to accept his pre-signed resignation, but, as in Lima, the council over the objections of the two Socialist members refused to accept the resignation.[61]

A similar series of events took place in Mount Vernon, Ohio. In April 1913 the Socialist local issued a statement accusing Socialist mayor Alfred Perrine of ignoring the party—charging that he seldom attended party meetings and, when doing so, acted though he wished he were somewhere else, and that at these meetings and on other occasions he arrogantly dismissed party recommendations on appointments and other matters. The local party considered him to be someone who knew nothing about the party rules that governed his conduct and did not care to know. It added, "Had he joined the party for the express purpose of disorganizing the Socialist Party in Mt. Vernon he could not have done a much better job of it."[62] Local party officials said he violated the state party's constitution and they had no choice but to present his resignation to the council. The mayor said he not the party, was running the city, and denounced this party's action. The council paid no attention to the resignation submitted by the party.[63] Perrine ran as an independent at the next election and won.

Lewis Duncan followed party rules when it came to making appointments—all his were cleared through the party's city central committee.[64] For him, the problem was that the local party changed directions and a hostile faction under the influence of the Industrial Workers of the World attempted to force his resignation.⁶⁵ This came shortly after he had defied the mine owners, won reelection, and was about to go to battle again with them. The state party was able to sidetrack the recall, but all this prompted an observation in the *Miners Magazine:*

> Such a condition of affairs well illustrates why the Socialist Party refuses to tolerate in its membership those who do not believe heartily in political action. Let a movement become honey combed with those who sneer at working for votes, office holding, and the plodding tasks of city administration and legal change and just when solidarity and mutual support are most needed, disruption and discord will bring all to a standstill.⁶⁶

The ability of local parties to institute a recall proceeding may have had a deterring effect influencing the decisions of Socialist mayors to do or not to do various things, but efforts to force resignations frequently failed because city councils refused to honor them. Socialist parties frequently used a fallback remedy of expulsion from the party. In George Lunn's case, long-standing tension between him and the local party in Schenectady, principally over patronage, eventually led to his being read out of the party by the state executive committee. He later charged, "Efficient Socialist mayors and other officials have been expelled from the Socialist organization all over this country because they refused to be controlled by a small coterie of the party machine. I do not know of a single case where they were expelled from the organization for inefficiency."⁶⁷ Mayors who were expelled generally continued in office, but their future, should they choose to run again, became a bit cloudier. Some ran as independents.

Some Socialist mayors were quick to defend the idea of party control. For example, following criticism for taking advice from local party leaders, Mayor Brueckmann of Haledon, New Jersey, responded, "My party elected me, and I intend to follow its advice whether this council likes it or not."⁶⁸ He and Seidel, who also stated that he planned to work with the party organization on appointments and policies, seemed to have largely avoided conflict with the local party. The advanced resignation system was regularly featured in Socialist campaigns as a guarantee that Socialist office holders were not going to be like those of the old parties—the grafters, liars, scoundrels, and thieves they regularly put into office. Some Socialists felt that the advanced resignation system was effective in avoiding these types of problems.⁶⁹ Along with calling for a resignation and expulsion, party members officially or unofficially simply denounced mayors of their own party who they felt had failed to protect the working class. In Grand Junction, Colorado, for example, party workers were applauded in Socialist circles for denouncing the Socialist mayor's decision to order all unemployed men out of town. Pulling no punches, one Socialist critic of the mayor declared, "The rank and file are all right, always have been right and always will be. It is high time the Grand Junction Socialists showed their so-called mayor that he has not delivered the goods to the working-class and shoved him back into the oblivion where he belongs."[70]

7. Being Mayor: Limitations, Opportunities, and Roles

What was it like to be a Socialist mayor? Mayor Duncan of Butte found it to be about as dangerous as it gets. He was stabbed three times by a fellow Socialist, finally shooting and killing the attacker.[1] For Mayor Seidel, intense personal criticism in the press, something he had not anticipated and prepared for, prompted him to flee to a secluded and quiet sanctuary, the location of which his wife and secretary refused to disclose, in order to withdraw and relax.[2]

For others there were varying degrees of work frustration that varied with the size and resources of the community served, the degree of political opposition, and individual temperaments. Here we look at some of the basic limitations of the job, focusing on Socialist administrations and political life in the places where Socialists were most successful: small towns. We also look at varying attitudes toward the job, and various roles customarily played by mayors.

THE ROUTINE AND BASIC LIMITATIONS

Generally, it can be said that Socialist mayors spent much of their time thinking about pressing municipal problems, involving such matters as finances, sewers, sidewalks, streets, sanitation, gambling, drunks, stray pets, and loose chickens. As historians John McCormick and John Sillito have suggested, many of them may have welcomed dealing with routine tasks as a way of demonstrating to voters that they were dedicated and capable administrators eager to stay in touch with the concerns and problems of their constituents no matter how small, rather than, as their political opponents warned, being out-of-control revolutionaries with crazy ideas.[3] While perhaps helping to demonstrate that they were up to the job, focusing on the routine tasks left little time for thinking about big plans or revolutionary action that would hasten the day of the cooperative commonwealth.

Socialist mayors in municipalities of all sizes who sought to go beyond the routine and pursue more basic policy objectives were often handicapped by problems of authority and finance. During the period under review, mayors throughout the country found that the lack of local home rule powers and their inability to get around unwanted state interference in local operations severely limited their ability to govern. Many sought to change state policy, publicly voicing the need for reform and lobbying state legislators. Compared to Democratic or Republican mayors, Socialists were at a disadvantage when it came to challenging state policy—they had but a few, if any, legislators to work with at the state level and few statewide office holders who shared their party affiliation.

Milwaukee was one of many localities where Socialists had very limited legal authority to undertake programs. Businessmen were satisfied with the existing restraints on the city and had used their ability to shoot down efforts in the state legislature to extend local power. They had turned back a drive to extend local home rule in 1908 and were confident of their ability to do so again if necessary. Socialists coming to power in 1910 and hoping to extend city activities had little choice but to go to the legislature to seek specific authority to do something. By the end of 1911 they had made over forty requests to take specific steps, most of which, including the authority to go after loan sharks and provide legal services to people who could not afford a lawyer, were turned down.[4] Socialists here as elsewhere were a force pushing for home rule but also were a prime reason why it was difficult to get it—the fear of Socialist control on the local level made the cause of home rule more difficult.

As the previous chapter indicated, two of the most difficult challenges facing Socialist mayors were getting along with the council and members of their own party. Socialists commonly found that although they held the office of mayor, they did not have enough council seats to effectively govern. The practice of holding elections at large contributed to the lack of council victories, though there were problems even when a district system was used, because district lines were drawn to discriminate against Socialist candidates.

THE SMALL-TOWN SETTING

The problem of implementing a reform agenda was especially pronounced in small towns or villages. In these places the governmental agenda had traditionally been very limited and the lack of finances, staff, and professional help were especially apparent. With limited help, the mayors did much of the administrative and management work that their counterparts in large cities delegated to others.

The fact that a community was small could under some circumstances, as indicated earlier, work to the advantage of getting a Socialist mayor elected. However, short terms of one or two years and sudden shifts in opinion (it took only a few malcontents in a small town to get things going), leading to frequent turnover in office, made it difficult for mayors to have enough time in office to make much of an impact. In the small town of Adamston, West Virginia, one finds a prime example of people simply voting for the candidate they liked best, regardless of what ticket they ran on, sudden shifts in sentiment, and constant turnover. From 1910 to 1915 the town was governed by six different mayors from five different political parties.[5] Nobody served very long. As Richard Judd found regarding Ohio, "In most cases Socialists simply were not afforded the time to demonstrate the advantages the party offered workingmen."[6]

In some places Socialists were well entrenched in the life of the community and well respected. In the working-class town of Star City, West Virginia, with just over three hundred residents, for example, the Socialist Party local, the Young People's Socialist League, and the leftward-inclined Local of the Glass Workers' Union were pillars of community life.[7] In various parts of the country the party provided a wide variety of party-sponsored community gatherings featuring dancing, games, picnics, and entertainers of various sorts.[8] Some locals had brass bands or even Socialist orchestras. As one might expect, one could find hard-liners denouncing such activities, insisting on strict devotion to the class struggle and the serious business of revolution. A hard-nose member of a Finnish local in Wisconsin complained, "It was said that if we had a hall, then we really would go to work. We now have a hall and we have started energetically—to dance!"[9] He had had enough of what was commonly referred to as "Hall Socialism." Socialist mayors, more appreciative of the value of social gatherings and aware of expectations as to their involvement, were generally kept busy attending, speaking, or presiding over not only party-sponsored activities, many of which were open to the public, but at a variety of other public events as chief representative of the municipal government.

In the friends and neighbor's community atmosphere, the fact that the mayor or someone else was a Socialist did not appear to be of any particular significance to most people or even most local newspapers. This seems to have been the case as far as the leading newspaper in Madrid, Iowa, which covered Socialist candidates and office holders such as George Crank, who was elected mayor several times starting in 1912, no differently than they covered the activities of candidates and office holders who were Democrats or Republicans.[10] Another example as far as newspapers are concerned involves Socialist John McKay, who in 1911 defeated a five-term incumbent for the office in Salem, Ohio, a town of some nine thousand people. A paper in a neighboring small town referred to McKay eleven times from December 1911 to April 1913 but identified him as a Socialist only in the first mention, one reporting his election, and then in just passing without comment.[11] Most of the coverage given the mayor involved his rulings in the mayor's court (see below) and personal items such as: "Mayor elect McKay quit work Wednesday at the Victor stove foundry and with his family will spend next week visiting relatives in other places before taking up the duties of mayor." In another issue came: "Mayor McKay has a dog that has such a fondness for milk that he slips upon the porches of neighbors and carries away full milk bottles. Then he noses in the paper top, tips the bottle and laps up the lacteal fluid."[12]

Newspaper coverage of Socialist mayors in small towns elsewhere also simply considered them as members of the community whose personal experiences, adventures, or activities, humorous or otherwise, were worthy of being briefly noted and passed along as items of gossipy interest. In the case of Socialist mayor Eric Dale of Rugby, North Dakota, for example, readers were given the following bits of information: May 3, 1912, "Mayor Dale of Rugby was arrested for speeding his auto"; August 16, 1912, "Mayor Dale of Rugby cuts the weeds on the streets of that fair city with his own team and mower"; and October 4, 1912, "Mayor Eric Dale of Rugby had his foot smashed while running a gasoline tractor."[13]

Neglecting to mention that the mayor was Socialist or playing it down may in some cases have reflected the feeling among small-town newspaper owners and managers that this fact was not all that salient in the prevailing climate of personal rather than partisan politics or no big deal because a Socialist was not likely to be willing or able to do much damage under existing legal, financial, and political conditions. It was also likely, perhaps more likely, that such information was not mentioned because local journalists did not want to mention it out of embarrassment or, with the backing of the local business community, out of fear that it would put a Socialist label on the town and, thus, scare off investors and hamper economic development. In Stillwater, Oklahoma, even some of a successful Socialist candidate's supporters wanted the local press to falsely publish that the candidate had run as independent in order to avoid damaging the town economically.[14]

On a day-to-day level, much of the time and effort of Socialist mayors was devoted to problems of law and order. In some states small-town mayors presided over what was known as the "mayor's court" or "police court," hearing civil and criminal cases involving municipal ordinances, which were somewhat like those heard by a Justice of the Peace.[15] Some indication of the activity in these courts is found in newspaper reports on the activities of Mayor McKay in Salem. Reports covering the 1911–1913 period show him hearing complaints from the ministerial association over the lack of enforcement of the city's blue laws prohibiting movies being shown on Sunday and over prize fighting being conducted in the city; warning the proprietors of "questionable joints" (bars, gambling dens, houses of prostitution) of possible actions against them; levying fines for drunk and disorderly conduct (disturbances occurring over the weekend left little time for anything else on Mondays); and listening to complaints about people permitting their chickens to run at large.[16] During his campaign McKay promised to clean up the town through a "rigid enforcement of the laws."[17] His eagerness to do so may have led to an unusually large collection of fines.[18]

Perhaps the most distinguishing aspect of their job was being close to the people. Mayors, especially those serving the smaller communities, then, as now, were far more likely than governors to directly hear from their constituents.[19] Whereas governors were insulated from many of their constituents by staff and long distances, mayors could hardly avoid them. Many of those who wished to make person-to-person contact with the mayor did so after shaking hands, but they also complained about taxes, refuse collection, stray dogs, and a variety of other matters. Sometimes the complaints came late at night. Compared to the typical mayor, the typical governor was a hermit.[20]

Small-town mayors went out of their way to touch bases, holding open office hours and appearing at various community functions. No matter what their party affiliation, they could be found on streets regularly making the rounds, greeting and visiting with just about everyone they encountered. Some of this is reflected in the report made by a Socialist writer following a visit in the summer of 1911 to his nephew in Red Cloud, Nebraska, a village of some two thousand people who had recently elected a Socialist mayor named Sam Foe. The writer said lots of people, including two newspaper editors and a barber, told him to "see the mayor and shake hands with a live Socialist in office." The writer and his nephew spotted the mayor but had a bit of difficulty making contact: "He was going up the street stopping here and there, first on one side of the street and then on the other and he went two blocks before we over took him." He described Foe as "a tall, slim man that appeared to be full of energy, sociability and Socialism."[21] Like many mayors of this period, however, Foe served but one year in office.

Laws sometimes limited the length of service, but the fact of the matter was that being mayor, while having some high points, was not all that attractive, and many did not want to serve more than one term. The office of mayor or a comparable office under another title in a small town, village, or borough offered little in terms of pay or, when it came to authority, finances, staff, and time. There was only a limited opportunity to do much beyond the routine. Nor did the job bring all that much in terms of prestige—mayors were often written off as glorified clerks. For many, the job was only a temporary civic duty they reluctantly assumed. During their one- or two-year service they focused on routine administrative jobs, doing much the same essentially caretaker type work as the office holders who came before them and those who were to follow. Small-town mayors and other office holders were regarded by some, including Socialist critics, as small-time players under the control of the dominant business-based elite—taking orders from them or seeking them out, hat in hand, for their advice and support.

The situation appears to have often been like that described in Montana in 1910: "In most instances the office seeks the man, and unfortunately it often happens that it experiences some difficulty in finding him, or persuading him to accept an honor that brings with it many embarrassments and considerable self-sacrifice. The office of mayor in a small town is a thankless job—one that is generally avoided by businessmen who prefer to devote their energies to their own personal affairs."[22] Another article regarding the retirement of a mayor (in this case officially known as a burgess) in Pennsylvania noted, "Being mayor of any small town where opinions differ in almost as many instances as there are citizens, makes it necessary for that official to keep a thick lining in the back of his coat."[23] All in all there may not have been much of an incentive to do try to do much. Being close to the people meant that there was likely to be an intense local blowback if something went wrong, something directed at the mayor personally from people he or she knew that would be difficult to ignore and could have long-lasting negative effects on his or her life in the community.

Small-town government generally meant little in terms of bureaucratization or professionalism, but much in terms of personal government, including considerable flexibility on a person-to-person basis in enforcing rules and regulations. Personal government meant face-to-face interaction between citizens and public officials as well as public expectations that the officials be readily accessible, friendly, humble, and willing to listen. For the mayor, it meant "knotting together one personal association with another until he (or she) has secured sufficient respect and support to put his (or her) measures through."[24] Though class lines could be found in a small town, these divisions may not have mattered much when measured against the forces leading to community unity. As writer Granville Hicks in a classic work on life in small towns saw it, "The truth is that in nine situations out of ten the class structure is overshadowed by a basic social equality that results from the smallness of the community and the sense of a common past. People who are thrown in constant contact over a long period of time learn to ignore distinctions that would make their relations difficult."[25] At the same time, though, in such communities there was little if any tolerance for those who held a minority view or were seen as troublemakers trying to move the town in a different direction.

Socialists differed from most other mayors in towns of all sizes by bringing new energy and ideas into the office and calling for change. If by chance a Socialist happened to win election as mayor in a small place dominated by an economic elite (most likely because they caught the elite napping), their tenure was likely to be uncomfortable and short. They were more likely than other mayors to be viewed as troublemakers and to arouse swift opposition. While Socialists saw capturing the office of great potential importance in building the party and the cause, many Socialist mayors became frustrated by the limitations of the office and with the political opposition they engendered by pushing for change or confronting business interests. Along with this, they became mired in immediate practical problems for which Socialist theory provided no answers other than a general decision rule to do what was best for the working class in any given situation.

Socialist mayors had varying degrees of qualifications for the job. Some had served on the council, though usually functioning there as outsiders pushing for change rather than those who controlled the law-making process. Some had been businesspersons, bringing with them administrative experience but also finding themselves in a new environment where it was far more difficult to direct those around them, including municipal workers protected by civil service and city council members who saw themselves as co-equals—many of whom were determined political enemies. Many of the Socialists who made it to the office came from a background of cause activity, for labor, the party, or both, and were not inclined toward compromise on basic principles.

Mayors in smaller, more isolated jurisdictions were more likely than those in larger jurisdictions to find themselves in a parochial environment where there was an emphasis on ignoring outside experts or intervention in favor of solving their problems their own way. Each mayor in this environment had their own set of local connections or confidants they could turn to for advice. In the case of Socialist mayor Duff Brace in Conneaut, Ohio, for example, there was a core of some twenty-five people who had been with him from the first, among whom were a newspaper editor, a few merchants, but mostly blue-collar workers who, like himself, were employed by the railroads.[26] While many small-town mayors primarily relied on local advisors they trusted, some, particularly those who were proactive like most Socialist mayors, reached out for help.

Socialist mayors and their supporters knew what they wanted to do in a general sense, but they also realized that they needed help in figuring the best way to do it. They needed substantive, procedural, and sound political advice. Those who recognized the need for assistance turned to books, reached out to Socialists in other cities or towns, hired experts who had worked in other Socialist cities, and took advantage of those affiliated with local universities who were willing to help. Some became involved in common projects with neighboring mayors who belonged to other parties or joined organizations such as a state league of cities or municipal leagues, where they interacted with an assortment of mayors and staff members employed by those organizations.

Some also utilized clearinghouse and information services provided by state organizations and the national Socialist Party. The national organization through its Information Department regularly responded to technical inquiries from party members holding office. Reporting in July 1913, for example, the head of the national bureau, Carl Thompson, wrote that among the many requests for help he had received was one from Mayor Brueckmann in Haledon, New Jersey, who said he needed legal assistance in his battle with the council over waterworks projects, and another from Mayor Kirkpatrick in Granite City, Illinois, who wanted information on reasonable rates for electricity.[27] Sometimes the national party offered help in the field. In 1913 the director, for example, in response to a request from a party local, traveled to Hamilton, Ohio, which had recently elected a Socialist mayor and conferred with elected officials and party members as to how to deal with their municipal problems.[28]

Small towns had more need than large towns of the technical services offered by the national party. Indeed, the national party often called upon the experts in the larger cities, such as lawyer Daniel Hoan when he was county attorney in Milwaukee, to provide the advice requested by mayors in smaller towns. Socialists in the larger cities not only were superior in terms of technical capabilities but also were involved in a larger network of contacts and relationships than those in smaller towns. Milwaukee, in particular, made considerable use of experts from the University of Wisconsin and high-priced ones from around the country. Milwaukee also provided many of the cues other jurisdictions acted upon. Mayor Lunn was among those who visited the city when Emil Seidel was mayor to study what was being done in his Socialist administration. In the Socialist world, the smaller towns were places where people went to give advice, and the larger towns were places where people went to find advice.

TEMPERAMENTS, TALENTS, AND ROLE PLAYING

Socialist mayors displayed varrying temperments and talents when it came to carrying out the job of mayor. One example of the determined revolutionary type was Scott Wilkins in St. Marys, Ohio, who was applauded by Socialists on the national level for his courage and eagerness to take action:

> Down at St. Marys, Ohio, they have a revolutionary mayor. His name is Scott Wilkins and he does not believe that his work as a Socialist ends when he calls upon the workers to unite at the ballot box. He believes in Socialism on the job as well as in the city hall. When he is confronted with a situation that demands action, he does not ask for a report by the city attorney as to just how far capitalist laws will let him go; he doesn't wonder how the middle class or small business men will regard him; he doesn't look in the scriptures for guidance. He simply decides what course of action is up to him to take as a representative of the working-class and then gets busy, preferring to lose control of the administration in behalf of his cause rather than hold on to political jobs by trimming his sails."[29]

Wilkins was close to the IWW and others doing battle on the industrial level, but he also saw political action of value in helping the workers in their fight against employers. He argued, "The worker should seek with his ballot to capture the machinery of government, especially in the industrial centers, so that he can prevent the importation of the thugs, who today pour into every strike district to assist the local police in defeating those who are fighting for more bread."[30] He also contended that no holds should be barred in the war with the capitalists: "The capitalist believes in Law and Order just as long as it conserves his economic interest. When it is used to destroy this interest, he despises and will not obey it, even if based on the Constitution. Witness our experience. So, I maintain the worker should despise and disobey the law whenever it becomes necessary to the advance of his economic interests."[31] Wilkins had a stormy and brief career as mayor, being defeated by a fusion candidate after one term.

Also destined for a short career as mayor, though it ended by choice, was J. Stitt Wilson. One of his contemporaries, a Socialist businessman who moved to Berkeley in 1911, said of Wilson: "I don't think of him as a good executive. In the first place, that was not really what interested him. He was interested in speaking and moving people and being before the people. He wasn't interested in the details. He was not very closely related to business and a mayor's job was a business job. His interest was promoting Socialism."[32] In refusing to run for reelection Wilson noted not only his reluctance to continue to do battle with people on the council "out of sympathy with my purpose and principles" but his eagerness to throw himself into the "movement of democracy—struggles of labor, local elections, campaigns for temperance and woman suffrage,— from which I have been withheld. I shall be able to respond to calls for special occasions throughout the country, wherever the battle rages most fiercely, or in the remote and way side places now neglected."[33]

Wilson was among those who appeared uncomfortable, if not totally frustrated, with being an insider—of being caught up in an environment where progress was slow in coming, where they had to deal with or somehow circumvent people who were definitely not on their side, a grinding process filled with conflict. Most Socialist mayors did not find themselves in a setting where they could overpower the opposition. To get anything at all, they had to compromise. While they might be able to claim some victories, the job was not all that much fun, and for some it was nowhere as exciting as agitating from the outside. Those seeking reelection and were able to do so not only seemed more comfortable with the nature of the work but, as indicated in the previous chapter, were more willing to follow a pragmatic and moderate "get what you can" approach.

Given his talents, Wilson could effectively use his office as a bully pulpit to speak out on issues. He, for example, made it widely known, with the cooperation of newspapers throughout the country, that he would not attend a banquet costing $3 a plate (considered a sizeable amount at the time) where he could hobnob with wealthy do-gooders and view movies of how poor people lived. In his letter to the sponsoring organization, he said he would prefer to stay home and send the $3 to a needy family rather than attend such a "vulgar" class or society function. The mayor declared:

> The supreme reason which I offer for not accepting your invitation is there is something positively vulgar and ostentatiously pagan in the spectacle of a group of citizens of a twentieth-century city sitting down to a $3 banquet while pictures are being shown displaying the hunger of the poor.... This picturing of the hunger and misery of the poor to overfed banqueters becomes the more reprehensible since it is now acknowledged by every social thinker and worker of any importance that these poor are made possible by unjust social economic conditions. They are victims of an unchristian and irrational industrial system that robs the people and enriches the exploiters of the people.[34]

Wilson too was well disposed to play the role of party building, a role also commonly assumed by other Socialist mayors. While there was considerable tension between party leaders and office holders, Socialist mayors frequently looked upon party building as a major responsibility—they gave back much to the party organization that helped put them in power. Many had strong ties to the party, as reflected in a history of active membership, holding a party office, working on a party paper, or going on tour as a party lecturer.

The mere election of a Socialist mayor often had a stimulating effect on party activity. Following the election of Socialist John Menton as mayor of Flint, Michigan, for example, Socialists in the city purchased a printing press, started a weekly working-class paper, produced a full line of revolutionary literature, and enjoyed an increase in their membership.[35] As part of his effort to build support for the party, Socialist J. P. Marchant, mayor of Girard, Alabama, wrote the editor of the *Appeal to Reason:* "As mayor of the town, I have a table in the council chamber which also is the mayor's court room, on which I keep Socialist papers for free distribution. If you have any samples that you want distributed, old or new, I will gladly hand them out to the best advantage."[36]

Mayor Duncan's election attracted numerous fellow believers to the city of Butte. He followed up by bringing in a stream of Socialist speakers from all over the country and circulating an unusually large amount of Socialist literature throughout the city. The editor of the *International Socialist Review* wrote in May 1913, "We in this office can testify that during the last two years Butte has circulated more scientific Socialist books in proportion to its population than any other city in the United States. Industrialist speakers from all over the country have found a hearty welcome and big audience in Butte."[37] On June 13, 1911, the thirty-third anniversary of the Butte Miners' Union, the city sponsored a monster parade of ten thousand people that culminated in a revolutionary address at an outdoor rally by Bill Haywood of the Industrial Workers of the World as the honored guest.[38]

May Day celebrations, sometimes with mayors playing prominent roles, were commonly used to build party and labor support. An example took place in Duluth, Minnesota, in 1906 when, following what was estimated to be a parade of some two thousand people, Socialist mayor Alexander Halliday of Two Harbors, Minnesota, spoke to the large number of them who crowded into an auditorium.[39] Socialist mayors also campaigned for other Socialists running for office not only locally but out of state. For example, both J. Stitt Wilson and Lewis Duncan campaigned in 1911 for Job Harriman in his unsuccessful bid for mayor of Los Angeles.[40]

Four years later, Thomas Van Lear went to New York City to speak on behalf of noted Socialist Morris Hillquit's bid for mayor. In 1911 party business and the need to prepare for the upcoming election brought Socialist mayors from "Berkeley, California, Butte, Montana, Coeur d'Alene, Idaho, Flint, Michigan, Girard, Kansas, Grand Junction, Colorado, and several other cities to a three-day conference in Milwaukee.[41]

Party business, including conferring with and often arguing with party officials, was a routine part of the Socialist mayor's life. But given the strength of the party organization in many places, it is difficult to think of the mayor as playing the role of chief of party. It is also difficult to think of the typical Socialist mayor as chief legislator given the common problems they had in dealing with council people. They have a stronger case for the title of chief administrator (in small communities being virtually the only administrator) and law enforcement chief due to their duties as judges and/or in the supervision of the police.

Being usually determined to shake things up, Socialist mayors were inclined to require much of those subject to their supervision. As an editor noted following Seidel's victory, "City employees who have been enjoying sinecures for years are fearful that they will have to do a lot of real work from this time forth." Mayor Seidel's first instructions to the employees were to "work diligently, persistently and conscientiously." In Seidel too we find what we would expect from a Socialist mayor—a pledge of openness or transparency to, in part, offset the charge commonly leveled at Socialist mayors, that the real decisions would be made behind the scenes by a secret party elite, and a commitment to an open-door policy when it came to access to the mayor, especially for those who had been ignored in the past. In the latter respect, Seidel notified the police who guarded the entrance to his office: "There is not a man, woman or child in Milwaukee who may not come into this office to see me. I want you to especially encourage people who have not the appearance of wealth. This is the office of the people of Milwaukee."[42]

Another role sometimes played with a distinct difference by Socialist mayors is that of chief of state—representing the city and, as part of this, hosting dignitaries on formal occasions. Socialist mayors gained nationwide headlines on various occasions for refusing to meet with dignitaries, including presidents, visiting their cities. Seidel did this to Theodore Roosevelt, citing the president's criticism of Socialism. He told the press, "Inasmuch as I am a Socialist and Roosevelt has designated Socialism as that which is against morals and religion, I am sure he will be pleased that I am not personally concerned with his reception."[43] For similar reasons, Mayor Duncan refused to meet with President William Howard Taft at a formal reception held in Butte.[44]

Mayor Hoan of Milwaukee received considerable national publicity by refusing to go along with the Chamber of Commerce's suggestion that he invite the king, queen, and crown prince of Belgium to his city while they were on tour of the United States. He was quoted as saying, "I stand for the man who works. To hell with the kings." He was not going to promote the cause of royalty.[45] One paper concluded, "The incident illustrates the difficulty of the radical in office. Practically he has to compromise with all sorts of institutions not approved by his cult, making an exception now and then where it seems to be good propaganda, The royal visitors, holding their position by virtue of the sovereign will of the people of Belgium, need not, and doubtless won't consider themselves seriously rebuffed.[46]

Finally, we find examples of Socialist mayors playing the role of emergency or crisis manager, commonly involving potential or actual labor strikes—an area where they stood out—and sometime riots, an area where Duncan of Butte was deemed to fall short. One example of crisis management that received considerable national publicity was Mayor Brace meeting a sudden coal shortage in his town of Conneaut, Ohio, by distributing coal on hold for the city's electric light plant directly to households at only slightly above cost to tide them over a shortage.[47] He took it upon himself to do what he could to supply coal to those in need when local dealers could not meet the demand. Small-town mayors suddenly became as important as their counterparts in large cities when it came to responding to a flood, fire, epidemic, or other emergencies threatening the town.

Overall, Socialist mayors played various roles, sometimes effectively and sometimes not so effectively, and often showed tendencies that made them distinctive. They were the most visible public official in their community and were considered to be more responsible than anyone else for what happened or did not happen while they were in office. They could not help but to be deeply involved in local politics. Their decisions or nondecisions had much to do with whether or how local conflicts were resolved. They also played a leading role in protecting and advancing the common interests of the community. Mayors lived in a relatively high pressure-packed political environment. They were in the best position to do something about community problems, to build up public support for action, and, as chief executive, to gather and coordinate the resources of the city to address problems. Even so, their ability to effectively respond to the demands upon them were compromised by problems of legal authority, finances, and political opposition. These problems were especially salient for most Socialist mayors, who were by inclination disrupters. Yet, while there were several obstacles to effective action, as the following chapters indicate, there also were several areas of accomplishment for these mayors.

8. Managing, Budgeting, Cleaning Up the Town

Throughout the country during the period under review we find variations not so much in the agendas of the Socialist mayors—even in small towns, honesty and efficiency, labor protection, and municipal ownership were central themes—but in the extent to which the objectives were pursued and reached. In this chapter we get into some policy areas where nearly all Socialist mayors had to take responsibility: hiring and firing of employers, managing finances, dealing with matters touching upon growth, and issues of law and order. Socialists encountered considerable difficulties, especially when it came to gaining control over the administrative process and municipal finances.

HIRING AND FIRING

While waiting for a Socialist mayor to take office, mayors who were still in charge sometimes followed the practice of securing the resignation of their appointees and quickly reappointing them for another term, thus blocking or at least delaying the ability of the new mayors to replace them. This happened, for example, in Hamilton, Ohio. Socialist mayors generally spent a great deal of time trying to get rid of previous appointees and putting their choices in office.

The hiring and firing of municipal employees was among the most important and (as suggested in the previous chapter) often among the most controversial decisions made by Socialist mayors. Mayors got into trouble with non-Socialist council members when trying to make appointments of Socialists to various offices and, often, with Socialists both on the council and in the party organization when they tried to appoint a non-Socialist.[1] Those who were fired often refused to leave. They hired a lawyer and went to court, arguing that they could not be dismissed because under civil service rules, due cause had not been shown.[2]

Some Socialist mayors, such as Parkman Flanders in Haverhill, Massachusetts, and John Lewis in Elwood, Indiana, appointed Socialists to virtually all offices.[3] Others saw the value of hiring at least some non-Socialists as evidence of their impartiality and their desire to get the best person for the job. This was also done in answer to charges that Socialists and their labor leader supporters were only interested in getting cushy public jobs. As a party leader remarked, the decision of Socialist mayor Charles Born in Sheboygan, Wisconsin, to appoint non-Socialists was "a good answer to those who see in the Social Democrats only a crowd of hungry labor leaders anxious to escape from manual labor."[4]

Mayor Emil Seidel of Milwaukee recognized the need for help in implementing his agenda and so brought in several experts, some at considerable cost from out of state and some of whom were nearby university faculty. Professionals found a home in the Bureau of Economy and Efficiency, the first of its kind in the country, which extended its work beyond economy and efficiency into making a general examination of living conditions in the city. In his search for experts Seidel frequently appointed non-Socialists to various positions, something for which he was applauded by Good Government types and the media.[5] Even so, he was criticized for appointing incompetent or unqualified people to office simply because they were Socialists.[6] Like other Socialist mayors, he felt considerable pressure from loyal party workers for appointments. In Conneaut, Ohio, Mayor Duff Brace made good use of his appointive power not only to reward party loyalists but to seduce left-leaning Democrats.[7]

When it came to appointments, Mayor George Lunn announced, "We shall prefer to have Socialists if we can get good and efficient men in sympathy with our organization, our aims, and our ideals; but, first of all, we want efficiency. If we have an engineering problem to solve, it is more important that we employ a good engineer than a good Socialist. In other offices it is the same." Still, he heard complaints that some of his appointees were not up to par when it came to having the proper experience for the job. Conceding this in some instances, Lunn said he planned to hire experienced experts as deputies to assist those in charge. In questioning some of Lunn s appointments, one writer noted, "The Comptroller, for instance, is a union molder who has had absolutely no experience in matters of finance. The new Superintendent of the Poor has done various odd jobs about town, but none of them would appear to have the remotest connection with training for the work which he will now have to undertake."[8] Also receiving some criticism was the decision of the Socialist mayor in Lackawanna, New York, to appoint a saloonkeeper as head of the fire department.[9]

From the viewpoint of the more committed Socialists, appointments of Socialists were important not simply because they rewarded worthy party members for their service, providing an incentive for others, but because the nature of the agency to which they were appointed gave the member an opportunity to do important work for the party or cause. Making this point in criticism of Mayor Born's appointments to a library board, a writer for a left-wing paper declared, "A library board is a tactical outpost in our war on capitalism. No true Socialist will fill such a position with capitalistic, labor hating politicians as Mayor Born did in Sheboygan."[10] Socialists may well have perceived a need for change. As one study suggests, libraries during the period under review provided little if any material coming from Socialist sources.[11]

Some of the more controversial decisions involved the hiring and firing of police personnel, a local function of special importance to Socialists and labor leaders. Mayor Harry Schilling of Canton, Ohio, came into office planning to discharge the entire police force.[12] He got as far as dismissing the police chief, charging that he was a habitual drunk, had accepted money from women engaged in prostitution in exchange for protecting them, and had commonly visited the places where they worked for reasons not connected with his official duties. A special commission, however, cleared the chief of all charges and reinstated him to his position.[13] Efforts on the part of Socialist mayor Corbin Shook in Lima, Ohio, and Socialist mayor Henry Stolze in Manitowoc, Wisconsin, to fire a police chief were also strongly resisted.[14] In Conneaut, Ohio, Socialists despised the holdover police chief but were divided "between those who wanted to get rid of him, and those who wanted to get rid of him immediately." When the Socialist mayor hesitated, those who wanted immediate action tried to expel the mayor from the party. Some suspected that those leading this effort were striking back because the mayor refused to appoint them to the offices they wanted.[15] For some time, Mayor W. E. Griffin of Beatrice, Nebraska, found his hands tied because the council refused to confirm three new officers. Once this stalemate was broken his party came after him because he gave some of the jobs to non-Socialists.[16] In Butte, Montana, Democrats and Republicans on the council got together and ousted all five police officers appointed by Socialist mayor Lewis Duncan.

Soon after taking office, Mayor Seidel appointed Milwaukee's first female police officer, a trained nurse who finished first in a competitive examination, whose primary task was to go on duty in factories to protect woman workers especially regarding sanitary conditions. In at least a couple of instances, Socialist mayors went out of their way to appoint a Black person to the police force. In Flint, Michigan, Mayor John Menton's appointment of a Black man, who happened to be a Republican, as police commissioner was turned down by the council. According to one report, "The aldermen turned down the appointment because they did not propose to place other than white men upon the board. They also took the position that Menton's appointment was only a grandstand play to catch the colored vote in this city, as it was figured beforehand that the council would not accept the appointment."[17] Around the same time, Mayor Duncan was able to secure the appointment of a Black man, also a Republican, to the Butte police force. Duncan reported, "His appointment raised a storm of protest, but it also opened the whole subject of race, color and creed distinctions inside the working-class movement. The controversy on this subject resulted in better education of non-Socialist working men. The Socialist support of the negro appointee demonstrated the sincerity of our party on the race question and our debates silenced all criticism inside the ranks of the working-class organization."[18]

FINANCIAL MANAGEMENT

Many Socialist mayors were elected in towns and cities that were in bad shape financially. For example, when he came to power in Victor, Colorado, Mayor J. B. Bitterly found "everything exploited to the limit" in this mining town of some four thousand people and a municipal government that was deeply in debt.[19] Socialists taking power in several Ohio towns were also confronted by budget emergencies.[20] In Butte the city was close to bankruptcy when the Socialists took over. For the Socialist mayor of New Castle, Pennsylvania, "Years of petty graft and neglect had left the city finances and records in shambles."[21]

Socialists in Milwaukee faced an inherited debt of some $200,000. They blamed previous administrations for playing the game of "keeping down taxes" by borrowing to fund operations, rather than raising taxes, a practice that drove the city deep into debt and made it nearly impossible for Socialists to fund new enterprises.[22] In trying to cope with finances, Mayor Seidel was constrained by a state law that limited the size of the city's annual budget and his inability to manage tax rates, assessments, and bonded indebtedness because the office of tax commissioner in charge of these functions was in the hands of a holdover appointee who belonged to an opposing party.[23] Socialist administrations sometimes found it difficult to borrow when it was discovered that the bonds were those of a Socialist administration. Such, for example, was the experience in Star City, West Virginia.[24]

Dealing with the council often meant budget battles. In Hamilton, Ohio, in 1913, for example, efforts of the Socialist mayor and Socialists on the council to reduce appropriations for the police department and a hospital controlled by the Catholic Church became major issues that were carried over in court suit and the November election.[25] Socialists in Hamilton, and often elsewhere around the country, felt that the police department was too large and that the money saved by reducing its size could be better spent on other activities.[26]

In many jurisdictions, frugality was expected, and what was perceived as overspending was punished. In Naugatuck, Connecticut, for example, Socialist mayor (with the official title of warden) A. Barton Cross Jr. was undoubtedly aware that his predecessors' spending thousands of dollars on a brick-paving street project raised such a hue and cry about extravagant spending that his reelection was out of the question.[27] Socialists sometimes felt the heat. Opponents, for example, in a story picked up by newspapers around the country attacked the Socialist administration in Granite City, Illinois, headed by Marshall Kirkpatrick for large increases in both spending and the tax rate. Socialists responded by shifting much of the blame to the city council, controlled by non-Socialists, and the ability of corporations to dodge paying taxes.[28]

Socialist mayors probably would have liked to spend more than they did, but most were very conscious of budgetary constraints. When the Socialists came to power in Hamilton, Ohio, for example, an observer from the national party who was invited into discussions involving spending plans noted that there was agreement among them that the wages of municipal employees should be raised, "but weight was given to the consideration that the budget made it impossible for the administration to spend more than a certain prescribed amount. On that account it was agreed that it might be better to raise the wages gradually, especially in view of the increasing number of the unemployed."[29] J. Stitt Wilson of Berkeley, California, was among those who gave special attention to the budget and the need to balance expenditures and revenues. He wrote, "I knew the city cash account better than my own. I balanced the various needs of the city with its possible and then its actual income. I must say that the non-Socialists in the council very soon graciously yielded to my judgment in city finances, and practically permitted me to make the second half-yearly budget, readjusting the city expenditures."[30]

Despite all the difficulties, several Socialist mayors took pride in successfully managing their city's finances. Mayor Duncan was able to reduce Butte's debt and restore its credit rating by raising taxes and cutting expenses (including by reducing the size of the police force). He claimed, with some justification, "We are running the city better than it has ever been run by either democrats or republicans, and are doing it at lower cost."[31] When it came to finances Mayor Wilson declared:

> One of the attacks made during our campaign was that the Socialists would ruin the finance of the city; that the candidate for mayor was a good 'talker,' but 'what business could he attend to?' This criticism was soon silenced. The finances of the city of Berkeley were never in better condition and everyone

knows it.... When I took charge, the total funds available from all sources was $32,000, but I left for my successor $60,000, besides $50,000 in the treasury for the incinerator."

Though Wilson did not raise taxes, he took pride in leading in the successful effort to amend the city charter so that future administrations would be able to do so if needed.[32] Lunn in 1913 took pride in reducing the size of the budget, declaring, "We were able to do this by cutting expenses at every point possible in the interest of true economy. Superfluous positions were eliminated." At the same time, he was able to raise the pay of city workers.[33]

In Milwaukee, the chief accomplishments on the fiscal front, and by no means insignificant ones, were the introduction of a modern budgeting system and accounting, purchasing, and book-keeping procedures, which enabled city officials to comprehensively track and evaluate income, expenses, cash flow, and unit costs and, with this information, reduce waste and duplication.[34] In contrast to municipal officials from other parties, Socialists running the town of Star City "issued regular financial statements for the town and closed the books in the black every year they held control."[35] Other Socialist mayors having some success in cleaning up their city's financial problems include those from Victor, Colorado; Daly City, California; Murray, Utah; and Martins Ferry, Saint Marys, and Mount Vernon, Ohio.[36]

Some Socialist mayors were fiscal conservatives who favored keeping taxes low and even cutting them, if necessary, to promote economic prosperity. Some considered that avoiding tax increases or even cutting taxes was important to their election prospects. However, those who took this approach ran the risk of being reproached by other Socialists. In Schenectady, New York, for example, Walter Lippmann criticized the Lunn administration for making a budget "on the principle that taxes must not be increased, because high taxes would alienate the property-holders whose votes decided the election." In doing this, he charged, the administration was following the lead of the Good Government reformers and ignoring the fact that "it is quite clearly the business of a Socialist administration to cut into the returns of property, [and] take as much of them as possible to be spent for social purposes."[37]

If there was a natural tendency among Socialist mayors when it came to the city budget, it was to raise taxes on the rich, use the funds for working-class programs, and avoid spending cuts affecting the working class. They felt Socialists had to give priority to basic social programs and that these should be paid for by those who could best afford to pay. To them, government had a more meaningful duty than cutting taxes. They had good political reasons to avoid tax increases—such action was likely to be given considerable negative attention in the mainstream media and the political campaigns of opponents. Still, Socialists commonly took pride in having the courage to raise taxes and, as far as possible, shift more of the tax load to businesses—actions the old parties were not inclined to take.[38]

Socialists hoped to pay for a great many services out of the general fund, which was based as much as possible on revenues collected from the wealthy, and provide services funded this way without charge to the general public. This included programs for streets, sanitation, and police and fire protection. For other programs, such as for water or electricity from a municipal plant, charges were to be levied on the consumer to recover the cost of providing the service. In providing these services the Socialists sought to protect the working class regarding rates and to make sure businesses paid their fair share. Socialists too generally sought to make sure that profits from municipally-run enterprises such as water and power plants be used for programs benefiting the broader community rather than to reduce taxes, especially on the wealthy.[39]

GROWTH AND THE IDEAL CITY

Many Socialist mayors were also interested in promoting economic growth. John Franklin Johnson, Socialist mayor of Fairhope, Alabama, provides a good example of a Socialist mayor who played the advocate role with considerable enthusiasm. As a reporter who interviewed Johnson in 1913 noted, "Mr. Johnson is a booster. He believes in Fairhope, talks Fairhope, and probably dreams Fairhope on nights when the moon is shining brightest on his beloved Mobile bay." At the time, he was working on transportation projects—better roads and the extension of railroad service.[40] The town, first populated by a colony of Henry George followers, was filled with artists and intellectuals, especially in the winter. Blessed with beautiful scenery, it survived by opening its arms to tourists. The attitude regarding growth was a bit more restrained by Socialists heading the small village of fishermen and ship builders of Gulfport, Florida. Here Socialist mayor E. E. Wintersgill, who came into office in 1910 when the town was incorporated, saw the dangers of uncontrolled growth being set off by a land boom and growing industrialization nearby, and sought to guide growth in order to make it compatible with the values and interests of people in the existing community.[41]

Mayor Seidel in Milwaukee, the Socialists' only large city, took note of the ill effects of growth and the lack of planning: "The modern city, while it has grown to large proportions, has increased its population until hundreds of thousands of souls are huddled together in small areas, has developed swamps of a different nature than those our forefathers drained. Some of these have become cesspools, the stench of which rises to the heavens. Men and women as well as innocent children, are wrecked and ruined in these swamps."[42] He set out to lay the groundwork for the "ideal city." In moving toward this, something a step up from "the city beautiful" being sought by other reformers, Socialists put a strong emphasis on more parks, playgrounds, and recreational facilities, and new and better schools.

Socialist mayors also put considerable emphasis on public health, safety, and slum clearance. In many Socialist-helmed cities there were efforts to protect the water supply; improve the sewage system; maintain clean streets; clean up the food supply through inspections of meats, milk, and other foodstuffs; conduct building and factory inspections; and actions to head off epidemics. Socialist administrations in locations such as Butte, Montana; New Castle, Pennsylvania; and Victor, Colorado, adopted measures that resulted in a reduction of the death rate and level of various diseases.[43] When it comes to public health, one study suggests that Socialist administrations far exceeded the work of the best Progressive administrations.[44]

Sometimes improvement came simply by substituting a Socialist administrator for a non-Socialist one. In Milwaukee, for example, the first semi-annual report of the Socialist coroner reported that it had handled thirty-three cases involving the death of railroad workers. The coroner charged railway companies with negligence in fifteen of these cases. In nine of the cases the district attorney was called in to make an investigation. In an annual report issued a year earlier by a non-Socialist coroner working for a different administration, there were forty-two cases and all these deaths were found to be "accidental."[45]

As one might expect, worker safety was a special priority. In Barre, Vermont, Socialist mayor Robert Gordon, for example, strongly urged the council to give priority to correcting conditions affecting the health and safety of workers in the granite industry over a program of tax cutting. In his address to the council, the mayor centered his argument on economic grounds, stating, "We hear of capitalists who won't invest in Barre on account of a high tax rate, but the time is coming when the workman will not sell his labor here on account of unhealthy conditions."[46] Gordon, a Scot who had come to Barre in 1880 at the age of fifteen and became a stonecutter a few years later, "understood the working class because he was, for his entire life, a member of it."[47]

Ironically, a few months after his call for safety legislation, ex-mayor Gordon was injured while operating a lathe at a local plant—his right hand got caught up in the gearing, badly injuring his right index finger and thumb. A local paper reported, "Mr. Gordon will not be able to assume work for some time."⁴⁸ As another bit of irony, the Socialist mayor of Oskaloosa, Kansas, in effect confirmed he was correct in ordering a young man be sent to quarantine because he had smallpox by, not long after conferring with the young man, coming down with smallpox himself.⁴⁹

LAW ENFORCEMENT

While there were some exceptions, the mayors examined for this book took a strong stand for law and order. This reflected in part a desire to demonstrate that contrary to charges commonly made against Socialists, they were not wild, dangerous radicals but responsible, respectable officials up to the task of governing. Socialist mayors were especially effective when working with a Socialist police chief, as in Minneapolis, Minnesota, where Mayor Thomas Van Lear teamed with his appointee, Lewis Harthill, a close ally who, like the mayor, had been associated with the Minneapolis Machinist Union; and in Grand Junction, Colorado, where Mayor Thomas Todd teamed up with S. B. Hutchinson, thought to be the first Socialist police chief in the country. A strong law-and-order stand seemed in many towns and cities to be a prerequisite to projecting an image of worthiness and winning an election. In some places, such as Martins Ferry, Ohio, both Socialist and non-Socialist mayors were judged by their ability to keep open vice and social disturbances at a minimum and were strongly encouraged by the local papers to do so.⁵⁰

Along with strict enforcement of the laws, Socialists put emphasis on the need for equality in enforcement. The party in Grants Pass, Oregon, declared, "The Socialists will stand behind no particular class. The pompous citizen will get the same Justice as Mike and Pat.⁵¹ Similarly, the Socialist administration in Grand Junction sent out the word that laws prohibiting the excessive use of alcohol were going to be implemented without regard to class status. To the mayor and his police chief Hutchinson, "a drunken banker looks the same as a drunken hobo." As far as the hoboes were concerned, however, the Socialists were a bit more sympathetic—they backed a program giving them a square meal every Sunday.⁵²

In 1906 the secretary of the Socialist Party in Minnesota reported, "The new Socialist mayor of Two Harbors is creating consternation in that burg by enforcing the laws something heretofore unknown. Every slot machine has disappeared." There was also a stern enforcement of the town's blue laws restricting certain activities on Sunday, including going into bars: "No liquor is sold contrary to law, and the police are held responsible for all violations. It was so dry last Sunday that it is reported the sidewalks cracked, and all kinds of labor was stopped except that which the law allows." The party secretary explained, "The comrades are not particularly favorable to the old blue laws, but, having pledged themselves to enforce the law, nothing short of changing them will save the natives from being compelled to obey laws they dislike."[53]

Some Socialists put their hearts and souls into moral crusades to clean up their towns morally as well as physically. One of the most prominent genuine moral crusaders was Arthur Le Sueur, president of the Minot, North Dakota, city commission who strictly enforced laws against gambling, liquor, and prostitution, taking on some deeply entrenched interests in the process. As a newspaper article in May 1912, reported (about a year after he had left office), Le Sueur "cleaned up Minot with a ruthless hand."[54] In Ohio, Socialist mayors actively crusaded: in Martins Ferry, they cracked down on crime and corruption, eliminating slot machines and other forms of gambling; in Lima they attempted to rid the town of vice, enforcing evening curfews and Sunday closing laws, denying liquor licenses, and imposing large fines in the mayor's court; in Lorain, they enforced Sunday blue laws against roller skating and dancing and shut down gambling places and houses of prostitution; and in Mount Vernon, they followed a similar path in regard to vice, including slot machines, illegal pool halls, and saloons.[55]

Further west, in Eureka, Utah, the Socialist mayor closed saloons on Sundays and put gamblers out of business completely. In Leavenworth, Washington, the Socialist mayor led a campaign to abolish the use of obscene language on the streets, while in Buena Vista, Colorado, saloons, pool halls, and all other places where any form of gambling was being carried on were required to close.

Socialists in Bicknell, Indiana, proudly reported there were fewer arrests in their city than in any other city of comparable size because they had closed the gambling houses, kept a close watch on the saloons, and had adopted a policy of forcing offenders to work on the streets as an alternative to fines or confinement. In Canton, Ohio, Mayor Harry Schilling set out to enforce the Ten Commandments. And in Minneapolis, Mayor Van Lear put together a semi-civilian "purity squad" to conduct a vice-cleanup campaign that shut down several establishments that had been ignored for years.[56] He promised, "When I enforce the law, I'll get the big fellows as well as the immoral women. . . . It is easy to enforce the law on the common people; they are accustomed to it," but the mayor wanted to go further and enforce the law "against the 'best' citizens," including those who owned the property where such activities flourished.[57] In remarking on Van Lear's efforts, the national party's *American Socialist* passed along the following observations:

A Socialist does not, as some people suppose, need nor cater for the support of the rough and tough elements. It has always been left to one of the old parties to enlist the aid of the denizens of the red-light districts and cheap lodging house sections of our cities. Socialism finds no friendly feeling in the ignorance to be found in the slums. It is the "reform" element in the old parties that often unites with the red-light district, the lodging house element and the slum population to defeat Socialism in its upward struggle.[58]

Socialist leaders, ideologues, and writers generally were highly critical of the liquor industry. As one left-wing editorialist put it, "The saloon influence is almost invariably wielded by those who live upon the labor of others."[59] To the Socialists this industry was not only an important component of the capitalist system and a foe to the party and its causes but also a peddler of a product that "debauched the workers, sapped their strength, demoralized their spirit, dulled their class consciousness, and prevented them from emancipating themselves from the evils of the industrial order."[60] In sum: "The man whose brain is debauched by drink is a poor soldier in the class war. He is worthless as a union man or as a Socialist. He seldom becomes either."[61]

Socialists, though, were not of one mind when it came to legal restrictions on the sale and use of alcoholic beverages. Some favored prohibition while others did not.[62] Still, if prohibition and other restrictions on the use of alcohol were on the books, Socialist mayors generally made a determined effort to enforce them. We do, however, find some Socialist mayors taking a soft approach when it came to cracking down on those who drank too much. Shortly after taking office in Granite City, Illinois, Mayor Kirkpatrick ordered the police when possible to take those who had too much to drink home rather than put them in jail. The mayor declared, "Men who drink are victims of temperament and not criminals."[63] In other statements he avowed that ordinary "plain drunks" were the victims of circumstances who do not deserve to be locked upon unless they were disturbing the peace.[64] The Socialist mayor in Flint also ordered police to take drunks home rather than put them in jail.[65]

In 1915 Socialist mayor Homer Whalen of Canton, Illinois, and the Canton council voted in favor of a mild prohibition ordinance. Whalen was soon widely criticized, even by some in his own party, for failing to crack down on so called "soft" drink establishments. One alderman complained, "When you pass those soft drink parlors the stench that comes from them almost knocks you down. . . . You see as many men reeling on the streets as ever."[66] The dry forces had their revenge by sweeping the Socialists, including Whalen, out of office in 1917.[67] As indicated in the following chapter, some Socialist mayors boldly toyed with the idea of putting their cities in the liquor business as a way of both curtailing the problem of excessive drinking and increasing city revenues. Some also thought in terms of higher liquor license fees. Mayor Fred Malzhan and his fellow Socialists in Bemidji, Minnesota, were among those favoring this route, seeing higher fees as a means of cutting down on the number of saloons and increasing the standard of operation for those that remained. They expected the higher fees would make up for the loss of revenue caused by saloon closings.[68]

On issues of morality, Socialists took the position that achieving Socialism itself would do away with many vices such as drunkenness and prostitution, because these were the products of economic and social conditions under capitalism. Socialist Party platforms commonly were sympathetic to women caught up in prostitution. The local party in Prescott, Arizona, for example, declared:

> We have no word of condemnation for the women who have been driven by economic causes inseparable from our modern civilization to seek their bread in the oldest profession in the world.... You will not end the traffic by an attack upon the woman. Nationally you will not be able to end the traffic until at least every working woman may have a fair day's wage for a fair day's work.[69]

Talking along similar lines in 1910, Socialist Joseph Warnock, who was elected mayor of Harbor Springs, Michigan, the following year, placed the blame on "so-called Christians, sincere in their beliefs, who hire girls at wages that compel the latter to sell their souls to save their bodies."[70] The Socialists of Perth Amboy, New Jersey, chimed in: "The Capitalist System is responsible for the thousands upon thousands of our daughters and sisters walking and selling their bodies for a miserable existence."[71]

While hoping for long-term solutions, Socialists in power at the local level sought to do what they could to control prostitution by, for example, confining the activity to a relatively remote district, limiting the sale of liquor in the district, putting activities there under close police supervision, and improving sanitary conditions. Most also called for increased law enforcement. Mayor Duncan in Butte concentrated on enforcing liquor laws and improving conditions in red-light districts.[72] In his war on sin he obtained a prohibition of sending messenger boys into these places and the power to revoke the licenses of saloons that were open to women.[73] A paper supportive of the first of these noted, "One of the telegraph companies refused to obey the law and took it to court on the ground that it interferes with business. What are boys to dividends? Private profit has no conscience."[74]

On the whole, Socialist mayors seemed less inclined than Progressive pioneers like Hazen Pingree and Sam Jones and to look the other way when it came to gambling, drinking, prostitution, and other moral problems.[75] Most Socialists believed that strong enforcement of laws regarding morality were part of a social uplift effort and also were in the interest of the community rather than the individual to clean up the town, making it more orderly and attractive; in addition, it showed their commitment to honesty and efficiency, demonstrating that Socialists could govern effectively at a high moral level worthy of respect.

9. The Working Class, Labor, and Business

Socialist recruiting and election campaigns commonly focused on the contrast between the lives of working people and the wealthy business or capitalist class that employed them. An example of a recruitment pitch is found in this quote from a left-wing labor newspaper: "If you as a working man are tired of voting for idle promises, rotten whiskey, stale beer and cheap cigars, cheap food, shoddy clothes, shacks for the poor, palaces for the rich, long hours of nerve racking toil for the workers, idleness, luxury and pleasure for the rich . . . join the working-class party, the Socialist Party."[1] On the campaign trail voters heard a similar message, such as one from Socialist Thomas Van Lear when running for Congress that "when fat, slick, well fed, well-dressed men, who never missed a meal in their lives, come down here and tell you workingmen that you should be patient and satisfied with things as they are, I think you ought to tell them to go to hell."[2]

While commonly more restrained in rhetoric, those Socialists who made it into office went out of their way to be helpful in small and big ways to working people and unions. Throughout the period under review, Socialist mayors also commonly engaged in combat with some of the nation's largest corporations, including Amalgamated Copper, US Steel, General Electric, General Motors, and privately owned local utilities that dominated the provision of basic transportation, water, gas, and electrical power services in their communities. Businesses, especially large ones, had much to worry about with the emergence of a Socialist administration: increased taxes and regulation, losing lucrative franchises or contracts with the municipalities, having to compete with new municipal enterprises, and facing a situation where the local government was now on labor's side in disputes with management. These worries were well justified.

LABOR PROTECTION

Given their party's deep historical, ideological, and political ties to the working class, Socialists routinely considered how various policy proposals affected the welfare of that class. Often there was debate within the party over what action was in the interest of the working class or over what was a working-class issue, and Socialists in power sometimes disagreed with party leaders on these matters. Nevertheless, much of what Socialist mayors did in terms of policy proposals and actions reflected their assumptions of how that stand affected the interest of the working class. In practice too, what was good for organized labor was commonly equated by party members and office holders with what was good for the working class.

Socialist administrations provided multiple educational and recreational benefits for working-class families, and better sanitation and sidewalks in working-class neighborhoods. They also commonly required the union label on all city printing, insisted on purchasing union-made goods, improved the wages and working conditions of municipal employees, put emphasis of employing only city workers on municipal projects, offered strikers protection from police during industrial disputes, and headed off or settled strikes to the advantage of the workers involved.[3] Socialists in Milwaukee and other places established free municipal employment bureaus to find work for the unemployed.[4] In spite of party boss Victor Berger's objections and some doubts about the legality of the action, the Socialist city council in Milwaukee adopted a measure giving washer women city water free of charge.[5] Emil Seidel's election as mayor also brought increased pay and an eight-hour day for city employees.[6]

According to a party source, the decision of Scott Wilkins in St. Marys, Ohio, to boost municipal workers' wages "had an immediate effect on employees working in private enterprises. The prevailing wage in the city had been $1.35 per day, and this now has been raised to $1.50."[7] Mayor Duncan in Butte, Montana, with the aid of two non-Socialist union members voting with the Socialists on the council, increased the pay of common city laborers to $3.15 per day and gave them an annual ten-day vacation with pay. The national party reported, "This is the first time in the history of this country for any administration to recognize common laborers as entitled to a vacation on pay."[8] Socialist mayors did a great deal for municipal employees. In giving municipal employees better pay and benefits, shorter hours, and improved working conditions they encouraged similar changes in the private sector.

Labor issues often pitted the Socialists against old party council members. In Haverhill, Massachusetts, Mayor Chase and Socialist council members favored having public works done directly by city workers rather than by private contractors, but Republicans held the opposite view and, being in control of the council, persisted in letting contracts.[9] However, Chase was able to come to the aid of city workers by increasing their wages and initiating a successful drive to reduce their hours of work from nine or ten down to eight.¹⁰ In Arma, Kansas, Socialist mayor Evan Morgan got caught up in some legal trouble by personally destroying a large portion of a sidewalk that was being constructed by a private contractor around the city park on the order of the city council after it had overridden his veto of the sidewalk contract.¹¹ In March 1908 in Red Lodge, Montana, Socialist mayor Ray Austin and Socialists on the city council were fighting what was thus far a losing battle with the combined forces of Democrat and Republican aldermen over putting police on an eight-hour day—the Socialists in favor of the move, their opponents defending the current practice of twelve hours and insisting on a total wage cut if the hours were cut back to eight.¹²

Organized labor—and those who were attempting to organize—likely most highly valued the actions of Socialist mayors regarding strikes. Socialists were eager to point out their importance in this respect:

> With the police power controlled by representatives of the proletariat, any just strike can be won in a week. With the police and military power in control of Democratic and Republican defenders of capitalism, the strikers have not one chance in a thousand to win. . . . Socialist administrations believe it is their duty to help win strikes: Republican and Democratic administrations believe it is their duty to aid the employers. Very simple isn't it?"¹³

When it came to strike activity, Socialist mayors were relatively free to act on their own, without council involvement, and willingly stuck their necks out time and again for the workers. They followed up on pledges by refusing to use police to break a workers strike and, more positively, providing police protection for striking workers. Mayor Wilkins in St. Marys, Ohio, went a step further by encouraging strike activity and assuring workers that they would be protected by the city should they go on strike.¹⁴ Mayor Kirkpatrick in Granite City, Illinois, felt it was impossible for a Socialist to be neutral in a strike situation: "There are certain things that the employers want done and that the strikers don't want done, and the mayor is forced to take sides. There is no middle ground. You must get on one side of the fence. We Socialists here have chosen to stay on our own side and be with workers."¹⁵ Success, he felt, was largely a matter of police protecting the right of strikers to picket and peacefully assemble at factory gates. He was fortunate in having a police chief who had allowed strikers to do so.

Mayor Lunn was twice arrested and jailed for coming to the defense of four thousand striking textile workers in the nearby town of Little Falls, New York.¹⁶ Following his arrest in November 1912, he held nothing back. He declared that manufacturers in Little Falls believed "in the divine right of money," were "drunk with power," and placed "property and profits over human life." He went on to call the city officials puppets in the hands of manufacturers and said the police were guilty of brutality to the striking workers, clubbing them on the street and after they got them to jail.[17] Lunn later got involved in a strike involving fifteen thousand General Electric employees, stemming from the company's decision to lay off union leaders. Under Lunn the strikers were allowed to picket. He declared, "The strikers will be given full protection. . . . There is no reason why they shouldn't be allowed to stop a person on the street and ask him to cease work."[18]

In 1913 the Socialist mayor of the borough of Haledon, New Jersey, William Brueckmann, assisted IWW leader Patrick Quinlan, who was heading a strike of silk workers in neighboring Paterson, by giving some thirty thousand striking workers the opportunity to hold meetings in Haledon after they had been told they could not hold meetings in Paterson. Brueckmann had a police department of one man who agreed with the mayor's views on labor. During strike meetings workers would occasionally call out, "What's wrong with the Haledon Police Department?" And respond: "He's all right!"[19] The mayor was later indicted for malfeasance in office, willfully ignoring his legal duties during the strike, but the case never went to trial because his opponents feared it would do more harm in publicity than good.[20] Following the experience, Quinlan declared that electing a Socialist mayor was the best way to avoid a policeman "batting you over the head with a club."[21]

In July 1918 Governor Joseph Burnquist of Minnesota warned Socialist Minneapolis mayor Thomas Van Lear that he had better do something to curb a strike of newsboys in his city, a strike he had been accused of encouraging by the local papers targeted by the strikers. The governor claimed the strikers were disruptive and dangerous—some, he contended, had attacked citizens, taking papers from them. He said he had no choice but to remove the mayor from office if he did not take immediate action. Van Lear denied that there was any serious problem requiring city intervention, that the situation had been overblown by newspapers politically hostile to him.[22] Fortunately for the mayor, the two sides were able to compromise, and the strike ended soon after the governor's warning was issued.

At times local officials found themselves caught up in disputes among rival unions. In Butte in June 1914, long-simmering divisions between miners associated with the IWW and miners associated with the Western Federation of Miners (WFM) led to a riot in which a Socialist councilman, taking up the challenge of restoring peace because Mayor Duncan was out of town and the acting mayor was on a fishing trip, was thrown out of a window on the second floor of the Miners' Union Hall and badly injured after falling to the street. The rioters proceeded to destroy the building with dynamite. The disruption was later put down by state troops. Mayor Duncan and the local sheriff were removed from office by a judge who concluded they had failed to do their duty of protecting the city from the rioters.[23]

Another incident involving the IWW took place in Grand Junction, Colorado, in April 1913. IWW leaders contacted Socialist mayor Thomas Todd and Socialist police chief S. B. Hutchinson, telling them that seventy-five members of their union on a trip from the California coast to Denver would like to stop off in Grand Junction on April 9 for a few days, doing some street speaking, and that they would appreciate the city's help in providing these people with food during their stay. The mayor and police chief were able to convince the council to host the group and appropriate funds to feed them when they arrived. The police chief promised that the IWW members would pay back the city for every cent spent on them by working off the debt.

The council's action produced a strong backlash. A local newspaper editor who was already a determined foe of the Socialist administration demanded to know, "What right have the city commissioners to make an appropriation to care for these worthless, country-hating, law-denouncing drones? . . . If any appropriation had to be made, it should have been an appropriation to provide extra police service to be utilized in running these foul trouble-breeders out of the community."[24] The editor called upon the citizens to defend themselves. Angered by what some declared an invasion of their city and the practice of IWW members speaking on the streets, business leaders, labor union members, and high school athletes joined in a citizens' protective organization to maintain the peace. A mass meeting of some five hundred people demanded that the sheriff drive the Wobblies out of town and called for the recall of the mayor if he refused to fire Hutchinson, who was widely blamed for his handling of the situation—not only did he refuse to arrest the IWW members, but he threatened to arrest anyone who attempted to interfere with their street meetings. Mayor Todd refused to fire the police chief, but the chief resigned, and the recall was avoided.[25]

Socialist-inclined mayor Reverend Harry Ferguson of Hoquiam, Washington, was less fortunate. He was recalled by voters in 1912 for being too sympathetic to the IWW by refusing to use the police to curb their activity during a strike in the city. Following his recall, Ferguson became an outspoken member of the Socialist Party.[26] Elsewhere around the country during the period under review, the Socialist mayor of Brockton, Massachusetts, refused company requests that police help break a strike and on another occasion forced a company to the bargaining table by warning that he would swear in two hundred strikers as policemen to preserve order; the Socialist mayor of De Ridder, Louisiana, rejected the demand of a lumber company that he prohibit a mass meeting of union members contemplating a lumber strike, and when the mayor refused, the company tried to run him out of town; the Socialist mayor of Camas, Washington, backed up his police chief, protecting workers on strike at a paper mill; and the Socialist mayor of Granite City, Illinois, stood up for workers picketing a steel plant, refusing company demands that they be arrested. The Socialist mayor of Hamilton, Ohio, swore in forty union members as policemen during a machinists' strike to protect the lives and property of the strikers; and in Coshocton, Ohio, the Socialist mayor stood behind workers on strike against a glassware company. In Manitowoc, Wisconsin, the Socialist mayor refused to allow the Aluminum Castings Company to hire armed guards in dispute with strikers; and in Eureka, Utah, the Socialist mayor cracked down on the use of Pinkerton detectives and gunmen by capitalists during strikes.[27]

CORPORATIONS AND BUSINESS REGULATIONS

Several of the early struggles of Socialists and their union allies were directed at the large corporations that dominated various towns or cities. One victory took place in 1903 in the company town of Anaconda, Montana, when the Socialist candidate for the office of mayor, John Frinke, came out ahead of the Democratic and Republican nominees. The victory rested on the support of unions and immigrant smelter workers.[28] The new regime did have some success, in, for example, working through the assessor's office to raise taxes on the Anaconda Copper Mining Company, the dominant employer in the city and part of one of the largest trusts in the country, the Amalgamated Copper Company.[29] Anaconda Copper struck back, firing and blacklisting anyone it felt might be a Socialist or Socialist sympathizer, eventually forcing some twelve hundred people out of town. With most of their supporters gone from the town, the Socialists, including the mayor, were easily swept out of office in 1905.

Mayor Finke left town following his defeat, moving to Tacoma, Washington. One of his comrades wrote not long after Frinke's departure:

> Comrade John W. Frinke left this evening for Tacoma on the 6:50 train. A few comrades and friends went with him to the railroad station to bid him farewell and wish him joy and liberty of conscience in his new home. Tacoma gains what Anaconda loses and he is and will always be in the ranks of the

proletarian army of the world, fighting against wrong and injustice. Comrade Frinke is of that type which is being developed by the economic conditions of our age, and as capitalism ripens more Frinkes will come to view.[30]

As for Anaconda, it soon became known in the Socialist press as "The City of Whispers," a place that

> stands as the epitome of oligarchic control.... The smelter which crowns the hills on the outskirts of the town dominates the entire mental, moral, physical, and spiritual life of the community. From this city emanates no thought that is not inspired by the sinister shadow of "The Company."... For the workers, who spend their days in the smelters... there is no freedom of speech, and scarcely of thought.[31]

Lewis Duncan's 1911 mayoral victory undoubtedly increased Amalgamated Copper's "fear that the principles of capitalism were not universally cherished in Butte."[32] Duncan showed his stripes by attempting to extend the city's boundaries so that it included Amalgamated Copper's mines—a move that would have led to increased city taxes on the company and, with the Socialists in control, an end to the practice of having the company's mine guards become deputy sheriffs through an arrangement with the county sheriff and thus able to act in this capacity during labor disturbances.[33] With the council controlled by the members from the old parties, this threat fizzled out.

One example of an extreme backlash involved Scott Wilkins, a letter carrier, considered by some in the press as a "serious minded sober chap whose entire sympathy has been enlisted in the cause of the toilers," who had campaigned hard to get himself elected mayor of St. Marys, Ohio, in 1911.[34] With the help of a supportive city council composed of seven Socialists, he wasted no time in going after privileged businesses. One target was the Saint Marys Machine Company, which was getting water from a city-owned plant for virtually nothing while others were carrying the load by paying much higher rates. Wilkins raised the rate on the company. After company officials resisted the rate hike, the city cut off its water. The company responded by shutting down and throwing people out of work. Not long after this, an angry crowd of the company's employees and their friends marched to city hall, threatening to hang the mayor. He barely escaped some rough treatment.[35]

A few years later the following comment appeared in the Socialist state party newspaper: Scott Wilkins "knows what it means to be a good Socialist mayor in a bad capitalist's town, for didn't the plutes of St. Mary's threaten to hang him?"[36] Hopes had been high for Wilkins in Socialist circles, but he and other Socialists were driven out of office and, indeed, in some cases out of town at or before the conclusion of their two-year terms.[37] The Socialist mayor of Martins Ferry, Ohio, took a similar action—he raised the rates local steel companies were paying the municipally owned electric plant—with less disastrous results, only prompting the company to come back at him when he stood for reelection, though its efforts fell short.[38]

In spite of opposition, the election of a Socialist mayor brought all kinds of public interventions in and checks on business activities. In Cameron, West Virginia, for example, a Socialist mayor ordered merchants and businessmen to remove all boxes, barrels, and other rubbish from the sidewalks, streets, or alleys in front of or near their establishments to improve the appearance of the town.[39] A similar notice was given by a Socialist administration in Sisseton, South Dakota.[40] Responding to consumer complaints, Socialist administrations in Victor, Colorado; Two Harbors, Minnesota; and elsewhere established municipal scales to assure that people received a just weight on coal and other commodities they purchased.[41] The new director of the weights and measures in Milwaukee found that "people had been robbed of hundreds of thousands of dollars through false scales and measures."[42] A Socialist city sealer in Schenectady, New York, also started off with a bang—in just twenty-two days he pursued more cases of false weights and measures than any previous office holder had pursued in a year.[43]

Much of the regulatory activity of Socialist mayors had to do with public utilities. They sought to get the best possible rates and services from those who held franchises or wished to have their franchises renewed. In Haverhill, Mayor Chase was able to negotiate a reduction in the rates charged by gas companies, and in Milwaukee, Mayor Seidel brought down the electric rates and implemented several campaign promises affecting the local streetcar company, for example, requiring that the company sprinkle the streets and provide a cross-town service.[44] In his 1916 campaign for mayor of Milwaukee, Daniel Hoan continued the attack on streetcar companies. He declared, "The main issue of this campaign is whether the flag of the streetcar company will float over the city hall, instead of the Stars and Stripes left there by Emil Seidel, former Socialist Mayor. I refuse to believe that it is necessary to sell out the city hall to the streetcar company and its black flag of monopolistic piracy in order to be American citizens."[45]

Mayors throughout the county, especially Socialist mayors, fought some fierce battles with utilities on franchise matters. Utilities commonly threatened to stop providing service unless they were given a franchise, be it a new one or a renewal, to their liking. Such was the case, for example, in Salem, Ohio; and Granite City, Illinois; regarding streetcars.[46] In New Castle, Pennsylvania, a private electric utility cut off power to the city street lights, forcing people to carry lanterns as they walked the streets at night, after Mayor Walter Tyler, a Socialist, refused to agree to give them a ten-year contract. Tyler did not want to tie things up that long. Like many Socialists, he wanted to move as quickly as he could to put the city in charge of providing electricity, either by building a new plant or purchasing a private one.[47]

Mayors bent on tightening up transportation franchises often ran into difficulty in the city council. They sometimes even found council members of their own party reluctant to be hard on the franchise holders because their working-class constituents were fearful of a loss of transportation and other services, something of vital importance to them. Socialist mayor R. A. Henning of Brainerd, Minnesota, for example, found this to be the case.[48] Henning vetoed various franchise agreements passed by the council in the belief that they did not provide adequate protection to the citizens and, more generally, that municipal ownership was the better way of providing the service.[49] Working with the support of the Information Department of the national party, Henning also vetoed against franchise offers made to the local gas company.

MUNICIPAL TAKEOVERS

Many, if not most, Socialist mayors followed the lead of the pioneer Massachusetts Socialist mayors Chase and Coulter in the late 1890s in pledging to do what they could to move in the direction of municipal ownership.[50] Socialists enjoyed some success in purchasing privately owned utilities for their cities. Success came, for example, through the efforts of Mayor Harry Gilham in Oswego, Kansas; Henry Stolze in Manitowoc, Wisconsin; William Thum in Pasadena, California; and George A. Huscher in Murray, Utah.

In practice, relatively few public utilities were purchased by Socialist administrations. Many faced the problem, as in so many areas of policy, that they lacked authority to act and state legislatures were unwilling to give them the necessary power. Thanks in part to the lack of state support, many also lacked the financial ability to make such purchases.[51] Barriers to municipal purchases as they developed in Chicago stemmed from doubts in the Good Government camp about the ability of the city to run large utility enterprises efficiently, and worries about corruption and the tremendous costs involved in acquiring properties and getting involved in lengthy legal battles.[52] The mere threat of public ownership sometimes produced better services and lower rates from the private providers.[53] But these improvements were likely to be only short term.

Even when mayors had authority, public ownership was a tough battle, and those who successfully got caught up in the struggle often had to wait several years for victory. Mayor Stolze came into office in 1905 calling for the city purchase of privately owned water and electric utilities but had to wait until 1911 when a public vote gave him the green light to make the water utility purchase. It took him three more years to purchase the electric utility.[54] Mayor Gilham waited several months before voters approved bonds necessary for the waterworks plant purchase he had proposed—concern over the price helped defeat the first vote, but the city and owner got together and lowered the cost to the city, and the voters went along with this the second time around.[55] Thum's focus in his 1911 campaign—which likely had a great deal to do with why he won—was on the need to acquire a water system for Pasadena. This he proceeded to do after hiring an expert, paying him out of his personal funds, to do an evaluation of the properties of the water company he wound up purchasing.[56] Thum, a leader in the municipal ownership cause, cautioned like-minded reformers to go slow, starting out with electricity and water and putting off other proposals "because asking for too much at once was likely to bring trouble."[57] Mayor Huscher won his battle for a municipal power plant only after a fierce battle with a privately owned utility.[58] As yet another example, Mayor Daniel Hoan of Milwaukee fought for many years for public ownership, including a fierce but ultimately lost battle with the Milwaukee Electric Railway and Light Company, and at the end of his long career could only point to city ownership of a stone quarry and streetlights.[59]

Overall, the drive for municipal ownership in the country had only limited success. The drive was most successful regarding the water-supply business. From 1880 to 1915 at least forty-eight plants changed ownership from private to public; twenty-seven did so after 1900. The transfer was most pronounced in cities over thirty thousand people. Privately owned waterworks remained relatively common in smaller towns, suggesting a special set of political and economic obstacles to ownership in these locations. The number of publicly owned power plants also increased in the early decades of the twentieth century. In these cases, we find considerable growth in the number of plants in the smaller jurisdictions. But these were small plants. In the country as a whole, the giant share of the electricity produced came from large privately owned utilities serving the larger cities. Private owners in larger cities had captured the major prizes.[60]

NEW MUNICIPAL ENTERPRISES

While purchases of private utilities were rare, Socialist administrations did frequently establish commercial enterprises providing such commodities as ice or coal that competed with private business. Much of this activity reflected the notion that governmental leaders have an obligation to do what they can reduce the high cost of living, especially for the poor. In Conneaut, Ohio, the Socialist mayor turned property the city already had into a fashionable municipal summer resort, where citizens could swim and have a meal at the municipal beach, dance at the municipal dance hall, ride in the municipal roller coaster, and sleep at the municipal hotel.[61] In Milwaukee, where the city was limited in its ability to undertake such functions, the city council asked for authority to engage in a variety of enterprises—ice plants, hospitals, packing houses, pawn shops (to protect against predatory lenders), and traditional public utilities—though having little success in the legislature.[62] The city was able to get into the dance hall business to provide an alternative to private halls, which were commonly considered places of "vice and low living." Early in 1911 the experiment appeared to be highly popular, particularly with church groups, and considered well underway toward making "all the private dance halls in that city unpopular and unprofitable."[63] Mayor Hoan followed up in Milwaukee with a system of public marketing that provided a wide variety of food at a reduced price in an effort to help to reduce the cost of living.

Getting into the liquor business was one of the few areas where there was considerable division within the Socialist movement. Some Socialists argued that to allow municipalities to go into the liquor business was as wrong as allowing them to go into the prostitution business, because these were parasitic forms of business that did great damage and should not exist, be they public or private in nature.[64] Socialist mayors in some places where drinking was allowed, however, had other ideas. Following the decision of voters in his county to "go wet," Socialist mayor John Wood of Coeur D'Alene, Idaho, toyed with the idea of getting the city into the saloon business in an effort to put some control on the problem, an idea that did not go down well with some Socialists and, more importantly, with business people who had already arranged to open saloons.[65] An experiment did get off the ground in Sisseton, South Dakota, under Socialist mayor John Knapp. In his plan, one person under a fixed salary was granted a license to sell liquor in the city, turning over all profits to the city. Because the saloon keeper shared none of the profits, he had no incentive to engage in improper or illegal activities—such as continuing to serve those who were already drunk, and selling to minors—and the city stood to gain considerably. The quasi-municipal saloon experiment in

Sisseton, the actual effects of which are unknown, came to an end in 1914 when the voters decided to return to prohibition.[66]

Socialists coming to power in Grand Junction, Colorado, where the city already owned and operated a successful water system, laid plans for the purchase of privately owned utilities providing electricity and gas, and street transportation, and establishing a municipal ice plant (producing a commodity much in demand in the days before electric refrigerators) and a municipal coal mine.[67] These grand aspirations failed to materialize for one reason or another, including public rejection of various proposals at the polls. For a time, the city did run a municipal woodpile enterprise, which provided jobs for homeless people in exchange for food and shelter and supplied fuel for people in the city who needed help in securing wood for cooking and heating their homes.[68]

George Lunn of Schenectady stood out among those mayors most eagerly engaged not only in calling for such commercial enterprises but in establishing them. He purchased two thousand tons of ice, which he began during the summer of 1912 to distribute to the poor for free and to others who could pay what it cost the city, asking for about 40 percent less than the private ice dealers were charging. The ice dealers complained that the city did not have a license to sell ice. Lunn countered that ice was nothing more than congealed water and the city had a license to sell water. The dealers got a court injunction ordering him to stop giving away or selling ice or "congealed water," but he and several associates, citing the need to come to the rescue of some ten thousand people who badly needed the product, got around the injunction by carrying on the work as a private enterprise. He used a similar arrangement in pursuing a program through which he dickered for cheap coal at the mines and sold it to residents of the city at a price lower than that being charged by local coal dealers. Along with these actions, Mayor Lunn established a municipal grocery store to provide food at cost or less, a municipal farm for itinerant workers, a municipal employment bureau, and a municipal lodging house.[69]

Following Lunn's failure to secure reelection in 1913, the anti-Socialist administration closed the municipal lodging house, which was intended for homeless men. This forced them to sleep in the corridors of the Milwaukee police department, on the cement floor without covering. Commenting on this situation, Lunn declared:

> I consider the closing of the municipal lodging house as an act of inhumanity, engendered by a gross ignorance of anything approaching fairness. I wish that all of the members of the present city administration could be compelled to go down stairs in the police station and stay there

for only 10 minutes and endure the stench of the city "lockup" where unfortunates, most of whom are out of work, are compelled to pass the night.[70]

Having campaigned against what he saw as corrupt city contracts with paving companies, Lunn while mayor also pushed for municipalization of the entire paving process. Unable to get the state legislature to change the state law requiring that such work be contracted out, he followed with a proposal to get around the state law and, in effect, put the city in the business as a competitor to the private paving companies; however, it failed to get the required two-thirds vote in the council. Lunn had to settle for the traditional contracting process, but he made sure that the contracting agreement was rigidly adhered too, withholding payments when he felt it was necessary.[71]

A central problem for some administrations hoping to directly provide products such as coal was finding a supplier. In December 1911 the Socialist administration in Two Harbors, Minnesota, set out to purchase coal to be resold to the public at cost, but the coal companies that dominated the supply refused to deal with the city. City officials responded by initiating a widely publicized inquiry into whether the coal companies had, in refusing to deal with them, entered into a combination in restraint of trade in violation of federal law.[72] After several months of investigation, the companies backed down and agreed to sell to the city.[73]

During the period under review, Socialist administrations around the country commonly sought to provide coal, ice, and various food products at cost to their citizens. In a tongue-in-cheek exercise, a writer for a left-leaning labor journal declared, "Those horrid Socialists at Star City, near Morgantown have shown their unfitness to live in this free country. They ordered two carloads of potatoes from Michigan and sold them for 75 cents per bushel, which was $1.75 below the local market. This criminal intrusion on business, and furnishing poor people with cheap potatoes, is bound to destroy the home. Officer, do your duty!"[74]

Conclusion

What can one say about the entry of Socialists into municipal politics? To provide some answers, this chapter reviews and further explores the difficulties encountered by Socialists who sought the office of mayor, and the frustrations, failures, and success of those who won the office. It also offers some observations about the performance and operation of the Socialist Party.

Socialists seeking office faced a variety of challenges, including an image of radicalism that made local boosters fearful about the economic consequence of a Socialist victory and the ability of Republicans and Democrats to fuse their tickets to defeat them. They also suffered from their party's third-party status. This often manifested in legal requirements that made it difficult to get on the ballot, imposed by members of the major parties who were anxious to avoid competition, and problems at the polls because of the reluctance of voters to sever their ties with the established major parties and the fears shared by many that they would be wasting their votes by casting them for candidates who had little chance of winning.

Socialists did their best to define the essential contest in which they were engaged as a simple one between the Socialist Party, representing the interests of the working class, and the two old parties, representing the interests of the capitalist class. The existence of a strong movement of left-wing Progressives within the old parties, however, muddled this picture and forced Socialists into a more challenging task of distinguishing themselves in terms of providing better government than left-wing progressive Democrats and Republicans or independents who, steeped in the cause of Municipal Socialism, put together similar reform packages. When Socialists became identified with a popular cause like municipal ownership, their opponents attempted to co-opt the idea and make it their own. They had considerable success in doing so.

Given these obstacles, Socialist mayoral candidates had little reason to be optimistic about winning office. Being realists and often well experienced at losing (many of those who won did so only after several attempts), they saw coming out on top as a long shot at best. Some preferred to look at campaigning as primarily an educational activity, a way of building for the future. They accepted the possibility of failure and often wound up as surprised as everyone else if they should happen to win.

Socialists initially felt they would do especially well in large cities because of the concentration of the working class in these places. As it turned out, several factors gave them a better chance in medium-sized and small towns. Whereas the size of the working class was not large enough as a percentage of the total population in most large cities to do much for the Socialists in city-wide elections, it was sometimes large enough in smaller places to have a significant impact on the Socialist vote for mayor. This was true in heavily industrialized and unionized small towns and mining camps, where Socialists enjoyed much of their success.

Overall, it was relatively easy for workers in these places to dominate the political process because of their numbers and their economic importance to the community. Workers and their political spokespersons could form social and political ties with local businesses and professionals they patronized and knew on a personal basis. They could find middle- and upper-middle-class citizens who sympathized with their resistance to the control and abuses of large corporations headquartered elsewhere. More generally, it was also far easier for Socialists to organize and conduct campaigns in smaller jurisdictions; the face-to-face personal nature of politics in these places greatly reduced the significance of partisanship ties, thus taking away a huge advantage enjoyed by major party candidates in larger jurisdictions, where party ties were virtually all that most voters knew about the candidates.

Successful Socialist mayoral candidates around the country commonly played off the failures of Republican or Democratic regimes and offered platforms that were adjusted to address immediate problems affecting everyday life in their localities. Socialists commonly stood for municipal ownership of utilities, improved roads, schools, water and sewer systems, honesty and efficiency in government, and moral crusades against drinking, gambling, and prostitution. Socialists were not misguided about the meaning of their electoral success when it came their way: they knew that much of the vote came in the form of protest against the status quo rather than a belief in Socialism. They knew that most voters had voted for experimentation, not revolution, and were waiting to see what the Socialists could do. Coming to power, Socialists often worked hard to assure the public that nothing disastrous was about to happen, particularly anything affecting the local economy, and that they were going to be cautious, and even conservative, in the changes they made.

At the same time, though, winning the office of mayor was a big deal for the Socialists. It offered the opportunity to demonstrate that they, as Socialists or members of the working class, or both, could do the job as well as or better than anyone else. Socialist mayors realized their tenure in office was not likely to do much to bring Socialism to their city or town but took some comfort in the thought that if they demonstrated their ability to govern, they could help lay the groundwork for the advancement of the party and the cause on the state and national levels, where Socialists would have an opportunity to accomplish much more. In the meantime, they set out to do what they could to improve the lives of ordinary people in their communities. In doing so, they were not acting in a revolutionary mode, but were nevertheless often highly disruptive of the status quo.

Socialist mayors were often in a position of having to choose between being what they and others felt was a true Socialist or being mayor. They ran the risk of violating Socialist principles to do what was necessary to win the office, and once elected mayor, of continuing to violate these principles by trying to please those who voted for them, most of whom were not Socialists. A strong dose of pragmatism was usually necessary to win office and survive. As was often predicted, many Socialist candidates for mayor watered down their platforms and sometimes were, like other politicians, guilty of promising things they could not deliver in a search for votes—something they may have had to do to win office but later put them in the unfavorable position of defending their record.

Yet, while there were opportunists among the Socialist mayors—a price the party paid as it became more popular—most Socialist mayors cannot be written off as politicians without any attachment to fixed principles or goals other than those relating to their personal pursuit of power. Once in power, Socialist mayors, adjusting to the pressures of the office, more practical political problems, and the necessity of having to work with others, tended to deemphasize doctrine. Indeed, most had already taken this course when running for office. Their performance in office, however, strongly indicates that they were still committed Socialists, individuals who continued to be dedicated to the interests of the working class and the goal of the cooperative commonwealth. They continued to see Socialism as the eventual cure for a variety of evils, be it poverty or immorality. They saw themselves as true believers in the revolutionary goals and viewed their pursuit of immediate reforms on the local level as a way of furthering the revolutionary agenda.[1]

Socialist mayors were not your typical politicians or mayors. Most came out of a movement, powered by religious zeal with a strong commitment to working people and the cause of organized labor. Though commonly drawn from the less ideological wing of the party, they were still far more driven by ideology than most municipal politicians. Even in the smallest towns, Socialist mayors viewed coming into power as providing an opportunity to do good things by shaking things up, by being a disruptor. They were more willing than the ordinary mayor to go to battle, or, one might say, less able to avoid conflict than the typical mayor. It also seems fair to say that Socialist mayors were less parochial, being more aware of and connected to the outside world, and more innovative than the ordinary mayor of the time.

Perhaps especially indicative of Socialist mayors and Socialists in general was their feelings of empathy for those who were suffering—in this case, those in the hard-pressed working class. As a delegate from Kansas declared at the party's unity convention in 1901, "I don't believe any man ever became a socialist that was worthy to be a socialist who did not first become such by having his indignation aroused over the wrongs wrought upon a class, as having his pity excited by the misery he saw about him."[2] Socialists in power lost some of their revolutionary zeal or found little time for revolutionary activity but retained their historic concern with labor and the welfare of working people. They looked forward to the cooperative commonwealth and doing what they could to promote the revolutionary cause.

While not expecting to usher in the cooperative commonwealth in one fell swoop, Socialists rejected the caretaker, limited-government model and fully expected to be change agents. They had ideas and plans. Many appeared to view honest government, sound fiscal management, and rigid enforcement of the law on issues of morality as the best ways to demonstrate they could govern. Beyond this, they planned to look for the opportunity to do what they could to promote and protect the interests of the working class and to move toward Socialism, especially through municipal ownership. With some fears, especially in the area of taxation, they proceeded to act upon this general plan while assuming that the voters were on their side or would be at election time.

They could, however, go only so far in implementing the plan. They often served in towns with severe problems (which is one reason they got elected) and places where the government, because of the size of the community, was ill-equipped to do much of anything or was historically disinclined because of its conservatism. Many operated within severe limitations imposed by the lack of authority, finances, staffing, time (short terms and term limitations), council opposition, and the resistance of significant groups within the community. They could not count on much, if any, support at the state level.

Council opposition was a major stumbling block. Only a relatively few Socialist administrations had councils controlled by members of their party. Even when they had control there was no guarantee that Socialist mayors could depend on the support of Socialist council members. Socialist had the additional problem of being associated with a party whose members felt they had the right to control the decisions of the office holders they helped put in office. The issue of party control surfaced in campaigns as a damaging argument against Socialist candidates. It also often became a severe problem for many of the Socialists who won the office of mayor.

Socialists had difficulty with success. The different factions within the party were able to hold together nominating candidates, frequently agreeing that electability should be a dominant consideration, and in putting together platforms and campaigns designed to win as many votes as possible from those who were unhappy with status quo. They shared a desire for power. Once they won an election, however, the consensus frequently fell apart as the various factions quarreled over what the Socialist office holder should do regarding appointments and policy matters.

Socialist mayors sometimes became frustrated with the difficulties of the job and the slow pace of reform. Many had spent years as cause-driven agitators railing against what they saw as a corrupt system and found it difficult to be patient, flexible, or compromising once they got into power. Many Socialist mayors decided not to run for reelection simply because they did not like the job. Others raised hell and were rejected at the polls. Only a relatively few adjusted to the demands and limitations of the office, accepted politics as the art of the possible, were willing to accept incremental change, eagerly sought reelection, and wound up serving several terms.

Despite all of these difficulties, Socialists could and did claim some accomplishments. Writing in 1914, a leading Socialist stated that Socialist administrations have "paved more streets, cleaned up more alleys, built more school houses, collected more taxes from the tax dodgers, [and] exacted more service from the private streetcar companies, gas light and power monopolies than the other parties ever tried to do." He went on to list some of the Socialists' accomplishments, citing numerous examples regarding public health and safety, education, welfare, public recreation, and a variety of other areas. In addition, he took special pride in Socialists doing well when it came to honesty: "No graft, no boodle, no thievery; absolutely honest. That means a great deal in this country, where every city government is a cesspool of political corruption."[3] Socialists did indeed appear to hold their own in terms of service provision and conduct.

Another thing that stood out for Socialist mayors was their status as great employers. They gave municipal employees better pay and benefits, shorter hours, and improved working conditions, and they protected workers in their efforts to unionize and bargain with employers. Their efforts encouraged similar changes in the private sector.

Socialist mayors could take some comfort in the thought that though the gains were not always spectacular, they were improving things. An indication of this is found in the following observations of a Socialist writer: "I saw Mayor J. Stitt Wilson look out of a window in the Berkeley city hall where workmen were putting the finishing touches upon a municipal playground where the children might come to play without fear of trespass or warning to be careful not to spoil the lawn. He was proud of that little bit of work; he knew what it meant, not in magnitude, but in DIRECTION!"[4] To some extent, there may have been, as the writer observed, a spirit that animated Socialist administrations, leaving mayors to believe that even little accomplishments were important because they were moving things in the right direction. Socialist mayors of the time seemed to enjoy being innovative and making changes, no matter how small. One observer of Mayor Emil Seidel found it remarkable that "scarcely a day passes that he does not do some sensible thing in a simple way that no one had thought of before."[5]

As predicted by left-wing critics, Socialist mayors in general did not accomplish much in terms of revolutionary action during their time in office. Most got into more trouble for what they said than for what they did. Still, their record in improving life for ordinary people in their communities was arguably as good or better than those of mayors who operated under similar or even fewer constraints. Electing a Socialist mayor made a difference—sometimes a huge difference—by bringing in new ideas, policies, and administrators who moved policy in a different direction. Socialist mayors embraced an ideology that encouraged them to seek more change than the typical mayor sought. They often wound up achieving less of what they sought or what was expected of them (or what they promised), but, it can be argued, this was as much if not more than the average mayor. Socialist mayors did exceptionally well when one considers the additional problems they faced because of their association with a third party and, more importantly, a badly divided third party, and one perceived as a threat by the business community.

Milwaukee, Wisconsin, provides the only example of how a Socialist administration might fare in a large city. Salient characteristics of the Milwaukee system were an emphasis on honesty and efficiency, modernizing and upgrading municipal administration, the inclusion of labor as a governing partner, greater labor protection and utility regulation, and an escalation in the provision of services. Scholars have commonly given Mayor Seidel high marks for his performance in these areas.[6] Milwaukee, it could be argued, was run as well as, if not better than, most Progressive cities.

As participants in the municipal reform movement, Socialist mayors and Socialists in general played a significant role in helping to spread the "Good Government" reforms of the time. Socialists generally differed from Good Government municipal reformers by placing more emphasis on democracy than efficiency and in opposing specific reforms such as nonpartisan elections and elections at large, which they felt were detrimental to the interests of the working class. Still, Socialist mayors outperformed the Good Government reformers at their own "honesty and efficiency" game. They also held their own with Progressive reformers on the left when it came to implementing a program of Municipal Socialism, and surpassed all mayors when it came to rising to the defense of working people in their struggles with employers. Socialist political action on the municipal level had positive results in improving the lives of ordinary people.

The number of Socialist mayors rose slowly in the early 1900s, hit a peak in 1911, following the breakthrough in Milwaukee, and steadily declined to a new low in the years following the entry of the United States into World War I and the harassment and repression of the Socialist Party for opposing that action. The municipal reform movement declined along with the general trend of Progressivism as the country entered the war period. Socialists faded away on the municipal level as the municipal reform movement ended.

Municipal ownership had been the best issue the party had going for it. As historian Ira Kipnis suggested regarding the Socialist experience in Haverhill, "Other platform planks, such as requiring the union label of government printing and using union labor on city projects, were put into effect with little difficulty. But these accomplishments were not great enough to maintain political enthusiasm at a high pitch over any length of time."[7] The municipal ownership issue, however, slowly lost its steam. By 1920 the rush for municipalization had run its course and was no longer much of an issue. Lively disputes over utility regulation also disappeared on the local level as this function, with the encouragement of the utilities, was shifted to the state level. Structural changes in the municipal reform package changed the image and operation of local government, particularly in smaller and medium-sized places where the Socialists had been relatively strong, making the need for structural reform generally less salient as an issue. As the Socialists feared, certain Good Government reforms, such as elections at large, made it more difficult for them to get a foothold in municipal politics.[8]

In the early 1900s Socialists saw themselves as effective municipal administrators in pursuing the interests of the working class; indeed, this was something even the capitalists were willing to acknowledge. The problem, Socialists argued, was that there were just not enough Socialist municipal administrations, a problem they largely blamed on the workers: "They do not know as yet how to handle and man their party, how to line up on a class ballot, how to quit voting and working for the party and the system which oppresses them and turn the power of a vote into a power to establish working-class control of every community."[9] Other complaints about the lack of support from workers during this period are not difficult to find. In Colorado a Socialist Party leader complained, "Too much must not be expected from Colorado because of the terrible school which her workers have been attending. It seems to require something more than persecution to make socialists."[10] From Utah a Socialist editor lamented, "We are of the laboring class, and their fight is our fight. But it is just about as the attorney said: 'If you help a laboring man he will kick you, but if you kick him, he will help you.'"[11]

Constance McLaughlin Green's study of workers in Holyoke, Massachusetts, found they had been somewhat attracted to the Socialist Party but had turned away by the early 1900s. The workers, she wrote, had concluded "that Socialism was still too theoretical to be immediately useful to them."[12] The party, capturing Milwaukee and turning increasingly to the right, did enjoy a large boost in worker support early in the second decade of the twentieth century, but this was to drift way, partly because of the gains Socialists helped bring about on behalf of working people, which reduced worker demands for reform and their need for Socialists.[13] Rather than class consciousness, the Socialists along with the forces of mainstream labor helped develop a sense of "job consciousness" among the workers, reflecting their pure and simple concerns with wages, working conditions, and job security.[14]

The rise and fall of Socialists at the local level is consistent with what we might expect from third-party theory. Like other third parties, the Socialist Party rose in response to the failure of established parties and the appeal of their message, only to decline when the conditions favorable to them disappeared.[15] The party itself, however, did not disappear. As events beyond the years covered in this study demonstrate, the Socialist Party did not turn out to be a one-shot, short-term party, like the Populist or People's Party that came and went. Rather, the Socialist Party established itself as a party that, depending on leadership and conditions, had the potential to move in and out of meaningful participation in the election system, being held together in periods of political inactivity by a relatively small band of true believers and, when politically active, as in the period under review, capable of furthering the cause of positive government, not only as an agenda builder and a crusading force keeping those in power on their toes, but as a governing party.

Appendix 1: Biographies of Featured Mayors

First in time among the prominent Socialist mayors featured in this study, and serving as a model for all those to come, is John Chase (1870–1937), who was elected mayor of Haverhill, Massachusetts, on the Social Democratic ticket in 1898 and 1899. Born in a small New Hampshire town to a working-class family, he first went to work at the age of eight in a woolen mill, receiving but a few months of schooling each winter. He went on to find employment in a shoe factory, continuing his education by taking private lessons in the evening. In the shoe factory he became active in the Boot and Shoe Workers' Union and, because of this, was blacklisted by employers in the local shoe industry. In search of employment, he became a clerk in a cooperative grocery store he helped create in Haverhill.

Politically, Chase moved from the Populist Party to the Socialist Labor Party to the Social Democratic Party. Popular in Socialist as well as labor circles, he accepted his party's nomination for various offices but was not successful until 1898, when he was elected mayor of Haverhill. He is commonly regarded as the first Socialist mayor in the country. He had put together a popular platform that was picked up by other Socialists inspired by his victory. During his terms as mayor and for several years thereafter, Chase served as a national organizer and lecturer for the Socialist Party. Following his stint as mayor he unsuccessfully ran as the Socialist candidate for various offices, including those of governor in Massachusetts and New York.

While Socialist success was relatively limited in the decade following Chase's election (though, as this book indicates, it was perhaps far more successful than commonly assumed), a major breakthrough came when Emil Seidel (1864–1947) became mayor of Milwaukee, Wisconsin, in 1910, and gave the Socialist Party its first victory in a major US city. This set off a flood of victories the following year.

Born in Pennsylvania to German immigrants, Seidel moved with his family when an infant to Wisconsin in 1867, eventually settling in Milwaukee. He left school at age thirteen and went to work as a woodcarver. He later declared that dropping out of school was "the greatest disappointment of my life . . . but I was the eldest of eleven and had to go to work."[1] He later spent several years in Germany developing his woodcarving skills and while there became an active Socialist. Seidel noted in his autobiography that in the shops in Germany where he worked, it "seemed as if every carver was a Socialist; and they made no bones about it their politics.... I was born republican though by this time a pretty wobbly one.... I wanted to know more about Socialism and read what I could get hold of."[2] Returning to Wisconsin in the early 1890s, he joined the Socialist Labor Party in Milwaukee and gradually moved on to the Socialist Party of America, of which he became a founding member. He failed in a bid for governor in 1902 but began his political career in Milwaukee by getting elected to the city council in 1904 and going on to serve several terms. His status as a bilingual labor unionist, speaking German in German wards, made him an ideal candidate for office.[3]

Following his failure to win reelection, in 1912 Seidel became the national party's nominee for vice president of the United States, running on a ticket with Eugene V. Debs as the presidential candidate. He lost a bid for reelection as mayor in 1914 but became a member of the city council in the next election and continued in that capacity for several years. Debs, whose relations with Seidel were somewhat strained at the time, suggested in a 1914 letter that Seidel, while sincere and a good speaker, suffered from "over seriousness" and being too slow in debate.[4] One scholar has suggested that Seidel was less successful than Daniel Hoan, another Socialist who became mayor of Milwaukee, because he was basically an ideologically driven Socialist, far less pragmatic than Hoan.[5]

Three of the most prominent Socialists elected as part of the wave engendered by Seidel were George Lunn of Schenectady, New York; Lewis Duncan of Butte, Montana; and J. Stitt Wilson of Berkley, California.

George Lunn (1873–1948) was born on a farm in Iowa into a devoutly religious family. He was one of six children. Like Chase and Seidel, he quit school, in his case, to sell newspapers in Des Moines. After deciding to become a minister, he went back to school, eventually receiving a college degree and completing his seminary training as a minister. Following several years as a pastor in a small town in Nebraska, brief service as an US Army chaplain during the Spanish-American War, and additional seminary training, he became an ordained Presbyterian minister in New York, starting in Buffalo and moving on to Schenectady, where he preached the social gospel for six years as pastor of the First Reformed Church. He resigned after several members complained about his diversion into politics. Taking several members of his congregation with him, he and others organized a new church, the United People's Church, which united with the Congregationalists, and continued to speak out to a largely working-class audience against evils in the social order.[6] He also initiated a newspaper called the *Citizen* to spread his views and campaign against graft and corruption in municipal government, especially the corrupt ties between prominent local officials and the "paving ring" of contractors that had resulted in padded contracts bilking the city.

Lunn won election as mayor in 1911, lost in 1913, and won again in1915. A newspaper account of Mayor Lunn as he appeared in 1912 describes him as follows:

> Lunn controls the only Socialist newspaper in town and is its chief editor. He is the pastor of a Socialist congregation. He is the head and front of the copartnership which took over the municipal ice business when the Supreme Court forbade the city to go on with it. He is the man who dickers for cheap coal at the mines and arranges for its sale at cut prices to the people.[7]

Lunn had been a Republican but joined the Socialist Party shortly before he accepted its nomination of him for the office of mayor. Lunn fell out with the Socialist Party during his second term. Joining with the Democratic Party, he won election in 1917 as its nominee for Congress. He returned to the office of mayor in Schenectady as a Democrat in 1919 and 1921. Later, in 1923–1924, he served as lieutenant governor of New York under Democrat governor Al Smith.

Lewis Duncan (1857–1936), twice elected mayor of Butte, Montana, was born in St. Louis, Missouri, and moved with his family to Quincy, Illinois, where he attended public schools. His first career choice was that of a public accountant, but he later decided to become a lawyer and, after he had done so, made the ministry his central concern. As a report on his death noted, "He was always of a religious turn of mind and after two years at the bar gave up his law practice to become a Unitarian minister."[8] His work as a minister moved him from two small towns in Illinois, to Milwaukee and, in 1902, to Butte. He was fired in Butte as a Unitarian minister for preaching Socialism. One of his related offenses was in opening his church door to anarchist Emma Goldman.[9] He responded to his firing by listing his occupation as "agitator."

Duncan actively worked to build up the Socialist Party in the state, served on the national committee of the Socialist Party, and was a well-known Socialist publisher, lecturer, and writer. He was elected Butte's mayor in 1911 and 1913 but was impeached and removed from office for neglecting his duties during riots in the city. Following his removal from power he found employment in the mines as a mine mucker, shoveling broken ore and waste rocks into ore cars or buckets. A sympathetic reporter wrote, "Two years ago he was mayor of Butte and candidate for governor of Montana, with the eyes of millions upon him. Today he's a mucker in the Butte mines, a tired man with blistering hands and feet. Only by taking refuge underground with an independent company has Louis J. Duncan thwarted the long arm of the copper kings, who have sworn to run him out of the district."[10] He found the mine labor too hard on him physically and gladly accepted a job in South Dakota working for the radical Nonpartisan League. He followed this with a move to Minneapolis, Minnesota, where he engaged in newspaper activity and, when that ended, offered private teaching services focusing on such subjects as business and public speaking.

J. Stitt Wilson (1868–1942)—his seldom-used first name was Jackson—was born in a small town in Canada, into a devout Methodist family. Like Lunn and Duncan, he became a Christian Socialist but also a follower of Henry George and his single tax plan, and was deeply influenced by the ideas of feminist reformers.[11] Immigrating to the United States, he settled in Evanston, Illinois, where he attended Northwestern University, graduated, and, after deciding to become a minister, enrolled in the theological seminary at the university. After his schooling he became a Methodist pastor and social worker in Chicago in a poor working-class area. Seeing the hardship and suffering around him, he turned to Socialism. As Wilson put it, "The injustices, misery, and wretchedness, and the unequal struggle of the workers against such frightful odds compelled me to study the underlying causes of this agony—and I became a Socialist."[12]

In the late 1890s Wilson joined others in an organization called the Social Crusade, which preached that Socialism was the pathway to true Christianity. He made Berkeley, California, his home in 1901 but spent much of his time traveling for the Social Crusade. Wilson established a reputation of being a well-educated, moderately progressive minister and public speaker.[13] As mayor he offered a moderate course of reform but was frustrated with the political obstacles he encountered. He did little to please those on the far left. During a lively debate early in Wilson's term, IWW leader Bill Haywood turned to Wilson and charged: "You are not a Socialist and I defy you to prove that you have done anything for the working class."[14] Elected mayor in 1911, he refused to run for another term. In 1915 he changed his mind and made another bid for the office on the Socialist ticket but went down to defeat. Two years later he left the party over its stand against the United States entry into World War I.

Daniel Hoan (1881–1961) stands out among the Socialist mayors elected to their office in 1916 or later who experienced what it was like serving during wartime. Born in Waukesha, Wisconsin, he served as Milwaukee's mayor from 1916 to 1940. Though he never had a city council where Socialists were in the majority, he established a productive and distinguished career that extended well beyond the period under study in this volume.[15] Prior to his election in 1916 he worked closely for a time with Socialist Party leader Victor Berger on a

Socialist newspaper and served as Milwaukee city attorney, leading a crusade against the street railways. He helped organize and manage a Socialist Club as a student at the University of Wisconsin in the early 1900s. Cooking was another of his passions, something he developed in his early teens and continued to do for a students' club at the university, restaurants in Milwaukee, and, after graduation in 1905, in Chicago, where he ran a restaurant and went to law school after working hours. He was admitted to the bar in 1908 and two years later ran for city attorney on the same ticket on which Emil Seidel was elected mayor. In 1936 he wrote, "All our efforts to make Milwaukee a better place in which to live has been purposely designed to make lighter the burden of those who toil. We have not and will not leave any stone unturned to continue to battle on their behalf."[16] Following his defeat for reelection in 1940, he joined the Democratic Party and ran without success for governor and mayor of Milwaukee as a nominee of that party.

Finally, mention has to be made of Thomas Van Lear (1869–1931), elected Socialist mayor of Minneapolis in 1916. Van Lear was born into a working-class family in the coal-mining town of Frostburg, Maryland. He had only limited schooling when we went to work in the coal mines as a boy. He joined the reform-minded Knights of Labor organization as a teenager and went on to serve four years in the US Army, including reenlisting for a year during the Spanish-American War. Leaving military service, he settled in Minneapolis, where he became a machinist by trade, an influential union leader who developed strong ties with members of various unions in the city, and an active Socialist. He spent much of his time trying to build up the union movement as well as the Socialist Party, which had not been much of a force in local politics. One biographer found him to be "a powerful orator whose fiery speeches thrilled his supporters and outraged his opponents."[17] After a couple of narrow defeats, he won the office of mayor in 1916, at the age of forty-seven, but accusations concerning his loyalty to the country growing out of his party's stand on the war contributed to his defeat in an attempt for reelection two years later. Van Lear was also expelled from the Socialist Party in 1919 for actions he had taken regarding the war but continued to be politically active through a new labor-Socialist party called the Municipal Nonpartisan League and, for a short time, a left-wing newspaper, the *Minnesota Daily Star*, in Minneapolis. He fell short in an attempt to regain the office of mayor in 1921.[18]

Appendix 2: Municipalities with Social Administrations, 1898–1920

Each entry lists the town name, followed by population (and year, in parentheses), name of mayor, and date of election or term.

ALABAMA (2)

Fairhope, 500 (1910), J. F. Johnson, 1912–1914.
Girard, 4,214 (1910), J. P. Marchant, elected in September 1912.

ARKANSAS (3)

Judsonia, 746 (1910), 899 (1920), Dr. J. C. Huntley, elected in fall 1916.
Hartford, 1,780 (1910), Peter Stewart, April 1912–April 1914, 1917.
Winslow, 289 (1910), 264 (1920), Charles F. Stauffer, elected in spring 1911.

CALIFORNIA (5)

Berkeley, 40,434 (1910), J. Stitt Wilson, 1911–1913.
Daly City, 3,000 (estimated 1912), 3,779 (1920), Bertram C. Ross, 1912–1916.
Eureka, 11,845 (1910), 12,023 (1920), Elijah Falk, 1915–1919.
Pasadena, 30,291 (1910), William Thum, 1911–1913.
Watts, 1,922 (1910), C. H. Dodd, elected in 1911.

COLORADO (14 MUNICIPALITIES, 17 MAYORS)

Anaconda, 300 (1900), George Hooten, reported elected in 1902.
Buena Vista, 1,041 (1910), H. J. Brown, 1913–1914.
Coal Creek, 676 (1910), Robert Tyson, reported elected in April 1907.
Coal Creek, 676 (1910), Harry Irwin, won the office of mayor in April 1912.
Crested Butte, 905 (1910), Dr. Orlando A. Oram, elected in 1914 and 1915.

Edgewater, 712 (1910), Eugene Bootz, won in 1913 and 1914, lost in 1915.
Grand Junction, 7,754 (1910), Thomas M. Todd, elected 1909, 1911.
Lafayette, 1,892 (1910), Seth Woods, 1913–1914.
Littleton, 1,373 (1910), John B. Mayers, 1912–1913.
Minturn, 241 (1910), Robert A. Bryant, 1912–1914.
Nederland, 446 (1910), Socialist mayor reported elected in 1911.
Oak Creek, 222 (1910), Dr. Charles A. Pankey, elected April 1912.
Oak Creek, 222 (1910), M. C. or M. A. Deering, elected in 1914.
Oak Creek, 222 (1910), 967 (1920), C. Tatman, elected spring 1916.
Ophir, 124 (1910), James Spurrier, elected in April 1912.
Paonia, 1,007 (1910), J. M. Haley, 1912–1916.
Victor, 1,007 (1910), J. B. Bitterly, 1911–1915.

CONNECTICUT (1)

Naugatuck, 12,722 (1910), A. Barton Cross Jr., 1913–1914.

FLORIDA (1)

Gulfport (no information on population), Elmer E. Wintersgill, elected in 1910, reelected in 1912.

GEORGIA (1)

Nicholson, 167 (1910), M. K. Nicholson, elected in 1916.

IDAHO (1)

Coeur d'Alene, 7,291 (1910), John T. Wood, 1911–1913.

ILLINOIS (17 MUNICIPALITIES, 18 MAYORS)

Buckner Hill, 1,046 (1910), 977 (1920), C. O. Harper, elected spring 1917.
Canton, 10,453 (1910), Homer Whalen, 1915–1917.
Davis, 352 (1910), J. J. Cleveland, 1911–1913.

Des Plaines, 2,348 (1910), W. M. Lawson, 1911–1913.
Dorrisville, 1,184 (1910), C. D. Brown, elected April 1911.
Granite City, 9,903 (1910), 14,757 (1920), Marshall Kirkpatrick, 1911–1915, 1917–1919.
Jerseyville, 4,113 (1910), A. C. Robb, 1913–1917.
Ledford, 599 (1910), Ewell Work, 1910, April 1912?
Lincoln, 10,892 (1910), 11,882 (1920), Herman Reetz, elected April 1915.
O'Fallon, 2,018 (1910), Dan L. Thomas, elected April 1911.
Pawnee, 1,399 (1910), Socialist mayor won in 1913 by a toss of the coin.
Riverton, 1,911 (1910), Socialist mayor reported elected in 1915.
Silvis, 1,163 (1910), 2,541 (1920), Fred O. Hartline, 1917–1919.
Silvis, 2,541 (1920), George Sleeth, elected April 1919.
Spaulding, 308 (1910), election of president of the board of trustees in April 1911 reported.
Thayer, 1,012 (1910), John Mainwarning, village president, elected in 1911, reelected in 1913.
Torrino, 514 (1910), Socialist mayor reported elected in 1915.
Venice, 3,718 (1910), J. E. Lee, 1911–1913.

INDIANA (6)

Bicknell, 7,635 (1910), 7,635 (1920), Tyler Lawton, elected November 1913, served January 1914 to January 1918.
Clinton, 6,229 (1910), 10,962 (1920), Morgan J. Tucker, 1911–1917.
Elwood, 10,790 (1920), John G. Lewis, elected November 1917.
Fairview Park, 630 (1910), Socialist victories in fall 1913 led to a Socialist administration.
Gas City, 2,870 (1920), Frank Leninaux, elected November 1917.
Staunton, 746 (1910), Socialist victories in 1911 and 1912 established Socialist administrations.

IOWA (6 MUNICIPALITIES, 7 MAYORS)

Boone, 10,347 (1910), C. J. Wilder, 1909–1911.
Davenport, 50,727 (1920), Charles Barewald, 1920–1922.
Madrid, 1,191 (1910), 1,783 (1920), George W. Crank, 1910–1912, 1916–1918, 1918–1920. Won in 1910, lost 1912 and 1914, won in 1916 and 1918.
Hiteman (no population data), full Socialist township ticket elected in 1900.

Hopkinton, 797 (1910), D. C. Ohler, 1912–1914.
Mystic 1,758 (1900), Joseph Wheeler, elected in spring 1904.
Mystic, 2,663 (1910), Socialist mayor reported elected in 1906.

KANSAS (12)

Arma, 327 (1910), Evan Morgan, 1911–1915.
Curransville, 773 (1910), James Perkins, 1911–1915, won in 1911 and 1913.
Dexter, 512 (1910), Dr. R. D. Williams, 1911.
Frontenac, 3,225 (1920), John Schildknecht, 1917–1921.
Girard, 2,446 (1910), H. P. Houghton, elected in spring 1911.
Hillsboro, 1,134 (1910), 1,451 (1920), Dr. H. Bruning, 1916–1922, was on council, was appointed to office after mayor resigned in 1916, won election to office in spring 1917.
Hoxie, 250 (1900), B. C. Decker, elected April 1900.
Liberal, 1,716 (1910), M. H. Jones, elected April 1912.
Osawatomie, 4,046 (1910), Charles Bates, 1911; was not elected as a Socialist but converted after elected.
Oswego, 2,208 (1900), 2,317 (1910), Harry Gilham, elected in spring 1905, reelected in 1906, lost in 1907.
Scammon, 2,233 (1910), Socialist mayor reported elected spring 1912.
Thayer, 542 (1900), J. M. Dunsmore, elected in 1900.

LOUISIANA (2)

DeRidder, 2,100 (1910), S. F. Presley, elected in 1912.
Winnfield, 2,925 (1910), Socialist reported elected in 1912.

MASSACHUSETTS (2 MUNICIPALITIES, 3 MAYORS)

Brockton, 40,063 (1900), Charles Coulter, 1899–1900, 1900–1901, 1902–1903; won in 1899, reelected in 1900, lost in 1901, won in 1902.
Haverhill, 37,176 (1900), John Chase, 1898–1899, 1899–1900; won in 1898 and 1899, lost in 1900.
Haverhill, 37,1761 (1900), 53,884 (1920), Parkman B. Flanders, 1903–1904, 1920–1923.

MICHIGAN (7)

Bear Lake, 504 (1910), Henry Chase, elected village president in 1912.
Flint, 38,500 (1910), John Menton, 1911–1913; won in 1911, lost in 1912.
Greenville, 4,045 (1910), Albert B. Thomas, 1911–1912; won in April 1911, lost in 1912.
Harbor Springs, 1,805 (1910), Joseph Warnock, elected in 1912.
Ishpeming, 12,448 (1910), W. J. Roberts, 1906–1908; lost reelection in April 1908.
South Frankfort, 681 (1910), Socialist reported elected village president in April 1911.
Traverse City, 10,925 (1920), Edward Lautner, 1917–1919.

MINNESOTA (10 MUNICIPALITIES, 14 MAYORS)

Bemidji, 5,099 (1910), Fred Malzhan, elected February 1912, lost February 1913.
Brainerd, 8,526 (1910), R. A. Henning, 1913–1915; won in 1913, lost in 1915.
Brainerd, 8,526 (1910), A. Ousdahl, 1909–1911; elected in spring 1909, lost in 1911.
Crookston, 7,559 (1910), H. L. Larson, elected November 1911, lost November 1913.
Dawson, 1,511 (1920), William Jackson, 1919–1924.
La Porte, 140 (1910), Andrew Gohres, elected in spring 1911.
Minneapolis, 301,408 (1920), Thomas Van Lear, 1917–1919.
St. Hillaire, 468 (1910), J. C. Dahl, 1911–1913.
Tenstrike, 250 (1910), James Sturdevant, 1911–1913.
Thief River Falls, 3,714 (1910), Lars Backe, elected in fall 1911, ousted in 1913.
Two Harbors, 3,278 (1900), 4,990 (1910), C. G. Rothfus, elected 1906.
Two Harbors, 4,990 (1910), Alex Halliday, March 1911, term expired April 1913.
Two Harbors, 4,990 (1910), 4,546 (1920), Ernst Gottfrid Strand, 1916–1917.
Two Harbors, 4,990 (1910), 4,546 (1920), William Towl, elected 1913 and again in 1915, resigned from office in 1916.

MISSOURI (5)

Cardwell, 874 (1910), P. A. Fitzgerald, 1911–1913.
Fornfelt, 1,209 (1910), unidentified, elected 1908.
Liberal, 800 (1910), M. M. Jones, 1912–1914.

Minden, 591 (1910), Fred Swain, 1911–1913; lost bid for reelection in 1913.
Rich Hill, 2,755 (1900), Lawrence Griffith, elected in spring 1903; lost in 1905.

MONTANA (4 MUNICIPALITIES, 5 MAYORS)

Anaconda, 9,453 (1900), John Frinke, 1903–1905; defeated 1905.
Butte, 39,165 (1910); Lewis Duncan, elected in 1911, reelected in 1913.
Butte, 39,165 (1910), 41,611 (1920), Clarence Smith, president of the council, filled in as acting mayor after Duncan was removed from office, 1914–1915. In April 1915 lost to a Democrat.
Missoula, 12,869 (1910), 12,068 (1920), Andrew M. Getchell, 1914–1916.
Red Lodge, 2,152 (1900), 4,800 (1910), Ray Austin, 1906–1908.

NEBRASKA (3)

Beatrice, 9,356 (1910), W. E. Griffin, 1911–1913.
Red Cloud, 1,686 (1910), Sam Foe, 1911–1913.
Wymore, 2,613 (1910), Edward Mauck, 1911–1913.

NEW JERSEY (2)

Rockaway, 1,902 (1910), William A. Matthews, 1911–1913.
Haledon, 2,560 (1910), 3,435 (1920), William Brueckmann, elected in November 1912, 1914, 1916; lost in 1918, had a comeback in the 1920s.

NEW YORK (2)

Schenectady, 72,826 (1910), 88,723 (1920), George R. Lunn, won November 1911, lost in 1913, won in 1915. Won another term as a Democrat.
Lackawanna, 17,918 (1920), John H. Gibbons, elected in November 1919, served 1920–1922.

NORTH CAROLINA (1)

East Spencer, 1,729 (1910), Howard Charles Bueck, elected in spring 1909.

NORTH DAKOTA (4)

Des Lacs, 433 (1910), O. H. Hoveland, 1911–1913.
Hillsboro, 1,237 (1910), Rev. J. L. Anderson, elected March 1912.
Minot, 6,188 (1910), Arthur Le Sueur, elected July 1909, served 1909–1911, resigned from office.
Rugby, 1,630 (1910), Eric Dale, 1912–1914.

OHIO (34)

Albany, 465 (1920), W. M. Higley, 1918–1920.
Amsterdam, 1,041 (1910), James Turvey, elected November 1911.
Barberton, 9,410 (1910), Charles Culler, elected November 1911.
Barnhill, 506 (1910), Eli Thorpe, 1912–1913.
Byesville, 2,775 (1920), D. L. Davis, 1917–1919.
Canton, 50,217 (1910), Harry S. Schilling, 1911–1913.
Canal Dover, 6,621 (1910), Lindsay Williams, 1913–1915.
Conneaut, 8,319 (1910), 9,343 (1920), Duff S. Brace, 1913–1917; won in 1913 and 1915.
Coshocton, 9,603 (1910), Lloyd N. Staats, 1913–1915.
Dillonvale, 1,519 (1910), Socialist reported elected in November 1911.
Fostoria, 9,557 (1910), William M. Ralston, 1911–1913; lost reelection in 1913.
Hamilton, 35,279 (1910), Frederick Hinkle, 1913–1915; lost reelection in 1915.
Jenera, 269 (1920), D. E. Hull, 1917–1921.
Kenmore, 1,561 (1910), Joseph Nice, 1913.
Lima, 30,508 (1910), Corbin Shook, 1911–1913.
Linden Heights, 991 (1910), Thos. M. Fleeheart, elected in fall 1911.
Lorain, 28,883 (1910), Thomas Pape, 1911–1913.
Martins Ferry, 9,133 (1910), Newton Wycoff, 1911–1915; elected in 1911, 1913, lost in 1915.
Massillon, 17,428 (1920), Henry H. Vogt, 1919–1920.
Midvale (no population information), full ticket said to have been elected in 1911.
Mineral City, 1,082 (1910), Socialist said to have won in 1911.
Mineral Ridge, 759 (1910), E. E. Robinson, 1911–1913.
Mount Vernon, 9,087 (1910), Alfred Perrine, won in 1911, reelected in 1913 as an independent.
New Boston, 1,858 (1910), 4,817 (1920), J. S. Davis (a.k.a. Sam Davis), elected in fall 1913.

New Knoxville, 537 (1920), H. L. Kattman, 1918–1920.
Osnaburg, 448 (1910), Socialist mayor reported elected November 1911.
Piqua, 15,044 (1920), Frank B. Hamilton, 1918–1919; elected in 1917, took office January 1918.
Salem, 8,943 (1910), John S. McKay, 1911–1913.
Shelby, 4,903 (1910), 7,000 (1920), Daniel Howe, 1913–1915.
Silverton, 795 (1920), William Kunhell, 1917–1919.
St. Marys, 5,732 (1910), Scott Wilkins, 1911–1913; elected in November 1911, took office in January 1912; lost reelection in 1913.
Sugar Grove, 368 (1910), S. D. Hansley, elected November 1911.
Toronto, 4,271 (1910), Robert Murray; elected December 1911, reelected in 1913.
Warsaw, 512 (1910), W. B. McClure, elected in fall 1913.

OKLAHOMA (9 MUNICIPALITIES, 10 MAYORS)

Antlers, 1,273 (1910), Tom Johnson, 1911–1913.
Chant, 882 (1910), Socialist mayor said to have been elected in 1913.
Cleveland, 1,3010 (1910), Socialist mayor reported elected in 1915.
Coalgate, 2,921 (1900), John Ingram, 1904–1905.
Coalgate, 3,225 (1920), Socialist said to have elected mayor in spring 1910.
Collinsville, 1,324 (1910), Socialist said to have won in April 1913.
Fort Cobb, 382 (1910), Socialist mayor reported elected in 1915.
Krebs, 2,884 (1910), J. A. Nixon, 1915–1917.
Peoria, 135 (1910), general ticket said to have won in spring 1914.
Stillwater, 3,434 (1910), C. F. Rogers, 1909–1911.

OREGON (2)

Coquille, 1,398 (1910), J. E. Quick, 1910–1912; did not run in 1912.
St. Johns, 4,872 (1910), A. W. Vincent, 1914–1916; defeated in 1915.

PENNSYLVANIA (16 MUNICIPALITIES, 17 MAYORS)

Beaver Falls, 12,191 (1910), entire ticket said to have been elected in November 1913.
Broad Top, 478 (1910), Socialist reported to have won in 1911.
Connellsville, 12,847 (1920), Samuel Lee, 1911–1915.

Garrett, 859 (1920), William Martin, 1917.
Hazeldale, 1,168 (1910), Socialist reported to have won in 1911.
New Castle, 36,280 (1910), Walter V. Tyler, 1912–1916, elected in November 1911.
Pitcairn, 4,975 (1910), Socialist burgess reported elected in November 1913.
Pitcairn, 4,975 (1910), 5,738 (1920), James A. Cox, elected in November 1917.
Roscoe, 1,450 (1910), elected a Socialist burgess November 1913.
Shamokin, 19,588 (1910), Socialist mayor reported elected November 1913.
Stoneboro, 1,074 (1910), clean sweep by Socialists reported November 1913.
South Connellsville, 12,845 (1910), Samuel Lee, 1911–1915.
Turtle Creek, 4,995 (1910), Socialist burgess reported elected in 1913.
Union City, 3,850 (1920), A. F. Young, 1918–1920.
West Brownsville, 2,036 (1910), Socialist said to have won office of chief burgess in November 1913.
Wheatland, 955 (1910), Harry Vaughn, elected November 1911.
Whitaker, 1,547 (1910), Socialist reported to have taken over in 1909.

SOUTH DAKOTA (1)

Sisseton, 1,397 (1910), John Knapp, elected in 1913 and 1914.

UTAH (9 MUNICIPALITIES, 11 MAYORS)

Bingham, 2,881 (1910), Anton Christenson, elected in November 1905, along with rest of the ticket. Did not run in 1907.
Cedar City, 1,705 (1910), Daniel T. Leigh, served 1906–1907, elected previous November 1905.
Cedar City, 1,705 (1910), Donald C. Urie, served 1912–1913, elected in fall 1911.
Eureka, 3,416 (1910), Andrew Mitchell, 1908–1913; elected in 1907, lost in 1909, won again in 1911, lost again in 1913.
Eureka, 3,008 (1920), Major Church, 1918–1921, elected in November 1917.
Joseph, 127 (1910), Socialist mayor reported elected in 1911.
Mammoth, 1,771 (1910), N. J. Hanson, 1912–1913, elected in all 1911.
Manti, 2,423 (1910), full ticket reported elected in 1911.
Murray, 4,057 (1910), George A. Huscher, 1912–1915, elected in fall 1911 and 1913.
Stockton, 258 (1910), Gus Anderson, 1912–1914, elected in fall 1911.

Salina, 847 (1900), Jonas Mattson, elected town board president in 1901, served 1902–1903.

VERMONT (1)

Barre, 10,008 (1920), Robert Gordon, 1916–1917.

VIRGINIA (1)

Brookneal, 504 (1910), 583 (1920), B. F. Ginther, 1916–1918.

WASHINGTON (12 MUNICIPALITIES, 16 MAYORS)

Bremerton, 2,993 (1910), D. L. Cady, 1914–1916, elected December 1913.
Burlington, 1,302 (1910), Neal Munro, 1913–1915, elected December 1912.
Camas, 1,843 (1920), O. T. Clark, elected November 1916, took office in 1917.
Camas, 1,125 (1910), 1,843 (1920), W. E. Farr, 1917–1920.
Colville, 1,512 (1910), W. L. Sax, elected December1909, won again in 1910, lost in 1911.
Concrete, 945 (1910), Socialist mayor said to be elected in 1912.
Edmonds, 474 (1900), Allen M. Yost, 1903–1905.
Edmonds, 1,114 (1910), W. H. Cook, 1910–1911.
Edmonds, 1,114 (1910), Hale E. Dewey, 1911–1912.
Hamilton, 405 (1910), H. A. Livermore, elected in 1912.
Hillyard, 3,276 (1910), Jared Herdlick, 1913–1914.
Leavenworth, 1,551 (1910), S. C. Woldenburg, elected in December 1913.
Northport, 787 (1900), George Stillinger, elected in 1901.
Northport, 476 (1910), Charles Adams, elected in 1907.
Pasco, 2,083 (1910), 3,362 (1920), Andrew M. Johnson, won in December 1913.
Tukwila, 361 (1910), Jacob Guntert, 1911–1913.

WEST VIRGINIA (8 MUNICIPALITIES, 10 MAYORS)

Adamston, 1,200 (1910), Henry Schutte, 1915–1916, reelected in 1916 on another party ticket.
Adamston, 1,200 (1910), Walter Boyles, elected in 1912.

Cameron, 1,660 (1910), Thomas Smith, elected in 1914.
Eskdale (no population given 1910), 1,003 (1920), T. L. Tincher, 1914–1916.
Hendricks, 640 (1910), R. S. Dayton, 1913–1915.
Miami (no information on population), E. S. (or E. E.) Crawford, elected January 1912.
Ridgeley, 1,709 (1920), J. C. Chase, 1919–1921, elected in 1918.
Star City, 318 (1910), William Shay, elected January 1911.
Star City, 318 (1910), John F. Higgins, 1915.
Weston, 2,213 (1910), 5,701 (1920), Matthew Holt, 1913–1915.

WISCONSIN (12 MUNICIPALITIES, 13 MAYORS)

Allouez (not listed in census), Enrich Wiese as chairman of the town, April 1912.
Bancroft (not listed in census), H. L. Kellogg said to have been elected chair of village in April 1912.
Brantwood (no population information), Socialist victories reported in April 1912 and 1914.
Eau Clair, 18,310 (1910), W. H. Barns, elected April 1912.
Kiel, 924 (1900), H. J. Ammann, spring 1903.
Manitowoc, 11,786 (1900), 13,027 (1910), 17,563 (1920), Henry Stolze Jr., 1905–1907, 1911–1917; elected in 1905, lost in 1907 and 1909, won in 1911, 1913, and 1915.
Marinette, 14,610 (1910), James Larson, 1911–1913.
Milwaukee, 373,867 (1910), Emil Seidel, 1910–1912.
Milwaukee, 457,147 (1920), Daniel Hoan, 1916–1940.
New Rhinelander, 6,654 (1920), S. G. Perringer, elected in April 1920.
Sheboygan, 22,962 (1900), Charles A. Born, elected 1903.
Washburn, 3,830 (1910), G. A. Herring, elected in April 1910.
West Allis, 6,645 (1910), David Love, 1916–1920.

NOTES

ABBREVIATIONS USED IN THE NOTES

ATR   *Appeal to Reason* (Girard, KS)
ISR   *International Socialist Review* (Chicago, IL)
LAT   *Los Angeles Times*
NMR   *National Municipal Review* (various locations)
NYT   *New York Times*
SDH   *Social Democratic Herald* (Chicago, IL)
SPP   Socialist Party Papers (Duke University, Durham, NC)

INTRODUCTION

1. Untitled item, *Republican-Atlas* (Monmouth, IL), May 26, 1910, 4.

2. The term *cooperative commonwealth* was first used by Socialist writer Laurence Gronlund in a volume published in 1884. It "was frequently borrowed by other socialists in order to downplay the dangerous connotations of Marxism, and it survived well into the twentieth century as a catch-phrase for the socialist goal." See Mark Pittenger, *American Socialist and Evolutionary Thought, 1870–1920* (Madison: University of Wisconsin Press, 1993), 60.

3. Letter to Eugene V. Debs, December 14, 1909, found in J. Robert Constantine, ed., *Letters of Eugene V. Debs*, vol. 1 (Urbana: University of Illinois Press, 1990), 311–314, at 311 and 313–314, note 1.

4. Marvin Wachman, *History of the Social-Democratic Party of Milwaukee, 1897–1910* (Urbana: University of Illinois Press, 1945), 10.

5. Henry Bedford, *Socialism and the Workers in Massachusetts, 1886–1912* (Amherst, MA: University of Massachusetts Press, 1966), 61.

6. Among others, this view of Socialist parties was held by political scientist V. O. Key in *Politics, Parties, and Pressure Groups*, 5th ed. (New York: Thomas Y. Crowell, 1964), 255, 267–269. See also Neil A. McDonald, *The Study of Political Parties: Short Studies in Political Science* (Garden City, NY: Doubleday, 1955), 31–32.

7. A. B. Edler, a Socialist leader in Utah, "A Reply to Opportunists," *Utah Labor Journal*, April 17, 1902, 1.

8. "Political Parties Not Endorsed by Us," *Industrial Worker*, August 12, 1909, 3.

9. "Hopeful Signs and New Duties," *Colorado Socialist Bulletin*, July 1910, 1.

10. See, for example, Bruce Rodgers, "Political Socialists vs. Socialist Politicians," *Washington Socialist* (Everett, WA), April 15, 1915, 4.

11. "Socialist Victories and Splendid Gains," *ATR*, April 15, 1911, 1.

12. "Municipal Problems," *Montana News* (Helena and Lewistown, MT), October 5, 1911, 2.

13. "A Socialist Mayor's Program," *Literary Digest*, January 14, 1899: 34–35, quote at 35.

14. See commentary of Richard S. Childs, *Civic Victories: The Story of an Unfinished Revolution* (New York: Harper & Brothers, 1952), 76.

15. Eugene V. Debs, "Danger Ahead," *ISR* 11 (January 1911): 413.

16. Ira Brown Cross, "Socialism in California Municipalities," *NMR* 1 (1912): 618.

17. Benjamin Parke De Witt, *The Progressive Movement* (Seattle: University of Washington Press, 1915), 97.

18. Walter Lippmann, "On Municipal Socialism," in *Socialism and the Cities*, ed. Bruce M. Stave (Port Washington: Kennikat, 1975), 184–196.

19. "Matchett and Maguire," *ATR*, August 15, 1896, 1.

20. Todd J. Fulda, "Daniel Hoan and the Golden Age of Socialist Government in Milwaukee," *American Journal of Economics and Sociology* 75, no. 1 (January 2016): 249.

21. There are several books on Socialist activity on the local level during the period under review in specific cities or states but no full-length book on activity around the country since the one by Richard W. Judd, *Socialist Cities* (Albany: State University of New York Press, 1989).

22. For a discussion of the failure see Seymour Martin Lipset and Gary Marks, *It Didn't Happen Here: Why Socialism Failed in the United States* (New York: W. W. Norton, 2000).

23. Socialists are largely if not completely ignored in the standard works on the municipal reform movement, such as Ernest S. Griffith, *A History of American City Government: The Progressive Years and Their Aftermath, 1900–1920* (New York: Praeger, 1974); Clifford W. Patton, *The Battle for Municipal Reform, 1875 to 1900* (College Park, MD: McGrath, 1969); and Kenneth Fox, *Better City Government: Innovation in American Urban Politics, 1850–1937* (Philadelphia: Temple University Press, 1977). Among the few academic books written during the period under review commenting on Socialist involvement—and then only in a limited descriptive fashion—is Charles A. Beard, *American City Government: A Survey of Newer Tendencies* (New York: Century, 1912).

24. The dispute among Socialists over the distribution of power was comparable in many respects to one that later surfaced among academics. For a critical review of the academic literature on community power see, for example, Robert A. Dahl, *Who Governs?* (New Haven, CT: Yale University Press, 1961); and Nelson W. Polsby, *Community Power and Political Theory* (New Haven, CT: Yale University Press, 1963).

25. In the United States the Socialist Labor Party (SLP), whose roots went back to the 1870s, joined other left-wing groups in backing Henry George's impressive but unsuccessful bid for mayor of New York City in 1886, but the alliance did not last because of doctrinal disputes between theorist Henry George's followers and the Socialists. Starting in the 1890s under the leadership of Daniel De Leon the party became rigidly Marxist in orientation and critical of political action. In June 1897 the

American Railway Union headed by Eugene V. Debs changed its name to the Social Democracy of America, which was joined by several radical groups. This party had some interest in forming cooperative colonies but also had a political action wing. The party lasted only a short time, splitting up in 1898. Some members went on to form the Social Democratic Party (SDP) of America, led by Victor Berger, which in 1898 enjoyed the success of electing the first Socialist mayor in the United States, John Chase, in Haverhill, Massachusetts. In 1901 the SDP and a faction of the SLP joined the Socialist Party of America (SPA).

26. Chief among the other sources were Jack Ross, *The Socialist Party of America: A Complete History* (Lincoln, NE: Potomac, 2015), appendix B, Socialist Elected Officeholders, 1897–1960; and Weinstein, *The Decline of Socialism in America, 1912–1920* (New York: Monthly Review Press, 1967), table 2, Cities and Towns Electing Mayors or Other Major Municipal Officers, 1911–1920, 116–117. For material from national party sources see Ira Kipnis, *The American Socialist Movement, 1897–1912* (New York: Columbia University Press, 1952), 345–346.

27. This list includes members of the Socialist Party who did not run for the office on a Socialist ticket but ran as independents or on a ticket with another name such as Public Ownership. Excluded from the list are Socialists who temporally held the office during the absence of a mayor. One example was Henry Lawrence, commissioner of finance and public affairs in Salt Lake City, Utah. Another was George Millar of Medford, Oregon, a member of the city council who briefly held the office while the mayor and all the other council members were out of town. Reporting on this event, a writer for a local newspaper noted: "Millar is busy receiving congratulations from his friends on becoming Medford's first Socialist mayor. Several radical changes have been suggested to him but there has been nothing doing." "Local and Personal," *Medford Mail Tribune*, August 14, 1912, 2. A third example is Mrs. Estelle Lawton Lindsay in Los Angeles, believed to be the first woman Socialist mayor, but only for a day, falling into the job when both the mayor and the president of the council were out of town. "Woman Socialist Mayor," *Northwest Worker* (Everett, WA), September 23, 1915, 1. Also excluded from the list are those who became Socialists after serving as mayor. One example is Reverend Harry Ferguson, who as mayor of Hoquiam, Washington, was considered inclined toward Socialism but did not become a Socialist until after he was recalled from office.

28. Eric Thomas Chester, *True Mission: Socialists and the Labor Party Question in the U.S.* (London: Pluto, 2004), 83.

CHAPTER 1. THE PARTY FRAMEWORK

1. J. Stitt Wilson, "The Story of a Socialist Mayor," *Western Comrade* 1 (September 1913): 186.

2. "Has the Party Been Over-Organized?" *Montana News* (Helena and Lewistown, MT), August 3, 1904, page 2. Related comments are found in "Nevada List Growing,"

Nevada Forum (Sparks, NV), September 21, 1908, 4; and "Kershaw Had Twinkle in Official Eye," *Bridgeport* (CT) *Evening Farmer*, December 2, 1910, 3.

3. Arnold Kaltinick, "Socialist Municipal Administration in Four American Cities: (Milwaukee, Schenectady, New Castle, Pennsylvania; and Conneaut, Ohio), 1910–1915" (PhD diss., New York University, 1982), 27.

4. Power of the Press," *Commonwealth* (Everett, WA), September 25, 1913, 4; C. H. Pierce, Secretary, Local Loon Lake, "A Plea for Solidarity and Effective Organization," *Commonwealth*, November 6, 1913, 2.

5. See generally Maurice Duverger, *Political Parties: Their Organization and Activity in the Modern State* (London: Methuen, 1954).

6. Bedford, *Socialism and the Workers in Massachusetts*, 6.

7. "At War with the Party: The Tyranny of Socialism," *Minneapolis Morning Tribune*, October 25, 1916, 6.

8. W. J. White, "Our Elected Servants," *ISR* 13 (June 1913): 868–869.

9. From the platform preamble of the Coeur D'Alene, Idaho, Socialist Party, as found in "News and Views, from the Coeur D'Alene."

10. Statement of Socialist in Grants Pass, Oregon, in "Socialists Advocate Municipal Reforms," *Rogue River Courier* (Grants Pass, OR), October 27, 1911, 1.

11. For a complaint about how Socialist Party practices were perceived, see, for example, "Where Was Clay," *Washington Socialist* (Everett, WA), April 8, 1915, 1.

12. Robert F. Hoxie, "The Rising Tide of Socialism," *Journal of Political Economy* 19 (October 1911): 624.

13. In California "a strong tradition of respectable middle-class Socialism, Fabian and Bellamyite, as opposed to the more proletarian and revolutionary varieties in vogue in Eastern industrial centers, helped make nonthreatening, even respectable, such notions as the public ownership of utilities, prison and hospital reform, social welfare, public housing, workmen's compensation, and other social programs eventually enacted by the Progressives." Kevin Starr, *Inventing the Dream: California through the Progressive Era* (New York: Oxford University Press, 1985), 207.

14. Hoxie, "The Rising Tide of Socialism,"624.

15. See, for example, discussion of the party in Conneaut, Ohio, by Kaltinick, "Socialist Municipal Administration," 372.

16. "Convention Echoes Red and Yellow," *Commonwealth*, March 28, 1913, 1.

17. Ralph Chaplin, *Wobbly: The Rough-and-Tumble Story of an American Radical* (Chicago: University of Chicago Press, 1948), 85.

18. Elizabeth Gurley Flynn, "Industrial Workers of the World (IWW)," Address, Northern Illinois University, November 8, 1961. Occasional Papers Series No. 24 (1977), American Institute for Marxist Studies.

19. Norman H. Clark, *Mill Town: Social History of Everett, Washington* (Seattle: University of Washington Press, 1970), 122.

20. One example of a request for advice from the national party on what to put into local platform is found in a letter from John J. Scholtes, Propaganda Secretary Local

Alliance, Ohio Socialist Party to Socialist Headquarters (no one in particular), received July 22, 1913, SPP.

21. 1904 SP convention, 258, SPP.

22. 1904 SP convention, 241.

23. 1904 SP convention, 243.

24. On the recommendations made, see appendix K, "Report of Committee on Municipal and State Program," Proceedings of the 1912 National Convention of the Socialist Party, SPP, 214–217.

25. Letter from John J. Scholtes, Alliance, Ohio, to CDT, November 7, 1913, SPP.

26. "News and Views, Idaho State Convention."

27. "Socialist Platform," *Bennington* (VT) *Evening Banner*, March 18, 1911, 7.

28. For an early statement on the problem, see F. P. O'Hare, "The Red Card Organization and State Election Laws," *ISR* (April 1912): 668–669.

29. "Time for Action," *Scott County Kicker* (Benton, MO), August 15, 1908, 1.

30. Remarks of Del. Ambrose (Montana), John M. Work, editor, National Convention of the Socialist Party, May 10–17, 1908, Chicago, 290–291, SPP.

31. "Duncan Addresses Large Crowd," *Daily Missoulian* (MT), September 14, 1912, 12.

32. "City Happenings and Personal Mention," *Palatka* (FL) *News and Advertiser*, February 24, 1911, 6.

33. See Errol Wayne Stevens, "Heartland Socialism: The Socialist Party of America in Four Midwestern Communities, 1898–1920" (PhD diss., Indiana University, 1978), 233–236.

34. "Socialists Name Ticket," *Barre* (VT) *Daily Times*, February 7, 1914, 1.

35. Stephen Cresswell, "When the Socialists Ran Star City," *West Virginia History* 52 (1993): 59–72.

36. "Record of Socialists," *Indianapolis News*, January 3, 1918, 4.

37. "Socialists Will Probably Name Ticket Sunday," *Medford* (OR) *Mail Tribune*, November 29, 1912, 1.

38. "Socialist Victories and Splendid Gains," *ATR*, April 15, 1911, 1.

39. R. W. Madison, "Millionaire Thum, Elected Mayor of Pasadena, Is Also Strong Exponent of Municipal Ownership," *Detroit Times*, April 19, 1911, 1.

40. J. W. Wood, *Pasadena, California, Historical and Personal* (N.p.: author, 1917), 215.

41. "Former Tramp Now Mayor" *ATR*, March 14, 1914, 4.

42. "Lecture at Armory Tonight," *Daily Capital Journal* (Salem, OR), February 7, 1912, 2.

43. Clark, *Mill Town*, 119.

44. Louise Overacker, *Money in Elections* (New York: Arno, 1974), 47,109, 145.

45. See, for example, "I.W.W. Moves on Denver," *Grand Forks* (ND) *Daily Herald and the Evening Times*, May 9, 1914, 1.

46. Duverger, *Political Parties*, 63, 67.

47. Quoted material from a letter from a presumed Socialist identified only as F. B. in "Free Press Worth It," *Day Book* (Chicago, IL), November 17, 1916, 22.

48. See, for example, "Reactionaries Attempt to Use Socialist Party," *Butte* (MT) *Daily Bulletin*, September 14, 1920, 1; and J. W. Sawyer, letter to the editor, *Daily Sentinel* (Grand Junction, CO), October 28, 1902, 3.

49. Hulet M. Wells, "The State Convention Echoes," *Commonwealth*, April 11, 1913, 1.

50. George D. Davis, "Comrade Davis Discusses S.E.C.," *Commonwealth*, March 7, 1913, 2.

51. Wachman, *History of the Social-Democratic Party of Milwaukee*, 67.

52. Arthur E. DeMatteo, "Socialist Municipal Administrations in the Progressive Era Midwest: A Comparative Case Study of Four Ohio Cities, 1911–1915," www.ohio academyofhistory.org/wp-content/uploads/2013/04/DeMatteo.pdf.

53. "Socialists Spend Little to Win," *Madison* (SD) *Daily Leader*, November 20, 1911, 4.

54. "Millionaire Is Mayor," *Medford* (OR) *Mail Tribune*, April 19, 1911, 3.

55. "The Socialist Mayor's Plan," *Cairo* (IL) *Bulletin*, April 21, 1911, 3.

56. "News and Views, Victory at St. Marys, Ohio." *ISR* 12 (December 1911): 377.

57. A. W. Ricker, "The Coming Battle at Flint," *ATR*, February 3, 1912, 2.

58. Frank Dawson, "St. Mary's Fighting Mayor," *ISR* 13 (June 1913): 874–876.

59. "Socialist Loses Job," *ATR*, April 28, 1917, 3.

60. "Rejected Selections Schildknecht Made," *Pittsburg* (KS) *Daily Headlight*, June 7, 1917, 2.

61. "Power of the Socialist Press," *Commonwealth*, September 25, 1913, 4.

62. "My Call Is the Call of Battle," *Commonwealth*, August 28, 1913, 4.

63. See, for example, "Same Trick of Silence," *Socialist* (New York, NY), September 21, 1902, 3, reprinting a letter from D. W. Smith, a Socialist writing from Payette, Idaho, September 15, 1902, to *Socialist Seattle*.

64. "News and Views, Socialist Politics in Toledo," *ISR* 12 (November 1911): 316.

65. Letter from Bradford, editor of the party-owned *Arizona Socialist Bulletin* (Phoenix, AZ), June 6, 1913, to Carl D. Thompson, SPP.

66. See views of Peter J. Holt, State Secretary Utah to Carl D. Thompson, June 7, 1913, SPP.

67. See, for example, Melvin Dubofsky, *Industrialism and the American Worker, 1865–1920* (Arlington Heights, IL: Harlan Davidson, 1975), 97.

68. "State Secretaries," *ATR*, September 5, 1903, report by state secretary E. H. Thomas from Wisconsin.

69. Sally M. Miller, *Victor Berger and the Promise of Constructive Socialism, 1910–1920* (Westport, CT: Greenwood, 1973), 36.

70. David Paul Nord, "Minneapolis and the Pragmatic Socialism of Thomas Van Lear," *Minnesota History* 45, no. 1 (Spring 1976): 2–10.

71. "Butte Unions Plan Meeting," *Searchlight* (Culbertson, MT), May 12, 1911, 3; "Girard Doing Things," *ATR*, May 20, 1911, 4.

72. William Mailly, editor, Proceedings of the National Convention of the Socialist

Party held at Chicago, May 1 to 6, 1904, issued by the National Committee of the Socialist Party, Chicago, 37, found in SPP.

73. Leonard D. Abbott, "The Socialist Movement in Massachusetts," *Outlook* (New York, NY), February 17, 1900, 411.

74. "Socialists Advocate Municipal Reforms," *Rogue River Courier*, October 27, 1911, 1.

75. "Van Lear Advocates Practical Politics, Socialist Mayor-Elect of Minneapolis in Talk Gives Advice to Party Members," *Northwest Worker* (Everett, WA), December 7, 1916, 1.

76. Paul H. Douglas, *The Coming of a New Party* (New York: McGraw-Hill, 1932), 203.

77. "Socialist Convention," *Sequachee* (TN) *Valley News*, March 26, 1914, 1.

78. A complaint of this nature was made, for example, by Socialists in Rockford, Illinois. See "Five Aldermen Elected to Rockford, Ill., Council," *Northwest Worker*, May 3, 1917, 1.

79. See, for example, Frederick A. Barkey, *Working-Class Radicals: The Socialist Party in West Virginia, 1898–1920* (Morgantown: West Virginia University Press, 2012), 86.

80. "Business Good," *Butte* (MT) *Daily Bulletin*, January 27, 1919, 3.

81. Molly Ann McClennen and Stephen Edward Cresswell, *Socialists in a Small Town: The Socialist Victory in Adamston, West Virginia* (Buckhannon, WV: Ralston, 1992); Ken Fones-Wolf, *Glass Towns: Industry, Labor and Political Economy in Appalachia, 1890–1930s* (Champaign-Urbana: University of Illinois Press, 2007), 113–145.

82. "Probably Misinformed," *St. Johns* (OR) *Review*, February 26, 1915, 1.

CHAPTER 2. MUNICIPAL REFORM

1. Frank Bohn, "The Socialist Party and the Government of Cities," *ISR* 12 (November 1911): 275.

2. Bohn, 275–276.

3. Initially, the business community showed little support for municipal reform, especially the Municipal Socialist component as reflected in the programs of Sam Jones of Toledo and Tom Johnson of Cleveland, who they viewed as radicals far too friendly to labor. Some too were worried that Good Government reforms would disrupt the relations they had been able to work out with local political machines and local officials, sometimes involving on outright bribery, without offering any guarantee of an alternative way of securing the favors they needed; see James Weinstein, "Organized Business and the City Commission and Manager Movements," *Journal of Southern History* 28, no. 2 (May 1962): 167–168. While leaders of large corporations, especially those that had lucrative public franchises or enjoyed favorable local tax policies, had special reason to worry about Municipal Socialism and the moves of Good Government advocates to end corruption, smaller enterprises, not benefiting from the status quo and picking up much the tax load, saw things differently; see "The

End of Municipal Reform," *Municipal Research Reports*, Municipal Research Bureau of the Socialist Party, 1930, SPP, 202. Over time, though, even large business found that seeking benefits through bribery or campaign contributions was troublesome: "They were expensive; they were wasteful; they were uncertain" (Samuel P. Hays, "The Politics of Reform in Municipal Government in the Progressive Era," *Pacific Northwest Quarterly* 55, no. 4 (October 1964): 167). Honest government came to have considerable appeal to much of the business community, as did the goal of greater tax-saving efficiency in municipal operations through sound business management, as exemplified in the commission and city manager forms of government.

4. Melvin G. Holli, *Reform in Detroit: Hazen S. Pingree and Urban Politics* (New York: Oxford University Press, 1969), 171.

5. On municipal reform organizations, see Patton, *The Battle for Municipal Reform*.

6. Patton, 32–33.

7. William L. Riordan, *Plunkitt of Tammany Hall* (New York: E. P. Dutton, 1963), 17.

8. Bradley Robert Rice, *Progressive Cities: The Commission Government Movement in America, 1901–1920* (Austin: University of Texas Press, 1977).

9. For example, the National Municipal League—the premier national Good Government group—did not endorse a policy of municipal ownership of utilities. See Frank Stewart, *A Half Century of Municipal Reform* (Berkeley: University of California Press, 1950), 37, 40.

10. Holli, *Reform in Detroit*, 162. This view was shared by academics such as political scientist Frank Goodnow. See Lurton W. Blassingame, "Frank J. Goodnow: Progressive Urban Reformer," *North Dakota Quarterly* 40 (1972): 23–30; and Fox, *Better City Government*, 118–119.

11. See Hays, "The Politics of Reform," 157–169.

12. Report of James Boyle, United States Council at Liverpool, April 25, 1902, as reported in "Public Ownership: Great Britain's Experiment in Municipal Socialism," *Freeland* (PA) *Tribune*, June 18, 1902, 4. The full report may be found in James Boyle, "The Increase of Municipal Socialism in England," *Barton County Democrat*, September 5, 1902, 6.

13. In his most noted work, *Progress and Poverty*, 1879, Henry George wrote: "It is true that wealth has been greatly increased, and that the average of comfort, leisure, and refinement has been raised; but these gains are not general. In them the lowest class do not share. . . . It is as though an immense wedge were being forced, not underneath society, but through society. Those who are above the point of separation are elevated, but those who are below are crushed down. . . . This association of poverty with progress is the great enigma of our times" (from reprint by Robert Schalkenbach Foundation, 1955, 8, 10). In a latter work he wrote, "Production has increased by leaps and bounds. But there has been something grievously at fault with its distribution. It has gone in great part for the enrichment of a few. As if by magic, it has piled up amazing fortunes; as though some possessed loadstones drawing to them a very large portion of the wealth and leaving to others only sufficient to afford subsistence and

barely encourage a continuance of production." Henry George, *The Menace of Privilege* (New York: Macmillan, 1905), 9.

14. The influence of George on Cleveland reform mayor Tom Johnson was especially strong. See Tom Johnson and Elizabeth J. Hauser, eds., *My Story* (New York: B. W. Huebsch, 1911); and Alexandra W. Lough, "Tom L. Johnson and Cleveland Traction Wars, 1901–1909," *American Journal of Economics and Sociology* 75, no. 1 (January 2016): 149–192. George's influence on "New Idea" Progressive reformers in New Jersey, George Record and Mark Fagin, is noted in Ransom E. Noble, *New Jersey before Wilson* (Princeton, NJ: Princeton University Press, 1946). Some indication that George's influence on the activities of another "New Idea" mayor, Fred R. Low of Passaic, New Jersey, 1908–1909, is found in Michael H. Ebner, "Redefining the Success Ethic for Urban Reform Mayors," in *The Age of Urban Reform*, ed. Michael H. Ebner and Eugene M. Tobin (Port Washington, NY: Kennikat, 1977), 86–101. One also must note his influence on Progressive mayors Hazen Pingree and Sam Jones, and Socialist J. Stitt Wilson. See discussion by Stephen E. Barton, "Berkeley Mayor J. Stitt Wilson: Christian Socialist, Georgist, Feminist," *American Journal of Economics and Sociology* 75, no. 1 (January 2016): 193–216. Reading *Progress and Poverty* left a permanent effect on Robert La Follette; see Robert Maxwell, *La Follette and the Rise of the Progressives in Wisconsin* (New York: Russell & Russell, 1956), 12. Another reform governor, John Peter Altgeld of Illinois, was an admirer of George, though he had some doubts about the single tax idea. He too had made much of his fortune through real estate activities George would have condemned. See Waldo R. Browne, *Altgeld of Illinois* (New York: B. W. Huebsch, 1924), 204; and Harry Barnard, *Eagle Forgotten: The Life of John Peter Altgeld* (New York: Duell, Sloan & Pearce, 1938), 5, 382.

15. Howard H. Quint, *The Forging of American Socialism* (Columbia: University of South Carolina Press, 1953), 72–102; and Bedford, *Socialism and the Workers in Massachusetts*, 12–15. For contemporary accounts see "Bellamy Is In It," *Advocate* (Meriden, KS), November 19, 1890, 10, referring to an article in *Northwest Reform Journal*.

16. On Christian Socialists and Social Uplifters see Russel B. Nye, *Midwestern Progressive Politics* (Lansing: Michigan State University Press, 1959), 159.

17. George Hodges, "A Mighty Influence," *Pittsburg* (PA) *Dispatch*, June 30, 1889, 15.

18. Hodges, "A Mighty Influence."

19. Hodges.

20. Though a Baptist minister, Walter Rauschenbusch, stood out as an important theologian of the movement. See David W. Noble, *The Progressive Mind, 1890–1917*, (Minneapolis, MN: Burgess, 1981), 76.

21. "Peter W. Collins Makes Hit," *Labor World* (Duluth, MN), December 20, 1913, 5.

22. Quint, *The Forging of American Socialism*, 107.

23. On McKay and Murray, see Judd, *Socialist Cities*, 74.

24. See, for example, "Can a Catholic Be a Socialist," *Northwest Worker* (Everett, WA), September 30, 1915, 2; and, regarding Mormonism, John S. McCormick and John R. Sillito, *A History of Utah Radicalism* (Logan: Utah State University Press, 2011), 109–120, 369–370, 382–443.

25. "News and Notes," *Meridian* (OK) *Sun*, October 3, 1912, 2. Bakeman, a Christian Socialist, was Lunn's assistant manager at the United Peoples Church. After leaving this position and joining Lunn, he wound up in jail for a short period along with the mayor for interfering in a strike in Little Falls, New York. Bakeman later broke with Lunn, joining the Schenectady Socialist leftists who sought to oust Lunn from the party; see Kenneth E. Hendrickson Jr., "Tribune of the People: George R. Lunn and the Rise and Fall of Christian Socialism in Schenectady," in *Socialism and the Cities*, edited by Bruce M. Stave (Port Washington, NY: Kennikat, 1975) 77, 87–88.

26. Also meriting mention as pioneer Progressive mayors on the left, though they served in later periods, are Mark Fagin, of Jersey City, New Jersey, working with the guidance of George L. Record, the leader of the "New Idea" progressive leaders in the state in the early 1900s; Edward Dunne, mayor of Chicago, 1905–1907, who later became governor of Illinois; and Brad Whitlock, Jones's protégé and successor in Toledo, serving 1906–1914. An especially useful discussion of Fagin is found in Noble, *New Jersey before Wilson*. On Dunne, see Richard Allen Morton, *Justice and Humanity: Edward F. Dunne, Illinois Progressive* (Carbondale: Southern Illinois University Press, 1997).

27. "Mayor Pingree Again Beats the Detroit Ring," *New Nation* (Boston, MA), July 1, 1893, 327.

28. Holli, *Reform in Detroit*, 138, 140.

29. See generally, Alexandra W. Lough, "Hazen S. Pingree and the Detroit Model of Urban Reform," *American Journal of Economics and Sociology* 75, no. 1 (January 2016): 58–85; Holli, *Reform in Detroit*; and Patton, *The Battle for Municipal Reform*, 51.

30. On Jones see Marnie Jones, *Holy Toledo: Religion and Politics in the Life of "Golden Rule" Jones* (Lexington: University Press of Kentucky, 1998); and Ariane Liazos, "Ministering to the Social Needs of the People: Samuel Jones, Strong Mayor Government, and Municipal Ownership, 1897–1904," *American Journal of Economics and Sociology* 75, no. 1 (January 2016): 86–115.

31. Patton, *The Battle for Municipal Reform*.

32. "A Practical Radical," *Outlook* (New York, NY), January 28, 1899, 206–207.

33. Samuel Jones to Debs, December 30, 1898, in Constantine, *Letters of Eugene V. Debs*, Vol. 1, 128.

34. From letter quoted in "Jones to Debs," *Topeka* (KS) *State Journal*, October 1, 1900, 1.

35. See "Mayor Jones's Golden Rules," *LAT*, March 12, 1902, A1.

36. "Mayor Jones's Golden Rules."

37. Quint, *The Forging of American Socialism*, 260; and Hoyt Landon Warner, *Progressivism in Ohio, 1897–1917* (Columbus: Ohio State University Press, 1964), 37–41.

38. "The Golden Rule Mayor," *Social Democracy Red Book*, January 1900, 103.

39. Elizabeth Hauser in introduction to Johnson, *My Story*, xxvi.

40. Elizabeth Hauser in introduction to Johnson.

41. See generally Lough, Tom L. Johnson and Cleveland Traction Wars, 1901–1909."

42. Quote from Charles Zueblin, *American Municipal Progress* (New York: Arno, 1974), 51.

43. See generally Lough, "Tom L. Johnson," 149–192.

44. Johnson, *My Story*, 202–203.

45. Untitled entry, *Commoner* (Lincoln, NE), November 13, 1903, 4.

46. "General News: Elections in Central States," *Orleans County Monitor* (Barton, VT), April 20, 1903, 2; "Out Looking for Candidates," *Billings* (MT) *Gazette*, April 14, 1903: 2.

47. On coming from opposite directions as far as the economy is concerned, see De Witt, *The Progressive Movement*, 90. On class agitation differences, see, for example, Cross, "Socialism in California Municipalities."

48. "Berkeley Mayor J. Stitt Wilson," 203.

49. See Starr, *Inventing the Dream*, 207–218; Tom Sitton, "John Randolph Haynes and the Left-wing of California Progressivism," in *California Progressivism Revisited*, ed. William Deverell and Tom Sutton (Berkeley: University of California Press, 1994), 15–33; and Tom Sitton, *John Randolph Haynes: California Progressive* (Stanford, CA: Stanford University Press, 1992).

50. "Socialists Rejoice Over Many Victories," *NYT*, November 9, 1911, 1. See also Warner, *Progressivism in Ohio*, 306.

51. "Plagiarism Charged by Ohio Socialists," *Stark County Democrat* (Canton, OH), May 15, 1908, 5.

52. Maxwell, *La Follette and the Rise of the Progressives in Wisconsin*, 200–201.

53. Miller, *Victor Berger*, 31.

54. "Socializing Society," *Day Book* (Chicago, IL), January 10, 1917, 24.

55. Donald Drew and Stow Persons, eds., *Socialism and American Life*, vol. 1. (Princeton, NJ: Princeton University Press, 1952), 298.

56. "News and Views, Socialist Politics in Toledo."

57. David D. Anderson, *Brand Whitlock* (New York: Twayne, 1968), 49.

58. Letter from Brand Whitlock to Octavia Roberts, Toledo, July 20, 1909, in Allan Nevins, ed., *The Letters and Journal of Brand Whitlock* (New York: D. Appleton-Century, 1936), 118.

59. "The End of Municipal Reform," 202.

60. "The End of Municipal Reform," 2.

61. "Worsley Pleads for Voters Who Are Not Well Educated," *Arizona Democrat* (Phoenix, AZ), June 6, 1912, 5.

62. Clifton Rodgers Woodruff, "American Municipal Tendencies," *NMR* 1 (1912): 15. The class struggle theme also irritated if not outraged some Christian Socialists who were active in the cause of Municipal Socialism. See Quint, *The Forging of American Socialism*, 126.

63. See Cross, "Socialism in California Municipalities."

64. On the resources of business groups in local politics, see, for example, William A. Schultze, *Urban and Community Politics* (North Scituate, MA: Duxbury, 1974), 115–121, citing, in part, Robert A. Dahl, "The Analysis of Influence on Local Communities," in *Social Science and Community Action*, ed. Charles R. Adrian (East Lansing: Michigan State University, 1960).

CHAPTER 3. THE SOCIALIST MUNICIPAL PROGRAM

1. Platform of principles adopted by the Socialists of Mt. Pleasant, Utah, found in "Municipal Socialism," *Iron County Record* (Cedar City, UT), November 7, 1903, 8. Similarly, in 1902 from a local in Washington: "We pledge our candidates, when in office, to always make the answer to this question their guiding rule of conduct. 'Will this act or legislation advance the interests of the producing class.' If it does our candidates are for it; if it does not, they are absolutely opposed to it." From "Yakima County Platform," *Socialist* (New York, NY), September 21, 1902, 3. As another example, in 1914, a county convention of Socialists in Washington declared, "The Socialist Party, when in Office, shall always and everywhere, until the present system of wage slavery is utterly abolished, make the answer to this question is guiding rule of conduct: 'Will this legislation advance the interests of the working-class and aid the workers in their class struggle against capitalism? If it does, the Socialist Party is for it. If it does not, the Socialist Party is absolutely opposed to it.'" From "Proceedings of the Kitsap County Convention," *Washington Socialist* (Everett, WA), August 13, 1914, 2.

2. "The Socialists, What That Party Would Do if Given Control," *Perth Amboy* (NJ) *Evening News*, October 9, 1912, 10.

3. "The Socialists, What That Party Would Do if Given Control."

4. Platform of the Socialist Party of Yuma, County, Arizona Territory, found in "Socialist Selections," *Arizona Sentinel* (Yuma, AZ), October 15, 1902, 1.

5. Kipnis, *The American Socialist Movement*, 347, 348.

6. City platform of Richmond, Indiana, Socialist Party, in "Socialists Urge All Charity Be Given by Police," *Richmond* (IN) *Palladium and Sun-Telegram*, June 18, 1917, 3.

7. City platform of Richmond, Indiana, Socialist Party.

8. "The Socialists, What That Party Would Do if Given Control."

9. "MT Pleasant Utah Platform, Municipal Socialism," *Iron County Record*, November 7, 1903, 8.

10. Found in Daniel Frederick Wolfson, "A History of the Socialist Party of Los Angeles" (PhD diss., University of Southern California, 1964), 12.

11. "Strikes About the Right Idea," *Montana News* (Helena and Lewistown, MT), February 1, 1905, 1.

12. See remarks of the Socialist mayor Woldenburg of Leavenworth, Washington, in "Large Crowd Attends New Council Meeting," *Leavenworth* (WA) *Echo*, January 1914, 1.

13. "Chicago and Public Ownership," *Labor World* (Duluth, MN), March 17, 1906, 4.

14. Liazos, "Ministering to the Social Needs of the People," 94.

15. Quoted in Christopher Webster, "Growth of Socialism as Observed in this County," *Hopkinsville Kentuckian*, April 14, 1906, 6. Patterson became commissioner of public works under Mayor Dunne in Chicago but resigned in 1906, expressing the feeling that the mayor's municipal ownership program was far too limited for a Socialist to accept. See "Resigns Because He Is a Socialist: Mayor Dunne's

Commissioner of Public Works Gives Up," *Hartford* (CT) *Courant*, March 3, 1906, 10. Patterson, becoming somewhat more conservative, went on to be the publisher of the *Daily News* in New York City.

16. De Witt, *The Progressive Movement*, 92.

17. See, for example, the local platform cited in "Great Falls Socialists, Put Up a Full Ticket for the Spring Municipal Campaign, Dead against Any Fusion," *Kalispell* (MT) *Bee*, February 24, 1903, 7.

18. Carman F. Randolph, *Opinion on Municipal Ownership of Public Utilities* (New York: De Vinne, 1907), 6. The author also noted: "A sweeping denunciation of the programme as 'Socialistic' is a somewhat childish performance in the face of a movement too big and too earnest to be checked by an epithet—which, moreover, is often misused. . . . Scrutiny of municipal ownership abroad by localities does not disclose a uniform connection with the Socialist propaganda" (Randolph, 6).

19. Stevens, "Heartland Socialism," 241.

20. "Socialist Platform," *Bennington* (VT) *Evening Banner*, March 18, 1911, 7.

21. John Morrissey, "Some Suggestions."

22. These examples are drawn from "Read Carefully before You Vote," includes Socialist Party Platform adopted by the Socialist Party at Great Falls, Montana, March 1911, SPP; "Municipal Socialism," *Iron County Record*, 8; "The Socialists, What That Party Would Do if Given Control," *Perth Amboy Evening News*, October 9, 1912, 10; "Great Falls Socialists, Put Up a Full Ticket for the Spring Municipal Campaign, Dead against Any Fusion," *Kalispell Bee*, February 24, 1903, 7; and City platform of Richmond, Indiana, Socialist Party, in "Socialists Urge All Charity Be Given by Police," *Richmond Palladium and Sun-Telegram*, June 18, 1917, 3.

23. "Schenectady Leads Them All," *ATR*, November 18, 1911, 11.

24. "Seidel Tackles Cost of Living," *Richmond Palladium and Sun-Telegram*, December 25, 1910, 2.

25. Cresswell, "When the Socialists Ran Star City."

26. "Urges City to Make Ice," *Tacoma* (WA) *Times*, February 23, 1912, 7.

27. Carl D. Thompson, "Middleman Eliminated," *Labor Journal* (Everett, WA), October 7, 1910, 1.

28. "A Socialist Mayor," *Oregon Union* (Corvallis, Benton County, OR), January 6, 1899, 1.

29. Platform of Socialist candidates in Fond Du Lac, Wisconsin, in handbill, "This Is the Program of These Three Candidates," SPP.

30. Thompson, "Middleman Eliminated."

31. Study for Socialist Party of Connecticut, State Executive Committee Minutes, Connecticut Socialist Party, March 30, 1913, SPP.

32. "Socialist Party of Missouri," SPP. This is a message regarding a proposed amendment to the state constitution providing for the initiative and referendum sent by Otto Vierling, state secretary of the Socialist Party of Missouri, to party leaders in the various locals sometime in 1913.

33. J. B. Gay, "The Poll-Tax Evil," *Texarkana* (AR) *Socialist*, January 9, 1913, SPP;

"Socialists Fight Poll Tax," *Topeka* (KS) *State Journal*, July 22, 1911, 4; and "Socialists against Collection of Poll Taxes," *Ogden Standard* (Ogden City, UT), October 28, 1915, 7.

34. "This Socialist Would Pay No Poll Tax," *Medford* (OR) *Mail Tribune*, February 13, 1911, 8 (on Biloxi); "From Jail to Run for Mayor," *Abilene* (KS) *Weekly Reflector*, March 30, 1911, 4; "The Socialist Movement," *Scott County Kicker* (Benton, MO), April 29, 1911, 1. On Socialist opposition to the poll tax, see also Gay, "The Poll-Tax Evil."

35. "Socialist Work Largely Perfunctory," *Daily Arizona Silver Belt* (Globe, AZ), October 4, 1908, 1.

36. "Strikes About the Right Idea," *Montana News*, February 1, 1905, 1.

37. For these points and an attempt by a Socialist to devise a local governing system with the proper balance between efficiency and democracy, see Thompson, "The Vital Points in Charter Making from a Socialist Point of View," *NMR* (July 1913): 416–426.

38. John J. Hamilton, *The Dethronement of the City Boss* (Freeport, NY: Books for Libraries Press, 1971), 50–57.

39. Austin F. Macdonald, *American City Government and Administration* (New York: Thomas Y. Crowell, 1956), 191.

40. Report to State Executive Committee, Minutes, Connecticut Socialist Party, March 30, 1913, SPP.

41. On the places mentioned, see "Socialists Attack Commission Plan," *Watertown* (WI) *Leader*, April 21, 1911, 3, on Sheboygan; Untitled item, *Washington Standard* (Olympia, WA), April 19, 1912, 2, on Everett; "Socialist Speaker Takes Crack at Commission Plan," *Bridgeport Evening Farmer*, April 6, 1915, 12, on Bridgeport; Statement issued by Idaho party, City Central Committee Socialist Party, "Fellow Citizens," February 1913, in report filed by D. J. O'Mahoney, SPP, on Pocatello; Daniel Allardyce Cornford, "Lumber, Labor, and Community in Humboldt County, 1850–1920" (PhD diss., University of California, Santa Barbara, 1983), 546, on Eureka; "Keller Speaks at Beatrice," *Omaha* (NE) *Daily Bee*, October 1, 1911, 3, and "Beatrice to Try New System of Government," *Norfolk* (NE) *Weekly News-Journal*, October 6, 1911, 1, on Beatrice; Barkey, *Working-Class Radicals*, 58, on Wheeling; Warner, *Progressivism in Ohio*, 450–451, and Judd, *Socialist Cities*, 145–148, on Dayton; and Clark, *Mill Town*, 122–124, on Everett.

42. See Proceedings of the National Convention of the Socialist Party 1912: general discussion in SPP, 46–55, and Appendix C, which contains a report made on the commission system, 179–217.

43. On national party action regarding municipal reform proposals, see Kipnis, *The American Socialist Movement*, 234.

44. Remarks of Delegate Bernard Berlyn (Illinois) in Proceedings of the National Convention of the Socialist Party 1912, 54. Found in SPP.

45. "Appendix C, Report of Committee on Commission Reform of Government," SPP, 186. See also general discussion on 46–55, and report made on the commission system, 179–217.

46. See, for example, Thompson, "The Socialist Argument against Non-Partisan Elections."

47. Thompson, "The Socialist Argument against Non-Partisan Elections."

48. "Old Party Politicians in Panic Over Non-Partisan Repealer," *Pennsylvania Socialist* (Reading, PA), July 16, 1919, 1, found in SPP.

49. "Wisconsin Notes: Socialist Kill Non-Partisan Bill," *Labor Argus* (Charleston, WV), June 22, 1911, 1.

50. See remarks of J. Stitt Wilson in Rice, *Progressive Cities*, 76–77.

51. Proceedings, National Convention of the Socialist Party, 49, SPP. A similar theme was advanced in "News of Socialism," *ATR*, January 6, 1912, regarding the ability of Socialists to win in Minneapolis should the city adopt a commission plan calling for nonpartisan elections.

52. "Milwaukee's Socialist Reverse," *Literary Digest* (New York, NY), April 13, 1912, 740; Fulda, "Daniel Hoan," 258.

53. "Another Socialist Mayor," *ATR*, December 16, 1916, 2.

54. Cresswell, "When the Socialists Ran Star City."

55. "Sixth District Notes," *Topeka State Journal*, August 18, 1902, 3.

56. See, for example, remarks by Major Church, Socialist mayor of Eureka, Utah, 1918–1921, in McCormick and Sillito, eds., *A History of Utah Radicalism*, 192.

CHAPTER 4. SOCIALIST MAYORS

1. Untitled editorial in the *Topeka* (KS) *State Journal*, December 8, 1898, 4.

2. Kipnis, *The American Socialist Movement*, 77; "First Socialist Mayor in America," *Rocky Mountain News* (Denver, CO), December 1898, found in the SPP; "Two Socialist Mayors in Massachusetts," *Outlook*, December 16, 1899, 904; "Municipal Victories for Socialism," *Literary Digest*, December 16, 1899, 731; "Socialist Capture Haverhill, Mass.," *Herald* (Los Angeles, CA), December 16, 1898, 7.

3. Bedford, *Socialism and the Workers in Massachusetts*, 4.

4. "A Socialist Mayor's Program"; "First Socialist Mayor in America"; and "Socialist Capture Haverhill, Mass."

5. Bedford, *Socialism and the Workers in Massachusetts*, 8.

6. Bedford, 161.

7. The Socialist Defeat in Haverhill," *Outlook* (New York, NY), December 22, 1900, 958–959.

8. The vote stood: Kendrick, Republican, 1,869; Garfield, Democrat, 1,849; Coulter, Socialist, 3,394. See "Two Socialist Mayors in Massachusetts," *Outlook*, December 16, 1899, 904.

9. Bedford, *Socialism and the Workers in Massachusetts*, 125.

10. Bedford, 127, 131.

11. "Great Socialist Gains Everywhere," *ATR*, April 18, 1903, 1; "State Secretaries," *ATR*, September 5, 1903, 1; "How the Battle Was Waged," *SDH*, April 5, 1903, 1; and William Mailly, National Secretary, "Victory!!!," *SDH*, April 11, 1903, 1.

12. Allan Patek, "The 1911 Election of Socialist Mayor Henry Stolze, Jr., of Manitowoc," Manitowoc County Historical Society, monograph 74 (1996): 1–16.

13. W. G. Henry, "News and Views: Grand Junction's Socialist Mayor," *ISR* 10 (June 1910): 1139–1141.

14. "Socialist Mayor Elected," *ATR*, November 13, 1909, 6.

15. Thomas F. Jorsch, "Radical Municipal Socialism in Madrid, Iowa, 1903–1920," *Socialist History* 56 (2019): 66–88.

16. In 1910 Seidel pulled in 27,622 votes, compared to 20,515 for his Democratic opponent and 11,262 for the Republican nominee. Frederic C. Howe, "Milwaukee—A Socialist City," *Outlook*, June 25, 1910, 411–421.

17. Sally M. Miller, "Seidel, George Lukas Emil," American National Biography Online, February 2000. http://www.anb.org.ezproxy1.1ib.asu.edu/articles/06/06-00588.html.

18. "First Socialist Mayor of America," *Valentine* (NE) *Democrat*, May 5, 1910, 3.

19. This view of Berger was shared by Eugene Debs: "Berger thrives only when he is the boss, with (the) spotlight (full) upon him. I have heard him admit . . . that he was a boss, admitting it with warmth, and then emphasizing it by saying that the Socialist Party like every other party had to have (its) bosses." Letter from Debs to Carl D. Thompson, December 5, 1910, in Constantine, ed., *Letters of Eugene V. Debs*, vol. 2, 339. "Critics charge that Victor Berger 'is the big Socialist boss' and gives orders to Hoan." See Edward Thierry, "Socialist Mayor May Lead Party Campaign," *Ogden* (UT) *Standard-Examiner*, May 9, 1920, 12.

20. Wachman, *History of the Social-Democratic Party of Milwaukee*, 11.

21. Wachman, 58.

22. Wachman, 59.

23. Voting information from Wachman, appendix C, 82.

24. "First Socialist Mayor of America," *Valentine Democrat*, May 5, 1910, 3.

25. Wachman, *History of the Social-Democratic Party of Milwaukee*, 62.

26. Kipnis, *The American Socialist Movement*, 233.

27. Wachman, *History of the Social-Democratic Party of Milwaukee*, 47.

28. Melvin G. Holli, *The American Mayor* (University Park: Pennsylvania State University Press, 1999) 64.

29. Miller, *Victor Berger*, 36.

30. Some thoughts along these lines were expressed by reformer Frederick C. Howe in discussing Seidel's victory in Milwaukee in 1910. See Howe, "Milwaukee—A Socialist City," 413.

31. "A Poor Advertisement for Coquille," *Daily Capital Journal* (Salem, OR), May 13, 1910, 2.

32. These estimates are drawn from information collected for this study. In 1911 Socialist mayors emerged victorious in Arkansas (Winslow), California (Berkeley, Nederland, Pasadena), Colorado (Victor), Idaho (Coeur'd Alene), Illinois (Buckner, Davis, Des Planes, Dorrisville, Granite City, O'Fallon, Spaulding), Kansas (Arma, Curransville, Dexter, Girard), Michigan (Flint, Greenville), Minnesota (Crookston, La Porte, St. Hilaire, Thief River Falls, Two Harbors), Missouri (Cardwell, Minden), Montana (Butte), Nebraska (Beatrice, Red Cloud, Wymore), New Jersey (Rockaway),

Ohio (Amsterdam, Barberton, Canton, Cuyahoga Falls, Fostoria, Lima, Linden Heights, Lorain, Martins Ferry, Mineral City, Mineral Ridge, Mount Vernon, Piqua, Salem, St. Marys, Sugar Grove, Toronto), Pennsylvania (New Castle), Utah (Murray, Eureka, Mammoth)Washington (Edmonds), West Virginia (Star City), and Wisconsin (Manitowoc, a reelection).

33. As Richard Judd pointed out, "Most 'Socialist' towns were located either in the Miami River valley, where machine shops, paper mills, and textile factories provided an industrial base for small communities, or in the mining and steel-producing regions of the North and East." Judd, *Socialist Cities*, 74–75.

34. "Press Comments on Election," *Montana News* (Helena and Lewiston, MT), April 6, 1911, 2.

35. A. G. Edmunds, "Butte Socialists Hand Smashing Blow to Capitalistic Ring Rulers," *California Social Democrat*, August 26, 1911, 2.

36. Lewis J. Duncan, "Socialist Politics in Butte, Montana," *ISR* 12 (November 1911): 287. See also Lewis J. Duncan, "The Trouble in Butte, Mayor Duncan's Statement to the Socialist Party and Press of America," July 21, 1913, SPP. For assessments of the victory, see "Socialists Carry Butte by Large Pluralities, Great Gains All Over the Country," *Montana News*, April 6, 1911, 1; Jack Keister, "Why the Socialist Won in Butte," *ISR* 11 (June 1911): 731–733; James W. Calvert, *The Gibraltar Socialism and Labor in Butte, 1895–1920* (Helena: Montana Historical Society Press, 1988); and David M. Emmons, *The Butte Irish* (Urbana: University of Illinois Press, 1989), 265, on Duncan's appeal to the Irish working class in Butte.

37. "Berkeley Socialist Wins Mayoralty," *Camas Prairie Chronicle* (Cottonwood, ID), April 7, 1911, 6. See also "Berkeley, Cal., College City of 45,000, Elects Socialist Mayor J. Stitt Wilson," *Detroit* (MI) *Times*, April 14, 1911, 13.

38. "A Socialist Mayor, Berkeley the First California Town to Have One," *Arizona Republican* (Phoenix, AZ), April 2, 1911, 1.

39. Kipnis, *The American Socialist Movement*, 347.

40. Cross, "Socialism in California Municipalities," 616.

41. Contemporary accounts of Lunn's election are found in "An Election-Day of Rebukes," *Literary Digest*, November 18, 1911, 897–898; Henry Farrand Griffin, "The Rising Tide of Socialism," *Outlook*, February 24, 1912, 438–448; "The Reds Raise Hell," *Labor Argus* (Charleston, WV), November 9, 1911, 1; and "The Socialist Vote," *Philip* (SD) *Weekly Review*, November 23, 1911, 3.

42. Hendrickson, "Tribune of the People."

43. Kaltinick, "Socialist Municipal Administration," 80.

44. "The Reds Raise Hell," *Labor Argus*, November 9, 1911, 1.

45. Griffin, "The Rising Tide of Socialism," 445.

46. A study by Robert Hoxie, University of Chicago economist and labor historian, found twenty-eight elected local chief executives (mayors, village presidents, and township chairmen) around the country (Hoxie, "The Rising Tide of Socialism"). Around the same time, a Socialist researcher, W. J. Ghent, found thirty local chief executives. Ghent's counts were based on press reports and private information. In

May 1911 he noted that his report "does not pretend to be strictly accurate" and asked readers to provide corrections or additions. See "Slow but Steady Growth of the Party Is One of the Most Favorable Signs of the Times," *Labor World* (Duluth, MN), May 13, 1911, 8; and "Socialists in Office," *ATR*, May 20, 1911, 3. In June he upped the number to thirty-three. W. J. Ghent, "Socialist Officials," June 19, 1911, found in SPP.

47. Annual Report of the National Secretary of the Socialist Party, January 1 to December 31, 1911, *Socialist Party Monthly Bulletin*, January 1912, cited by Kipnis, *The American Socialist Movement*, 346, note 63. By one count, twenty-seven new mayors had been elected in November and December. See Hoxie, "The Socialist Party in the November Elections," *Journal of Political Economy* 20, no. 3 (March 1912): 205–223.

48. Carl D. Thompson, "Have the Socialists Made Good in Office?," *Washington Socialist* (Everett, WA), June 18, 1914, 1, 4, citing the thirty-four number for 1913 and list of Socialists holding elective office in 1915, SPP.

49. H. A. Livermore, "In Skagit County," *Commonwealth* (Everett, WA), October 4, 1912, 7.

50. "Fight Desperately in Hamilton, Ohio," *Party Builder* (Chicago, IL), September 27, 1913, 4.

51. Emil Seidel, *Thy Kingdom Come: Some Sketches from My Life*, part 3 (Microfilm, State Historical Society of Wisconsin), 165. See also "Milwaukee Puts Socialism Aside, The Non-partisan Municipal Ticket Defeats Socialist Mayor," *El Paso* (TX) *Herald*, April 3, 1912, 5, and "Milwaukee's Socialists Reverse," *Literary Digest* (New York, NY), April 13, 1912, 740.

52. "The Spring Elections," *Scott County Kicker* (Benton, MO), April 13, 1912, 1. See also Judd, *Socialist Cities*, 106.

53. Later on, he declared in regard to the 1913 election: "I was defeated, and I felt I was defeated in large measure because of the fact, that the people knew that under the Socialist Party an elected official was supposed to be under the control of the Local rather than responsive direct to the whole population, as he should be." See George R. Lunn, *Testimony to the Special Investigative Committee of the New York State Assembly, January 28, 1920* (Albany, NY: J. N. Lyon, 1920), 352–366.

54. In Lima, Lorain, Canto, and Mt. Vernon, disputes among Socialists led to the mayor being expelled from the party; those who sought reelection did so under different labels. More commonly the Socialist incumbents, who had been elected in contests involving more than two candidates, were defeated in a one-on-one contest with a candidate supported by a coalition of Democrats and Republicans. See Judd, *Socialist Cities*, 76, 88; D. A. Donovan, "Keep Their Money in Purse, Other Parties Boast," *Morrow County Republican* (Mt. Gilead, OH), November 11, 1913, 3, notes that Socialists lost mayoral contests in Lorain, Lima, St. Marys, and Canton, had some solace in the election of a mayor in Hamilton, and elected their mayor in Coshocton, and reelected one in Martins Ferry.

55. "Straws of the Steam of Alabama Comment: Socialist Mayor in Alabama," *Birmingham* (AL) *News*, September 29, 1912, 13.

56. Gregory G. Kiser, "The Socialist Party in Arkansas, 1900–1912," *Arkansas Historical Quarterly* 40 (Summer 1981): 119–153.

57. "Our Visitors," *Party Builder*, November 1, 1913, 5.

58. "Socialist Victories in Recent Elections," *Commonwealth,* November 20, 1913, 1.

59. Kaltinick, "Socialist Municipal Administration," 372–373.

60. "Eskdale Carried by Socialists," *Socialist and Labor Star* (Huntington, WV), January 9, 1914, 1.

61. Cornford, "Lumber, Labor, and Community in Humboldt County," 550.

62. Nord, "Minneapolis and the Pragmatic Socialism of Thomas Van Lear," 10.

63. "Every Local Should Enter Municipal Campaign," *Ohio Socialist* (Cleveland, OH), June 1917, 1. See also James Weinstein, "Anti-war Sentiment and the Socialist Party, 1917–1918," *Political Science Quarterly* 74 (June 1959): 215–239; and "Ohio Socialists Claiming Victory," *Evening Capital News* (Boise, ID), November 3, 1917, 1.

64. See, for example, Paul H. Douglas, "The Socialist Vote in Municipal Elections of 1917," *NMR* 7 (March 1918): 131–139.

65. In September 1917 Tyler Lawton, Socialist mayor of Bicknell, Indiana, was one of these, leaving the Socialist Party and his public office because he disagreed with the party's stand. David Love, Socialist mayor of West Alliance, Wisconsin (1916–1920), also supported US entry into war and resigned from the Socialist Party. Mayor Duff Brace of Conneaut and former mayors J. Stitt Wilson of Berkeley and John Knapp of Sisseton, South Dakota, also broke with the party on the war issue. On Lawton, see accounts in "Socialist Mayor Recants Faith," *New York Tribune*, October 20, 1917, 7; "Socialist Steps Out of Party and Office," *Seattle* (WA) *Star*, October 13, 1917, 4; and "Socialist Mayor Quits His Party," *Richmond Palladium and Sun-Telegram*, September 11, 1917, 2.

66. Holli, *The American Mayor*, 66.

67. George William Shea, *Spoiled Silk: The Red Mayor and the Great Paterson Textile Strike* (New York: Fordham University Press, 2000).

68. Jorsch, "Radical Municipal Socialism in Madrid, Iowa," 66.

69. "Hold Big Anti-War Rally," *NYT*, February 11, 1917, 6.

70. "State Lawyers Ask Removal of Minneapolis Mayor for Antagonizing Government," *Bemidji* (MN) *Daily Pioneer*, August 10, 1917, 1.

71. "Van Lear Again Files for Mayoralty Race," *Bemidji* (MN) *Daily Pioneer*, May 18, 1918, 1. For criticism from the left for reversing his position, see "Mayor Van Lear Joins American Labor Alliance," *Labor World*, July 6, 1918, 1.

72. Iric Nathanson, "Thomas Van Lear, City Hall's Working-Class Champion," *Minnesota History* 64 (July 1, 2015): 224–233.

73. See "Minnesota Socialists Expel Van Lear for War Stand," *New York Call* (New York, NY), July 9, 1919, 6. Found at marxisthistory.org.

74. "Elect Socialist Mayor: Lackawanna Incumbent's Defeat Attributed to Steel Strikers," *NYT*, November 5, 1919, 3.

75. William Scheuerman, "The Politics of Protest: The Great Steel Strike of 1919–20

in Lackawanna, New York," *International Review of Social History* 31 (August 1986): 121–146.

76. "Socialists Win in Iowa," *Manitowoc* (WI) *Pilot*, April 8, 1920, 3.

CHAPTER 5. GETTING THERE, STAYING THERE

1. Frank Parker, "On an 8,000 Mile Swing," *Winfield* (KS) *Daily Press*, July 26, 1911, 2.
2. Woodruff, "American Municipal Tendencies."
3. "Socialists Advocate Municipal Reforms," *Rogue River Courier* (Grants Pass, OR), October 27, 1911, 1.
4. Kaltinick, "Socialist Municipal Administration," 182. The eleven cities or towns elected Socialist mayors noted by Kaltinick were Ashtabula, Canal Dover, Conneaut, Lorain, Martins Ferry, Massillon, and Piqua, Ohio; Elwood and Gas City, Indiana; Granite City, Illinois; and New Castle, Pennsylvania.
5. "Giving Votes to Debs," *Sistersville* (WV) *Daily Oil Review*, September 28, 1904, 6.
6. "Giving Votes to Debs."
7. "The Socialist Outlook," *ISR* 5 (1904–1905): 203–217, quote at 208.
8. Remarks of John Chase as reported in "Haverhill's Socialists, Their Ups and Downs Described by Their Ex-Mayor," *Indianapolis* (IN) *Journal*, February 19, 1902, 3.
9. Kevin Starr, *Inventing the Dream*, 212 (on Pasadena); "Progressive Municipality," *Arizona Socialist Bulletin* (Phoenix, AZ), December 27, 1912 (on Grand Junction).
10. Henry, "News and Views, Grand Junction's Socialist Mayor."
11. Hoxie, "The Rising Tide of Socialism," 619, 621.
12. McCormick and Sillito, *A History of Utah Radicalism*, 191.
13. See Dubofsky, *Industrialism and the American Worker*, 33; Herman G. Gutman, "The Worker's Search for Power, and Green, "The 'Salesmen-Soldiers' of the 'Appeal Army,'" in *The Gilded Age*, ed. Wayne Morgan (Syracuse, NY: Syracuse University Press, 1970), 31–53.
14. Gutman, "The Worker's Search for Power," 530.
15. This situation existed in "Middletown" (Muncie, Indiana) in the 1920s, as revealed in a pioneering study of small towns by Robert and Helen Lynd. See Robert Staughton Lynd and Helen Merrell Lynd, *Middletown: A Study in Modern American Culture* (New York: Harcourt, Brace, 1929).
16. See, for example, the discussion in Robert C. Wood, "A Re-examination of Local Democracy," in *Democracy in Urban America: Readings on Government and Politics*, ed. Oliver P. Williams and Charles Press (Chicago: Rand McNally, 1961), 109–125.
17. Hoxie, "The Rising Tide of Socialism," 617.
18. On the effects of having elected councilmen in Milwaukee, see Wachman, *History of the Social-Democratic Party of Milwaukee*, 62; and Howe, "Milwaukee—A Socialist City," 414.
19. Bedford, *Socialism and the Workers in Massachusetts*, 5, 6.
20. "How the Battle Was Waged," *SDH*, April 18, 1903, 1.

21. On the Ohio visits in Martins Ferry, St. Marys, and Mansfield, see, respectively, Judd, *Socialist Cities*, 80; "News and Views, Victory at St. Marys, Ohio," *ISR* 12 (December 1911): 376–377; and "Ohio Socialists in Action," *ISR* 12 (October 1911): 236–242.

22. "Ohio Socialists in Action."

23. Letter from John J. Scholtes, Alliance, Ohio, to CDT, November 7, 1913, SPP.

24. "What They Are Doing in Hamilton," *Party Builder* (Chicago, IL), October 4, 1913, 2.

25. From an article dealing with William D. Haywood, "Acquitted of Murder, Run for President," *Hawaiian Star* (Honolulu, HI), August 20, 1907, 5.

26. Bohn, "The Socialist Party and the Government of Cities."

27. On Duncan, see Emmons, *Butte Irish*, 103, 265.

28. See Patek, "The 1911 Election of Socialist mayor Henry Stolze, Jr., of Manitowoc."

29. Socialist mayors defeated by a fusion ticket included the mayors of Colgate, Oklahoma, 1905; Crookston, Minnesota, 1913; Edmonds, Washington, 1912; Flint, Michigan, 1912; Fostoria, Ohio, 1913; Girard, Kansas, 1914; Granite City, Illinois, 1915; Hamilton, Ohio, 1915; Hartford Arkansas, 1914; Haverhill, Massachusetts, 1900; Milwaukee, Wisconsin, 1912; Schenectady, New York, 1913; and St. Marys, Ohio, 1913. Many of these mayors initially won office with less than a majority of the votes in contests with three or more candidates. In some cases, the losing Socialist increased his share of the vote. In Girard, Kansas, for example, Socialist H. P. Houghton went from a victory where he captured 39.6 percent of the vote in a three-person contest in 1911 to a defeat where he collected 42.2 percent of the vote in a two-person contest in 1914. Mayors in some of these places, such as Schenectady and Granite City, came back to recapture the office after being ousted by a fusion candidate.

30. Report from an Edgewater Socialist called Comrade Kirkman in "They Hold the Fort, " *Party Builder*, August 9, 1913, 2.

31. Abbott, "The Socialist Movement in Massachusetts."

32. "Two Socialist Mayors in Massachusetts," *Outlook* (New York, NY), December 16, 1899, 904.

33. Kipnis, *The American Socialist Movement*, 77.

34. See reports from Socialist State Party secretaries in Colorado and Montana in "The Socialist Outlook," *ISR* 5 (1904–1905): 203–217.

35. Richard Hofstadter, *The Paranoid Style in American Politics* (New York: Vintage, 1967), 34. Hofstadter noted the special emphasis the far right placed on sponsoring appearances of ex-communists in the 1950s and 1960s.

36. "Thousands Hear the Debate between David Goldstein and Arthur LeSueur at Minot," *Bowbells* (ND) *Tribune*, May 3, 1912, 2.

37. "A Problem for Coeur D'Alene to Solve," *Coeur D'Alene* (ID) *Evening Press*, April 3, 1911, 1.

38. Editorial, "Will We Endorse Socialism?," *Coeur D'Alene Evening Press*, March 29, 1911, 2. Same theme in the editorial "Revolution or Government," *Coeur D'Alene Evening Press*, March 28, 1911, 2; and "Which Shall It Be?" *Coeur D'Alene Evening Press*, March 27, 1911, 2.

39. "Ring Rule Supreme," *Clarksburg* (WV) *Telegram*, February 15, 1912, 4.
40. Stevens, "Heartland Socialism," 111–112.
41. "Milwaukee's Socialist Reverse," *Literary Digest* (New York, NY), April 13, 1912, 740.
42. "Milwaukee's Socialist Reverse."
43. "Socialists Lose," *Irish Standard* (Minneapolis, MN), April 6, 1912, 1.
44. "Socialist Mayor Attacked," *Day Book*, September 30, 1913, 30.
45. "Mayor of Deplanes, Ill., Flees from Citizens," *Zion City* (IL) *Independent*, October 3, 1913, 2.
46. "Mayor Lawson Turns Tables on Enemies," *Day Book* (Chicago, IL), October 1, 1913, 30.
47. "4,000 Socialists Hold War Protest Meeting," *Sun* (New York, NY), August 9, 1914, 7.
48. "Minneapolis Mayor Delivers Message to Enormous Crowd in Auditorium," *Labor World* (Duluth, MN), February 17, 1917, 1.
49. "Socialists Abandon Parade at Bicknell, *Daily Tribune* (Terre Haute, IN), June 6, 1917, 1.
50. "Illinois Has New Big Bill," *Free Trader-Journal* (Ottawa, IL), September 17, 1917, 2.
51. "Defense Meetings for Piqua Socialists," *Ohio Socialist* (Cleveland, OH), November 20, 1918, 3.
52. "Frontenac," *Pittsburg* (KS) *Daily Headlight*, June 28, 1918, 11.
53. "School's Use Is Denied for Socialist Meeting," and "Mayor Is Denounced," *Indianapolis News*, November 25, 1919, 32.
54. Some political science research finds incumbent mayoral candidates winning reelection close to 80 percent of the time. See, for example, Albert K. Karnig and B. Oliver Walter, "Joint Electoral Fate of Local Incumbents"; and Clarke A. Hagensick, "Influences of Partisanship and Incumbency on a Nonpartisan Election System," *Western Political Quarterly* 17 (March 1964).
55. Richard A. Folk, "The Golden Age of Ohio Socialism," *Northwest Ohio Quarterly* 41, no. 3 (1969): 6.
56. The ability to deliver has also been offered among the explanations for the success of Progressive reformers such as Robert La Follette in Wisconsin. See John H. Fenton, *Midwest Politics* (New York: Holt, Rinehart & Winston, 1966), 47. Still, some have wondered whether the package of benefits commonly provided by the Socialists were of a nature to generate more than short-term support. See, for example, Kipnis, *The American Socialist Movement*, 77.
57. Quoted in David A. Shannon, *The Socialist Party of America* (New York: MacMillan, 1955), 14.
58. Fulda, "Daniel Hoan," 246.
59. Fulda.
60. Thierry, "Socialist Mayor May Lead Party Campaign."
61. Patek, "The 1911 Election of Socialist Mayor Henry Stolze, Jr."

62. Jorsch, "Radical Municipal Socialism in Madrid," 66.
63. Shea, *Spoiled Silk*, 102.
64. "That Vacation," *Scott County Kicker* (Benton, MO), July 15, 1911, 1.
65. "That Vacation."
66. On taxes see "Socialists Increase Taxes," *Catholic Bulletin* (St. Paul, MN), March 14, 1914, 2; "Do the Socialists Raise Taxes, A Stupid Capitalist Press Attack."
67. "More Seats Won by Socialists: Kirkpatrick Again Mayor of Granite City, Illinois," *Northwest Worker* (Everett, WA), May 3, 1917, 1.
68. Untitled entry, *ATR*, December 7, 1901, 3; "Editorial Talk," *Ellensburg* (WA) *Dawn*, December 21, 1901, 1. On the town, see "The Story of Northport," https://northportproject.com/northport-washington-history.
69. "Socialist Victory," *ATR*, December 14, 1901, 4.
70. Untitled item, *ATR*, February 8, 1902, 1.
71. "Socialists Rule North Port Town," *San Francisco* (CA) *Call*, January 19, 1902, 19.
72. Cresswell, "When the Socialists Ran Star City."
73. "Harry Schilling Socialist," *News-Democrat* (Canton, OH), November 8, 1911, 11.
74. Judd, *Socialist Cities*, 76, notes that there were five organizations involved in the 1911 election: "the Citizen's Independent, Democratic, Republican, Socialist Labor, and Socialist parties."
75. This comes from *Mahoning Dispatch* (Canfield, OH), December 8, 1911, 2. This description of the contest is also found in "Guess Decides Tie Vote," *NYT*, November 12, 1911, 1. The contest has also been described as being one deciding who came closest to predicting the number of kernels in a cup of corn. See "Mayor Says City Must Obey 10 Commandments," *Tacoma Times*, December 5, 1912, 4; and Judd, *Socialist Cities*, 86.
76. "Mayor Says City Must Obey."
77. See Judd, *Socialist Cities*, 76–77. The explanation given by the party was that he had been expelled because he had gone back on his word to abide by the ear-of-corn contest, "Mayor Says City Must Obey."
78. "Mayor Says City Must Obey."
79. "Mayor Says City Must Obey"; Judd, *Socialist Cities*, 77.
80. "Turnbull Declared Mayor," *Greenville Journal* (OH), May 8, 1913, 3.
81. Judd, *Socialist Cities*, 77.

CHAPTER 6. COMING IN, PROGRESS, AND PROBLEMS

1. "Socialist Mayor Surprised at Vote," *Star Press* (Muncie, IN), December 1, 1911, 10.
2. "A Socialist Mayor's Program," *Literary Digest* (New York, NY), January 14, 1899, 34–35. See also "A Socialist Mayor's Views," *Hartford* (CT) *Courant*, January 3, 1899, 2; "Haverhill has Socialist Mayor," *Times* (Richmond, VA), January 3, 1899, 2; Kipnis, *The American Socialist Movement*, 77.
3. Statements are from Seidel's inaugural address as reported in the Associated

Press report "Socialist Mayor Elect Declares against Bosses," *Los Angeles* (CA) *Herald*, April 7, 1910, 1; Untitled entry, *Goodwin's Weekly* (Salt Lake City, UT), April 23, 1910, 6–7; "Will Seek to Allay Fears," *Evening Times* (Grand Forks, ND), April 7, 1910, 1.

4. "Berkeley, Cal., College City of 45,000, Elects Socialist Mayor—J. Stitt Wilson," *Detroit Times*, April 14, 1911, 13; "Wilson Exults in His Election," *San Francisco Call*, April 3, 1911, 1, 2; "Wilson Tells of His Plans," *Medford* (OR) *Mail Tribune*, April 3, 1911, 1.

5. "Canton Socialist Mayor Announces Purpose," *Marion* (OH) *Daily Mirror*, November 9, 1911, 2.

6. Stevens, "Heartland Socialism," 154.

7. "A Pioneer Socialist," *Fort Scott* (KS) *Daily Tribune and Fort Scott Daily Monitor*, May 7, 1912, 2.

8. "Town of Edmonds Will Try a Socialist Mayor for Next Two Years," *Tacoma* (WA) *Times*, December 23, 1910, 4.

9. "Butte Elects a Socialist Mayor," *Daily Missoulian* (Missoula, MT), April 4, 1911, 6.

10. "To Reform Butte," *Fergus County Democrat* (Lewistown, MT), May 9, 1911, 2. See also "Smoky City Mayor Is Radical," *Daily Missoulian*, May 2, 1911, 5.

11. Letter from Duncan to Hiram Pratt, May 20, 1911, Duncan Papers, Montana Historical Society Archives, Helena.

12. "Former Pugilist to Take Office Monday," *Salt Lake Tribune* (Salt Lake City, UT), April 9, 1911, 2.

13. Judd, *Socialist Cities*, 103.

14. "Hoisting the Red Flag," *New York Tribune*, November 12, 1911, 2.

15. Hendrickson, "Tribune of the People," 83. See also Kipnis, *The American Socialist Movement*, 363; and Kaltinick, "Socialist Municipal Administration," 104.

16. Griffin, "The Rising Tide of Socialism."

17. Griffin, 441–442.

18. Griffin, 438–448.

19. Kaltinick, "Socialist Municipal Administration," 97.

20. Editorial statement, *Little Falls* (MN) *Herald*, November 10, 1911, 4.

21. "Sisseton and Vicinity," *Sisseton* (SD) *Weekly Standard*, April 25, 1913, 5.

22. From a review of newspaper responses to Chase's election in "A Socialist Mayor's Program," *Literary Digest*, January 14, 1899, 34–35.

23. "Election Returns," *Montana News* (Helena and Lewiston, MT), April 6, 1911, 2.

24. Untitled item, *Roundup* (MO) *Record*, April 14, 1911, 4.

25. "Berkeley as a Political Laboratory," *San Francisco Call*, April 3, 1911, 6.

26. Cross, "Socialism in California Municipalities," 617.

27. Untitled editorial, *Red Cloud* (NE) *Chief*, April 6, 1911, 4.

28. Untitled editorial, *Red Cloud Chief*, November 23, 1911, 4.

29. See, for example, the statement by Wisconsin party leader E. H. Thomas concerning the recent election of Socialist Charles A. Born as mayor of Sheboygan, in "Socialist Mayor Assumes Office," *SDH*, April 25, 1903, 1.

30. Letter from Carl D. Thompson to R. A. Henning, Brainerd, Minnesota, September 12, 1913, SPP. Thompson, a Congregationalist minister for many years,

became a convert to Christian Socialism, left the ministry, and became an active organizer, lecturer, writer, and spokesperson for the Socialist Party. He served in the Wisconsin state legislature, worked for the Seidel administration in Milwaukee, developed the national party's municipal program, and headed the national party's Information Department. He left the party because of its opposition to US participation in World War I. His history is comparable in many respects to mayors Duncan, Lynn and, even more, J. Stitt Wilson. (See appendix 1.)

31. Judd, *Socialist Cities*, 74, citing the *Cleveland* (OH) *Plain Dealer*, November 12, 1911.

32. Judd, *Socialist Cities*, 82, citing the *New Castle* (PA) *Free Press*, September 14, 1912.

33. D. L. Thomas, Mayor, O'Fallon, Ill., July 4, 1912, to Carl D. Thompson.

34. Letter, July 8, 1912, SPP.

35. Letter from W. M. Ralston to Carl D. Thompson, September 16, 1913, SPP.

36. E. E. Robinson to Carl D. Thompson, September 10, 1913, found in Judd, *Socialist Cities*, 88.

37. "Socialists on the Job," *ATR*, February 24, 1912, 3.

38. "Socialists on the Job," 3.

39. "News and Views, Flint Flashes," *ISR* 12 (August 1911): 119.

40. Jorsch, "Modernized Republicanism," 722.

41. "Socialist Mayor of Haledon, N. J. Wins," *Commonwealth* (Everett, WA), March 7, 1913, 4.

42. *Salt Lake Tribune* (Salt Lake City, UT), January 7, 1908, 9.

43. Kaltinick, "Socialist Municipal Administration," 250–251.

44. Letter, Walter V. Tyler to Carl D. Thompson, September 23, 1913, SPP.

45. "Socialist Mayor Tells Story of New Castle PA," *American Socialist* (Chicago, IL), September 26, 1914, 2.

46. "Commission Ousts Socialists," *Fairmont West Virginian*, December 5, 1913, 5.

47. J. Stitt Wilson, "The Berkeley Municipal Administration," in *The American Labor Yearbook* (New York: Rand School of Social Science, 1916), 116.

48. "Le Sueur Quits, Resigns as President of Minor Commission," *Evening Times* (Grand Forks, ND), May 16, 1911, 2; "Minot Socialists Ask President Le Sueur to Resign," *Ward County Independent* (Minot, ND), May 11, 1911, 9; Jackson Putnam, "The Socialist Party of North Dakota, 1902–1918" (MA thesis, University of North Dakota, 1956).

49. "City Government under Capitalism, Insurgent Mayor Fights Graft," *Montana News*, December 2, 1909, 1.

50. E. Francis Atwood, organizer, "Sisseton, South Dakota, Campaigns 1913 and 1914," April 1914, SPP.

51. "Socialist Mayor of Davenport to Leave the Party," *Grand Forks Herald and the Evening Times* (Grand Forks, ND), January 5, 1921, 2. See also "Davenport Mayor Cuts Socialist Ties," *Rock Island* (IL) *Argus and Daily Union*, January 5, 1921, 1; and William H. Cumberland, "The Davenport Socialists of 1920," *Annals of Iowa* 47 (Summer 1984): 451–474.

52. "Friction in Socialist Local Over Police Recall," *Coeur d'Alene* (ID) *Evening Press,* April 17, 1911, 1, 4.

53. "Socialists Demand Mayor Wood's Scalp," *Coeur d'Alene Evening Press,* June 5, 1911, 1.

54. Stanley S. Phipps, "Building Socialism in One City: Coeur d'Alene, Idaho's, 1911 Municipal Government," *Museum of North Idaho Quarterly Newsletter* 7 (Winter 1986): 1–5.

55. "Curt Comment of the Times," *Will Maupin's Weekly* (Lincoln, NE), May 19, 1911, 4.

56. "Nebraska Beatrice Socialists Ask Mayor to Resign," *Omaha* (NE) *Daily Bee,* December 15, 1911, 3, "Ask Socialist Mayor to Resign, Beatrice Man Charged with Violating Party Principles Will Not Vacate," *Abilene* (KS) *Weekly Reflector,* December 21, 1911, 14.

57. "Socialists Are at Outs in Berkeley," *San Francisco Call,* July 6, 1911, 1.

58. "Socialists in Family Quarrel," *Ronan Pioneer* (MT), February 19, 1915, 1; "Montana Squibs," *Cut Bank* (MT) *Pioneer Press,* February 19, 1915, 4; and "Missoula Local's City Officials Refuse to Accept Resignations Signed before Elected," *Labor World* (Duluth, MN), February 27, 1915, 6.

59. "Shook Refuses to Quit Office," *Marion Daily Mirror,* January 3, 1912, 5.

60. Statement from E. O. McPherron, Chair of Socialist Party of Ohio, March 19, 1913, SPP, 4.

61. In both Lorain and Lima some party members and leaders reportedly had evidence that the mayors elected on their tickets were using their appointment power to build up personal political machines to use for their advancement to another office. See Shannon, *The Socialist Party,* 17.

62. "To Whom It May Concern," *Democratic Banner* (Mt. Vernon, OH), April 1, 1913, 8.

63. "Spring a Sensation," *Democratic Banner,* March 28, 1913, 3; "The Mayor and His Party," *Democratic Banner,* April 4, 1913, 4.

64. Duncan, "Socialist Politics in Butte," 287–291. Duncan relates how he cleared appointments with the central committee of the Socialist Party in the city in a letter from Lewis Duncan to Mr. H. A. Barton, Many 12, 1911, Duncan Papers, SC2175, Montana Historical Society Archives, Helena, MT.

65. "Butte Socialists Break," *Willmar* (MN) *Tribune,* June 18, 1913, 2.

66. "The Lesson in Butte," *Miners Magazine,* July 10, 1913, 14.

67. From: "At War with the Party, the Tyranny of Socialism," *Minneapolis* (MN) *Morning Tribune,* October 25, 1916, 6.

68. Shea, *Spoiled Silk,* 42.

69. For defense of the system of party control, see, for example, "Socialist Officials," *Labor Argus* (Charleston, WV), December 14, 1911, 6.

70. "News and Views, Grand Junction Socialists All Right," *ISR* 12 (August 1911): 118.

CHAPTER 7. BEING MAYOR

1. "Mayor Duncan Shot Assailant," *River Press* (Fort Benton, MT), July 8, 1914, 1. On another act of violence involving a Socialist mayor, a newspaper noted, "The Socialist mayor of a Pennsylvania town, who failed to give satisfaction in his administration, was shot in his office by a too critical constituent. This simple and practical way of exercising the recall has, however, like all extremely simple methods, its disadvantages in highly civilized communities." Untitled item, *Bowbells Tribune* (ND), May 10, 1912, 4.

2. "Socialist Mayor Seeks Rest from His Enemies," *Washington* (DC) *Times*, April 11, 1911, 5. In a related article, the author wrote that Seidel had "broken down from worry over the newspaper attacks made upon his administration. . . . Those who have been 'keeping cases' on Mr. Seidel's administration will feel sympathy for him, for it is conceded by unbiased critics that the Socialists have done their best to conduct the municipal government in an unselfish and judicious manner." Still, the author suggested, Seidel should have been prepared, as he and other Socialists had done their share of criticizing those in power and should have expected the same when they came to power. See "Socialist Meeting," *Pierre* (SD) *Weekly Free Press*, June 1, 1911, 1, citing the *Yankton Herald*.

3. McCormick and Sillito, *A History of Utah Radicalism*, 192.

4. Carl Sandburg, "Otis Fakes About Milwaukee," *Labor Argus* (Charleston, WV), December 28, 1911, 4. Sandburg, the noted poet and author, had been employed by Seidel as his personal secretary. See also "Home Rue for Milwaukee," *New York Tribune*, December 21, 1910, 8.

5. See generally McClennen and Cresswell, *Socialists in a Small Town*; and "Quite Checkered Are the Results," *Daily Adamston* (Clarksburg, WV), January 5, 1912, 3.

6. Judd, *Socialist Cities*, 94.

7. Cresswell, "When the Socialists Ran Star City."

8. See, for example, on Milwaukee, Kaltinick, "Socialist Municipal Administration," 27; and Clark, *Mill Town*, 116.

9. John I. Kolehmainen and George W. Hill, *Haven in the Woods: The Story of the Finns in Wisconsin* (Madison: State Historical Society of Wisconsin, 1951), 125.

10. Jorsch, "Radical Municipal Socialism in Madrid, Iowa, 1903–1920," 83.

11. Based on eleven brief news reports mentioning the mayor by name, usually under the column heading "Salem," in *Mahoning Dispatch* (Canfield, OH) from December 1911 to April 1913. Actual dates in the paper: December 15, 1911, 1; December 22, 1911, 6; February 2, 1912, 6; April 5, 1912, 8; April 12, 1912, 6; July 26, 1912, 6; August 12, 1912, 6; November 15, 1912, 6; January 3, 1913, 1 (no Salem heading); April 18, 1913, 1.

12. "Salem," *Mahoning Dispatch*, December 19, 1913, 1; "Salem," *Mahoning Dispatch*, April 19, 1912, 6.

13. Sources, in order: "News of the State," *Bismarck* (ND) *Daily Tribune*, May 3, 1912, 8; "Flickertails Facts and Fancies," *Bottineau* (ND) *Courant*, August 16, 1912, 4; and "Flickertails Facts and Fancies," *Bottineau Courant*, October 4, 1912, 4.

14. "A Socialist Mayor," *Stillwater* (OK) *Gazette*, April 30, 1909, 4.

15. Some mayors valued this activity as an effective way of opening one's eyes to how the other half lives, but others scorned it as something that interfered with their more important duties and was best entrusted to others (on the first point see "Issues Statement to Preachers," *Fulton County Tribune* (Wauseon, OH), December 4, 1914, 9, for statement from a Democratic mayor who also happened to be a minister and, on the second point, a statement from Socialist mayor Walter Tyler from New Castle in "Snapshots at State News," *Citizen* (Honesdale, PA), March 21, 1913, 3. The practice could be abused, as in Medford, Oregon, where a mayor used his authority to levy a fine on a Socialist who was a political opponent of his in the council—someone he was trying to keep in line—a decision that was later reversed by a higher court. See "Eifert Finds Millar Guilty of Immorality," *Medford* (OR) *Mail Tribune*, March 31, 1913, 1, 2.

16. This information was drawn from eleven brief news reports mentioning the mayor by name, usually under the column heading of "Salem," in the *Mahoning Dispatch* from December 1911 to April 1913.

17. Judd, *Socialist Cities*, 74.

18. In January 1913 the mayor announced that in 1912, 422 arrests had been made in Salem and $1,099 in fines had been collected, just under $91 per month; see "Washingtonville Local Gleanings, *Mahoning Dispatch*, January 3, 1913, 1. In the small Ohio town of Conneaut, where Socialist D. S. Brace was mayor, fines averaged $28.50 a month. See "News in Brief," *Washington Socialist* (Everett, WA), March 25, 1915, 3. The population of the two towns in 1910 was close: Salem with 8,943, Conneaut with 8, 319. Other work suggests that the Socialist mayor of Lorain, Ohio, also imposed unusually large fines for relatively small offenses in his quest to clean up his city. See DeMatteo, "Socialist Municipal Administrations in the Progressive Era Midwest," 31.

19. Useful sources on small towns drawn upon were Duane Lockard, *The Politics of State and Local Government*, 2nd ed. (New York: Macmillan, 1969); and Alvin D. Sokolow, "Small Local Governments as Community Builders," *National Civic Review* 78 (September-October 1989): 362–370.

20. A remark of this nature was once made in comparing New York governors and mayors; see Lockard, *The Politics of State and Local Government*, 379.

21. Report of J. F. Kenworthy, Earlham, Iowa, "The Lure of the Jungle, Number Four," *Galena* (KS) *Weekly Republican*, July 21, 1911, 7.

22. "Mayors of Small Towns," *River Press* (Fort Benton, MT), March 23, 1910, 4.

23. "Retiring Burgess," *Fulton County News* (McConnellsburg, PA), January 1, 1912, 1.

24. Wood, "A Re-examination of Local Democracy," 111.

25. Granville Hicks, *Small Town* (New York: Fordham University Press, 2004 [1946]), 89. His remarks on the minimal significance of class conflict were all the more striking in that Hicks at the time of his settlement in the small town he wrote about was a member of the Communist Party, an affiliation he later renounced.

26. Kalinick, *Socialist Municipal Administration*, 371.

27. Along with this information the bureau sent copies of party platforms suitable

for small cities to various locals around the country. See "What They Want," *Party Builder* (Chicago, IL), July 12, 1913, 3.

28. "Starting Right," *Party Builder*, December 27, 1913, 4.
29. "A Revolutionary Mayor," *ISR* 12 (June 1912): 832.
30. Dawson, "St. Mary's Fighting Mayor," 875.
31. Dawson, 876.
32. Quoted by Stephen E. Barton, "J. Stitt Wilson, Berkeley's Socialist Mayor," *Newsletter of the Berkeley Historical Society* 29, (Summer 2011): 4.
33. Letter to Berkeley Socialists, Declining the Nomination for the Mayoralty of Berkeley, February 19, 1913. Found in collection of articles in Hathi Trust Digital Library, https://www.hathitrust.org, 33, 36.
34. "'Ostentatiously Paean' Declares Berkeley Mayor," *San Francisco Call*, January 31, 1913, 10.
35. "News and Views, Flint Flashes," *ISR* 12 (August 1911): 119.
36. Untitled entry, *ATR*, February 22, 1913, 3.
37. "Socialist Victory in Butte," *ISR* 13 (May 1913): 829.
38. Clarence A. Smith, "Miners' Union Day in Butte," *ISR* 12 (July 1911): 5–6.
39. "Duluth Socialists in Big Celebration," *Labor World* (Duluth, MN), May 6, 1911, 1.
40. "Socialist Vote in Los Angeles Heavy," *Labor World*, November 4, 1911, 1.
41. "Office-Holding Socialists Meet," *Chico* (CA) *Record*, August 13, 1911, 6.
42. "Instructs the City's Employees," *Daily Capital Journal* (Salem, OR), April 25, 1910, 4.
43. "Seidel Refused to Meet Teddy," *Weekly Chieftain* (Vinita, OK), September 9, 1910, 8.
44. "Socialist Mayor Wouldn't Meet Taft," *Daily Star-Mirror* (Moscow, ID), October 19, 1911, 1.
45. "To Hell with Kings," *Chattanooga* (TN) *News*, September 22, 1919, 4; "King Refused Invitation," *Cresco* (IA) *Plain Dealer*, September 26, 1919, 7.
46. "A Radical in Office, *Baraboo* (WI) *Weekly News*, October 9, 1919, 4, citing the *Springfield Republican*.
47. See, for example, "Socialist Mayor Bought Coal for People of Town," *Harrisburg* (PA) *Telegraph*, November 17, 1916, 21.

CHAPTER 8. MANAGING, BUDGETING, CLEANING UP THE TOWN

1. This happened, for example, in Cedar City and Eureka, Utah. The problems of Cedar City mayor Daniel T. Leigh are remarked upon in "Deadlock in Cedar, "*Inter-Mountain Republican* (Salt Lake City, UT), March 3, 1906, 9. On problems of mayor Andrew Mitchell of Eureka, see "Republicans Hold Up Socialist Names," *Salt Lake Telegram* (Salt Lake City, UT), January 1, 1907, 4.
2. This, for example, was a problem faced by Socialist mayor Gibbons, in

Lackawanna, New York. See "Rum Seller Is Fire Chief," *Sun* (New York, NY), January 3, 1920, 5.

3. "Keeps Pie for Socialists, Haverhill Mayor Decides to Appoint Collectivists Only to Municipal Posts," *Omaha* (KS) *Daily Bee*, July 3, 1903, 2; "Indiana New Brief" *Daily Tribune* (Terre Haute, IN), December 29, 1917, 4. Similar complaints were direct at Mayor G. A. Herring of Washburn, Wisconsin, early on in his administration for appointing only members of the Socialist Democratic Party, "Carrying Politics Too Far," *Washburn* (WI) *Times*, April 20, 1911, 8.

4. E. H. Thomas, "Socialist Mayor Assumes Office," *SDH*, April 25, 1903, 1.

5. See, for example, Cross, "Socialism in California Municipalities."

6. Kipnis, *The American Socialist Movement*, 361; Kaltinick, "Socialist Municipal Administration," 46–48.

7. Kaltinick, 372.

8. Griffin, "The Rising Tide of Socialism," 442.

9. See "Rum Seller Is Fire Chief."

10. "Other Than Socialists to Office," *Labor World* (Duluth, MN), November 21, 1903, 2.

11. Wayne A. Wiegand, *Main Street Public Library: Community Places and Reading Spaces in the Rural Heartland, 1876–1956* (Iowa City: University of Iowa Press, 2011).

12. "Socialist Mayor Plan Will Discharge Entire Police Force of Granite City, Establish Municipal Coal Yard," *Cairo* (IL) *Bulletin*, April 21, 1911, 3.

13. "Ohio State News Given in Brief, Find Police Chief Not Guilty," *Greenville* (OH) *Journal*, February 6, 1913, 2.

14. "Buckeye Notes," *Greenville Journal*, January 25, 1912, 6, and February 1, 1912, 3; "Stolze Comes in Open," *Ladysmith* (WI) *News*, December 22, 1906, 4.

15. Kaltinick, "Socialist Municipal Administration," 335.

16. "Special Officers in Beatrice," *Omaha* (NE) *Daily Bee*, May 12, 1911, 5; "Nebraska Beatrice Socialists Ask Mayor to Resign," *Omaha Daily Bee*, December 15, 1911, 3.

17. "Names Negro, Council Balks," *Detroit* (MI) *Times*, May 17, 1911, 2.

18. Duncan, "Socialist Politics in Butte," 287–291. The attitude of Socialist mayors toward Black Americans could not be fully explored in this study. At one end, one can find some Socialist mayors expressing white supremist views. An example is J. P. Marchant, mayor of Phenix City, Alabama; see Brad Alan Paul, "Rebels of the New South: The Socialist Party in Dixie, 1892–1920" (PhD diss., University of Massachusetts Amherst, 1999), 77. The endorsement of a Mayor Van Lear of Minnesota in his bid for reelection in 1918 by a group of Black citizens called the Colored Citizens' Volunteer Committee suggests Van Lear belonged at the other end of the scale. Their endorsement read, "Mayor Van Lear has shown a special interest in the Negro citizens, not as Socialists (because there is not one among them), but as a part of the civic family entitled to their share of rights and privileges. He has maintained an open door to all at all times, and in many instances has given evidence of his spirit of justice and sympathy. He appointed a member of our race on his Advisory Board and our first police woman and an assistant stenographer in his office. He stopped the display of

objectionable signs in public places, such as 'Colored Patronage Not Solicited,' etc. He urged our people to pass the civil service examinations, so that we might qualify for positions in the city departments. He has addressed several meetings, such as the National Association for the Advancement of Colored People, and the Farewell to the Drafted Boys, always making a clean and patriotic address, paying a high tribute to the valor and discipline of the Negro troops, with whom he had served, and words of praise in honor of our men and women. . . . He refused to permit the film 'The Birth of a Nation' to be shown, being the second Mayor in America to take such action." (Paid advertisement, "Why We Should Re-elect Mayor Thomas E. Van Lear," *Twin City Star* (Minneapolis, MN), November 2, 1918, 1.

19. Letter from J. B. Bitterly, Socialist Mayor of Victor, March 1913, to Carl D. Thompson, Information Department, SPA, SPP.

20. DeMatteo, "Socialist Municipal Administrations in the Progressive Era Midwest."

21. Kaltinick, "Socialist Municipal Administration," 153.

22. Sandburg, "Otis Fakes About Milwaukee."

23. Howe, "Milwaukee—A Socialist City."

24. Cresswell, "When the Socialists Ran Star City." On the other hand, Socialists elsewhere had no problem with the selling of bonds. See "Montana Municipal State Campaign," *Montana News* (Helena and Lewiston, MT), March 26, 1908, 1.

25. "Fight Desperately in Hamilton, Ohio," *Party Builder* (Chicago, IL), September 27, 1913, 4.

26. "Starting Right," *Party Builder*, December 27, 1913, 4.

27. Constance McLaughlin Green, *History of Naugatuck, Connecticut* (New Haven, CT: Yale University Press, 1948), 152.

28. See, for example, "Socialists Increase Taxes," *Catholic Bulletin* (St. Paul, MN), March 14, 1914, 2, and for the Socialists' response, "Do the Socialists Raise Taxes: A Stupid Capitalist Press Attack," *Party Builder*, March 7, 1914.

29. "Starting Right," *Party Builder*, December 27, 1913, 4.

30. Wilson, "The Story of a Socialist Mayor," 186.

31. Duncan, "Socialist Politics in Butte," 288. See also Lewis J. Duncan, "Socialist Administration: Butte, Montana," Socialist Party of America, Information Bureau Press Release (May 1, 1911–April 30, 1912), SPP; Duncan, "The Butte Municipal Administration," in *The American Labor Yearbook 1916* (New York: Rand School of Social Science, 1916), 116–117; "Butte Administration a Success," *Party Builder*, August 30, 1913, 2; and "In the Calcium Glow," *Western Comrade* (Los Angeles, CA), April 1913, 11.

32. Wilson, "The Berkeley Municipal Administration."

33. "Schenectady Municipal Administration," *American Labor Yearbook 1916* (New York: Rand School of Social Science, 1916), 120.

34. Thompson, "Have the Socialists Made Good in Office"; Kaltinick, "Socialist Municipal Administration," 49.

35. Cresswell, "When the Socialists Ran Star City."

36. Letter from J. B. Bitterly, Socialist Mayor of Victor, March 1913, to Carl D. Thompson, Information Department (on Victor); Cross, "Socialism in California Municipalities," 617, and Wolfson, "A History of the Socialist Party of Los Angeles, 7 (on Daly City); untitled article, *Party Builder*, November 15, 1913, 7 (on Murray); and Judd, *Socialist Cities*, and DeMatteo, "Socialist Municipal Administrations in the Progressive Era Midwest" (on Ohio towns mentioned).

37. Lippmann, "On Municipal Socialism." See also comments by Kipnis, *The American Socialist Movement*, 363. Lunn was later able to raise taxes on the major employers, General Electric and the American Locomotive Company, but Socialist assessors in the city were unable to do much to increase the assessment of corporate property (Kaltinick, "Socialist Municipal Administration, 378).

38. For the Socialist position in Montana, see "Municipal Problems," *Montana News*, August 24, 1911, 2.

39. Such pledges were found in party platforms. See, for example, "Strikes About the Right Idea," *Montana News*, February 1, 1905, 1, citing the city platform of the Socialists of Fitchburg, Massachusetts.

40. "Beautiful and Picturesque Fairhope Alabama," *Pensacola* (FL) *Journal*, October 5, 1913, 30.

41. Paul, "Rebels of the New South."

42. "City Beautiful Urged by Socialist Mayor, Emil Seidel Says Moral Cess Pools of Milwaukee Must Be Drained," *Atlanta* (GA) *Constitution*, April 8, 1910, 7.

43. Duncan, "Socialist Politics in Butte," 288; Duncan, "The Butte Municipal Administration"; Kaltinick, "Socialist Municipal Administration," 248–249; Letter from J. B. Bitterly, Socialist Mayor of Victor, March 1913, to Carl D. Thompson, Information Department.

44. Kaltinick, "Socialist Municipal Administration," 379.

45. "Wisconsin Notes," citing a report by K. H. Thomas, state secretary, Socialist Party of Milwaukee, *Labor Argus* (Charleston, WV), August 10, 1911, 6.

46. "Better Conditions for Workingmen Recommended," *Barre* (VT) *Daily Times*, January 24, 1917, 1.

47. Robert E. Weir, "Solid Men the Granite City: Municipal Socialism in Barre, Vermont, 1916–1931" *Vermont History* 83, no. 1 (Winter/Spring 2015: 52. See also Mark Bushnell, "Then Again: A 'Hotbed of Radicalism,' Barre Was First in Vermont to Elect Socialist Mayor," VTDigger, March 29, 2020, vtdigger.org/2020/03/29/then-again-a-hotbed-of-radicalism-barre-was-first-in-vermont-to-elect-socialist-mayor/.

48. "Talk of the Town," *Barre Daily Times*, June 29, 1917, 8.

49. "How the Mayor Proved His Case," *Oskaloosa* (KS) *Independent*, May 21, 1920, 7.

50. Judd, *Socialist Cities*, 82–83.

51. Promises made by the Socialist running for municipal offices in Grants Pass, Oregon: "Socialist Advocate Municipal Reforms," *Rogue River Courier*, October 27, 1911, 1.

52. "New Chief of Police Declares a Drunken Banker Looks Same As Drunken Hobo," *Montrose* (CO) *Daily Press*, No. 82, November 16, 1911.

53. J. E. Nash, Secretary State Socialist Party, "Finn Socialists of Hibbing Build Hall, Exceedingly Large Vote Polled for Socialist Candidates in St. Paul Election, Socialist Mayor of Two Harbors Gains Reputation for Enforcing All Laws," *Labor World* (Duluth, MN), May 26, 1906, 1. As a follow-up on this story, the Socialist mayor leading the blue law cause reportedly decided to do some repair work in his laundry in Two Harbors on a Sunday and was promptly arrested for violating the Sabbath. ("Two Harbors Sundayisms," *Cook County Herald* (Grand Marais, MN), June 8, 1907, 2; "Violated the Sunday Law," *Virginia* (MN) *Enterprise*, May 31, 1907, 1.

54. "Thousands Hear the Debate between David Goldstein and Arthur Le Sueur at Minot," *Bowbells* (ND) *Tribune*, May 3, 1912, 2. Some in Le Sueur's party, the more orthodox, preferred a direct attack on the capitalistic system, which, they felt, was the underlying cause of all this vice. See Putnam, "The Socialist Party of North Dakota," 104.

55. DeMatteo, "Socialist Municipal Administrations in the Progressive Era Midwest."

56. See, respectively, "Eureka Council Turns Down Socialist Mayor," *Salt Lake Tribune* (Salt Lake City, UT), January 7, 1908, 9; "Mayor Says City Must Obey; Lid Goes Down on Gambling at Buena Vista," *Salida* (CO) *Record*, November 14, 1913; "Record of Socialists," *Indianapolis* (IN) *News*, January 3 1918, 4; and "Socialist Mayor Opens Fight on Vice Resorts," *Labor World*, January 20, 1917, 1.

57. "Van Leer Promises Law Enforcement," *Labor World*, January 13, 1917, 1.

58. "No Aid to Socialism," *American Socialist* (Chicago, IL), February 17, 1917, 1.

59. "Saloons, Socialism, Labor," *Greeley* (CO) *Tribune*, April 14, 1910, 7.

60. James H. Timberlake, *Prohibition and the Progressive Movement, 1900–1920* (Cambridge, MA: Harvard University Press, 1963), 96.

61. "Saloons, Socialism, Labor."

62. The national Socialist Party in 1912 took a soft stand on the issues, only urging working-class people to be moderate in their drinking habits. In his study of the prohibition movement, James Timberlake suggested that several factors were behind the party's rejection of prohibition. These included "the influential role played by Germans in the party; the fear that prohibition would result in unemployment; the danger that the issue might disrupt party unity and solidarity; dislike of the sort of dry propaganda that crudely assumed that poverty was caused mainly by drink and that prohibition would eliminate poverty and help solve the social problem; and the desire to avoid any further extension of the police powers of the capitalistic states." Timberlake, *Prohibition and the Progressive Movement*, 97–98.

63. "Victims of Temperament," *Santa Fe New Mexican*, June 28, 1911, 8.

64. See "'Rule of Reason' for Victims of Drink," *Bisbee* (AZ) *Daily Review*, June 30, 1911, 8; and "Cops to Take Drunks Home: Intoxicated Man Is Not Necessarily Criminal, Mayor Says," *Topeka* (KS) *State Journal*, June 27, 1911, 3.

65. Untitled item, *Owosso* (MI) *Times*, February 2, 1912, 4.

66. Stevens, "Heartland Socialism," 156.

67. Stevens, 159.

68. "New Paper for High License," *Bemidji* (MN) *Daily Pioneer*, December 1, 1911, 4; "Has Socialist Mayor," *Irish Standard* (Minneapolis, MN), February 24, 1912, 3.

69. *Arizona Socialist Bulletin* (Phoenix, AZ), December 27, 1912, 3.

70. Untitled entry, *Detroit* (MI) *Times*, October 31, 1910, 3.

71. "The Socialists, What That Party Would Do If Given Control," *Perth Amboy* (NJ) *Evening News*, October 9, 1912, 10.

72. Duncan, "Socialist Administration: Butte, Montana."

73. "Boys and Dividends," *Ouray* (CO) *Herald*, December 8, 1911; "War on the Winerooms," *Wibaux* (MT) *Pioneer*, June 2, 1911, 1.

74. "All Around Town, Boys and Dividends," *Ouray Herald*, December 8, 1911, 3.

75. See, for example, Liazos, "Ministering to the Social Needs of the People," 87.

CHAPTER 9. THE WORKING CLASS, LABOR, AND BUSINESS

1. "Socialist Officials," *Labor Argus* (Charleston, WV), December 14, 1911, 6.

2. Nord, "Minneapolis and the Pragmatic Socialism of Thomas Van Lear," 4.

3. For an overview, see Thompson, "Have the Socialists Made Good in Office?"

4. On Milwaukee's highly successful program, see Kaltinick, "Socialist Municipal Administration," 48.

5. "Home Rue for Milwaukee," *New York Tribune*, December 21, 1910, 8.

6. Kaltinick, "Socialist Municipal Administration," 46.

7. "Doing Things At St. Marys Ohio," *Party Builder* (Chicago, IL), August 15, 1913, 2.

8. "Our Visitors," *Party Builder*, November 1, 1913, 5.

9. "Duty of Socialists," *ATR*, July 28, 1900, 1.

10. John C. Chase, "What Socialists Can Do in Office," *Chicago Daily Socialist*, March 26, 1910, 8. Available at www.marxisthistory.org/history/usa/parties/spusa/1910/0326-chase.

11. See, for example, "A Mayor's Veto too Violent," *Santa Fe New Mexican*, August 1, 1912, 4; "Fined Mayor of Arma $5," *Leavenworth* (KS) *Times*, August 15, 1912, 3; and "Arma's Mayor Arrested," *Topeka* (KS) *State Journal*, July 26, 1912, 5 (in this article he is incorrectly identified as John Morgan).

12. "Red Lodge Elections," *Montana News* (Helena and Lewistown, MT), March 26, 1908, 1.

13. "Two Viewpoints," *Socialist and Labor Star* (Huntington, WV), December 5, 1913, 4.

14. "A Revolutionary Mayor," *ISR* 12 (June 1912): 832. See also Dawson, "St. Mary's Fighting Mayor."

15. Remarks from a letter in "What Should a Socialist Administration Do in Time of Strike?," *Party Builder*, October 25, 1913, 3.

16. "Free Speech War," *Day Book* (Chicago, IL), October 19, 1912, 22; Hendrickson, "Tribune of the People." See also account in "Schenectady Strike Settled," *Party*

Builder, December 20, 1913, 2. Here the number of workers in the walkout was reported as fifteen thousand.

17. "Lunn Decries the Rich," *New York Tribune*, November 18, 1912, 4.

18. "Lunn Helps Strikers," *Party Builder*, December 6, 1913, 2; Hendrickson, "Tribune of the People," 87; "General Electric Workers Strike," *Newark* (NJ) *Evening Star and Newark Advertiser*, November 25, 1913, 5.

19. Shea, *Spoiled Silk*, 66.

20. Shea, 95–101.

21. "Quinlan Piles Up Sentences," *Barre* (VT) *Daily Times*, August 1, 1913, 2.

22. "May Oust Mayor, Governor of Minnesota Warns, Socialist Executive. Strike Blots Must Stop and Order Restored," *Topeka* (KS) *State Journal*, July 6, 1918, 2.

23. "Butte's Socialist Mayor Removed from Office," *Herald Democrat* (Leadville, CO), October 7, 1914 (no page), "I.W.W. Men Lead Riot against Butte Labor Leaders," *Barre Daily Times*, June 15, 1914, 3.

24. "Feeding Law-Defying Hoboes," *Salida* (CO) *Mail*, April 22, 1913, 4.

25. Contemporary sources relied upon for this account include "Ask to Have I.W.W. Driven from Town," *Norwich* (CT) *Bulletin*, April 12, 1913, 1; "Chief of Police Will Be Fired, Mayor of Grand Junction Hopes to Be Able to Save Himself," *Las Vegas Optic* (East Las Vegas, NM), April 12, 1913, 1; "Citizens Drive I.W.W. Out of Town," *Idaho Republican* (Blackfoot, ID), April 18, 1913, 4; and "Feeding Law-Defying Hoboes," *Salida Mail*, April 22, 1913, 4.

26. "Hoquiam Recall Fight at Climax," *Aberdeen* (WA) *Herald*, June 3, 1912, 8; "Tales of the Town Tersely Told," *Aberdeen Herald*, August 1, 1912, 5.

27. "Socialist Sets Example on Municipal Work," *Carson City* (NV) *Daily Appeal*, April 7, 1911, 1 (Brockton); "Ask to Have I.W.W. Driven from Town," *Norwich Bulletin*, April 12, 1913, 1 (Grand Junction); "State News," *Lower Coast Gazette* (Pointe-a-la-Hache, LA), March 22, 1913, 3, and Covington Hall, "With the Southern Timber Workers," *ISR* 13 (May 1913): 805–806 (DeRidder); "Washington Notes," *Northwest Worker* (Everett, WA), May 3, 1917, 2(Camas); "Mayor Kirkpatrick" and Kirkpatrick's account in a letter to Carl Thompson, April 29, 1915, with an attached article, "Socialism Repudiated in Granite City," SPP (Granite City); "As It Should Be," *Scott County Kicker* (Benton, MO), January 22, 1916, 4, article reprinted from the *Masses* (Hamilton); "Here's a Mayor That's with Labor," *Labor Journal* (Everett, WA), October 15, 1915, 2 (Coshocton); "Socialist Mayor Aids Workers," *Grant County Socialist* (Medford , OK), May 11, 1912, 1 (Manitowoc); and "Eureka Makes Progress," *Party Builder*, November 8, 1913, 2 (Eureka).

28. Duane A. Smith, *Rocky Mountain West: Colorado, Wyoming, and Montana, 1859–1915* (Albuquerque: University of New Mexico Press, 1992), 187.

29. "Notes from Yankee Land," *SDH*, August 15, 1903, 3.

30. "Correspondence," letter from by C. C. McHugh, May 16, 1905, printed in the *Montana News*, May 24, 1905, 3.

31. "Shall Butte Also Whisper?," *Butte* (MT) *Socialist*, April 4, 1915, 4.

32. Emmons, *The Butte Irish*, 247.
33. Emmons, 266.
34. "News and Views, Victory at St. Marys, Ohio," *ISR* 12 (December 1911): 376.
35. Contemporary accounts were found in "Doing Things at St. Marys Ohio," *Socialist and Labor Star* (Huntington, WV), August 15, 1913, 2; "Who Are the Anarchists?" *Socialist and Labor Star*, October 31, 1913, 2; and "Mob Socialist Mayor in Ohio, Angry Employees of Chain Company Resent Action in Shutting off Water," *Mitchell* (SD) *Capital*, October 9, 1913, 1.
36. "A Committee That Will 'Do,'" *Ohio Socialist* (Cleveland, OH), January 1917, 3.
37. See "News and Views, Victory at St. Marys, Ohio," and Judd, *Socialist Cities*, 85.
38. DeMatteo, "Socialist Municipal Administrations in the Progressive Era Midwest," 37.
39. "Cameron," *Wheeling* (WV) *Intelligencer*, February 28, 1914, 16.
40. "Notice," *Sisseton* (SD) *Weekly Standard*, November 28, 1913, 8.
41. Letter from J. B. Bitterly, Socialist Mayor of Victor, March 1913, to Carl D. Thompson, Information Department, SPA, SPP; "Notes of the Movement," *ATR*, January 20, 1912, 4.
42. A. W. Ricker, "Socialists at Work," *ATR*, September 2, 1911, 3.
43. "Which for You?," *Grant County Socialist*, May 4, 1912, 1.
44. See Chase, "What Socialists Can Do in Office," 8; Thompson, "Have the Socialists Made Good in Office?"; and Carl D. Thompson, "Socialist Try Hand at Regulation," *Labor Argus*, August 10, 1911, 6.
45. "The Socialist Attorney of New York, the Socialist Mayor of Milwaukee, the Socialist Councilman of Reading," in *The Labor World: Western Organ of the Socialist Party* (San Francisco, March 21, 1930), 73, as reprinted in SPP.
46. See "Socialists at Work," *ATR*, January 6, 1912, 3; and "Granite City in Fight with I.T.S.," *Urbana* (IL) *Daily Courier*, May 29, 1911, n.p.
47. "City in Darkness," *Party Builder*, October 18, 1913, 4.
48. R. A. Henning, Mayor of the City of Brainerd, Minnesota, letters to Carl D. Thompson, Manager, Information Department, national Socialist Party, August 8, 1913, August 26, 1913, September 7, 1913, and September 12, 1913, SPP.
49. "Brainerd Mayor Vetoed the Gas Franchise," *Little Falls* (MN) *Herald*, February 13, 1914, 5.
50. On the Massachusetts mayors, see Abbott, "The Socialist Movement in Massachusetts"; and "Municipal Victories for Socialism," and "Two Socialists," *Topeka* (KS) *State Journal*, January 15, 1900, 3.
51. On the legal and financial problems, see Gail Radford, "From Municipal Socialism to Public Authorities: Institutional Factors in the Shaping of American Public Enterprise," *Journal of American History* 90 (December 2003): 863–890.
52. Morton, *Justice and Humanity*, 10.
53. For debate over public ownership in New Castle, Pennsylvania, see Kaltinick, "Socialist Municipal Administration," 260–261.

54. Lloyd Velicer, *Municipal Ownership and the Manitowoc Wisconsin Socialists*, Manitowoc County Historical Society, occupational monograph 35, 1978, 35. See also account of Stolze's struggle in Thomas F. Jorsch, "Modernized Republicanism: The Radical Agenda of Socialists in Manitowoc, Wisconsin, 1905–1917," *Historian* 70 (Winter 2008): 716–731.
55. "Oswego Buys Water Works," *Parsons* (KS) *Daily Sun*, January 6, 1906, 1.
56. "Notes and Events, Mayor Thum's Administration," *NMR* 2 (1913): 493.
57. Madison, "Millionaire Thum."
58. See details in "Untitled Article," *Party Builder*, November 15, 1913, 7.
59. Radford, "From Municipal Socialism to Public Authorities."
60. These remarks draw upon statistical evidence presented in Evans Clark, "Municipal Ownership in the United States," *Intercollegiate Socialist* 5 (October-November 1916): 1–30.
61. "Here's a Town That Owns Its Own Resort," *Valdez* (AK) *Daily Prospector*, July 9, 1914, 1. This article was also found in other papers in other states.
62. "Home Rue for Milwaukee," *New York Tribune*, December 21, 1910, 8.
63. "A Socialist Experiment," *Washington Herald*, January 17, 1911, 6.
64. Timberlake, *Prohibition and the Progressive Movement*, 97–98.
65. "News of the Week," *Commoner* (Lincoln, NE), December 22, 1911, 10.
66. See "The City Saloon," *Herald-Advance* (Milbank, SD), November 28, 1913, 1; and "A Municipal Saloon," *Herald-Advance*, April 25, 1913, 1. For a positive evaluation of the experiment, see "The Liquor Question in a Socialist City," *Party Builder*, May 23, 1914, 4.
67. In Canton, Illinois, the Socialist mayor hoped to open a municipal coal mine but could not find one to lease that would supply coal at a price lower than currently being charged by private suppliers. See Stevens, "Heartland Socialism," 154.
68. See, generally, "Progressive Municipality," *Arizona Socialist Bulletin* (Phoenix, AZ), December 27, 1912; Jeanette Smith, "Walter Walker and His Fight against Socialism," *Journal of the Western Slope* 12 (Fall 1997): 1–18; and "Local History Thursday: When Grand Junction Had a Socialist Mayor," https://mesacountylibraries.org/2020/03/local-history-thursday-when-grand-junction-had-a-social.
69. Hendrickson, "Tribune of the People." For contemporary accounts, see "The Municipal Store, Farm, Ice Cart and Coal Wagon the Chief Ventures of the Rev. Dr. Lunn," *Sun* (New York, NY), October 13, 1912, 5; "City Enjoined from Giving Ice," *Municipal Journal* (New York, NY), August 1, 1912; and "Right of Municipality to Furnish Ice," *American City* (New York, NY), August 1912; "The City Is Fighting the Ice Trust," *Daily Capital Journal* (Salem, OR), July 15, 1912, 1; "Schenectady's Socialist Administration," *Washington Socialist* (Everett, WA), October 15, 1914, 2; and "Wasn't It Fierce to Make a Mayor of This Person: The Reverend Mayor Who Showed Em," *Tacoma* (WA) *Times*, August 13, 1912, 4.
70. "Close Lodging House," *Party Builder*, January 24, 1914, 3.
71. Kaltinick, "Socialist Municipal Administration," 132.

72. "Investigation of Certain Coal Companies, Two Harbors, Minn.," 62nd Congress, Second Session, House of Representatives, Report Number 918, to accompany H. Res. 577.1, June 21, 1912.

73. "City Can Buy Coal" Duluth Dealers Will Sell to Two Harbors, Minn.," *Fargo* (ND) *Forum and Daily Republican*, September 5, 1912, 1.

74. "'Officer, Do Your Duty!' Current Comments," *Labor Argus*, December 7, 1911, 2.

CONCLUSION

1. Duncan, Butte's socialist mayor, provides an example of this thinking. Writing in the left-wing *International Socialist Review* eight months after his election, he declared, "The Butte Socialists are all revolutionists; not mere reformers or parlor Socialists. We realize fully that, under capitalism and capitalistic laws, little more can be accomplished than superficial reforms. But our realization of that fact does not mean we are content to stop at that point. We are as determinedly revolutionary in office as we were before getting political power, and we hold mere political success very cheaply. Not for an instant do we relax our efforts for the entire revolutionary program." At the same time, however, Duncan contended that it was important to show the world that his Socialist city administration could successfully confront the "practical problems of city administration" and demonstrate "that working men can run a city government as well as 'business' men." He argued that by doing this, "we believe we are strengthening the party and the entire working-class movement, by banishing bourgeois fears, by winning the confidence and respect of all classes, and thus paving the way ... to future success. From Duncan, "Socialist Politics in Butte," 290–291.

2. Remarks of Mr. Clemens of Kansas, Socialist Unity Convention, Indianapolis, IN, July 29 to August 1, 1901, 14. Several statements of this nature coming from Socialists about their motives are found in David R. Berman, *Radicalism in the Mountain West* (Boulder: University Press of Colorado, 2007), 12. German economic historian Werner Sombart once contended, in the words of sociologist Rudolf Heberle, "that many non-proletarians became socialists out of a desire for social justice and because their aesthetic sense was offended by the squalor of the proletariat's existence" (Rudolf Heberle, *Social Movements* (New York: Appleton-Century-Crofts, 1951), 96). There is a large volume of literature suggesting the inclination of those on the political left to feel more empathy for the down and out than those on the political right. See, for example, the discussion and sources cited by Hasson, et, al., "Are Liberals and Conservatives Equally Motivated to Feel Empathy Toward Others?," *Personality and Social Psychology Bulletin* (October 2018): 1449–1459.

3. Thompson, "Have the Socialists Made Good in Office?," 1, 4.

4. Chester M. Wright, "The Socialist Spirit in the City," *Western Comrade* (June 1913): 93.

5. "Doing Sensible Things," *Iowa County Democrat* (Mineral Point, WI), July 21, 1910, 4, taken from *New York Evening Post*.

6. See, for example, Sally M. Miller, "Milwaukee: Of Ethnicity and Labor," in *Socialism and the Cities*, ed. Bruce M. Stave (Port Washington, New York: Kennikat, 1975), 65; Martin J. Schiesl, *The Politics of Efficiency: Municipal Administration and Reform in America, 1800–1920* (Berkeley: University of California Press, 1977), 124–125; and Kipnis, *The American Socialist Movement*, 360.

7. Kipnis, *The American Socialist Movement*, 77.

8. Studies suggest that the adoption of a commission system did sometimes do considerable damage to Socialists. In the city of New Castle, Indiana, the imposition of a modified commission plan imposed by the state ripped "the Socialist councilmen from office and emasculated the mayor" (Kaltinick, *Socialist Municipal Administration*, 294). It also had disastrous effects from the Socialist point of view in Passaic, New Jersey (Ebner, "Socialism and Progressive Political Reform").

9. "Montana Municipal State Campaign," *Montana News* (Helena and Lewistown, MT), March 26, 1908, 1.

10. "The Socialist Outlook," *ISR* 5 (1904–1905), 203–217, at 207.

11. "A Word of Appreciation," Annual Labor Review of the *Inter-Mountain Worker* (Salt Lake City, UT), June 19, 1915, n.p.

12. Constance McLaughlin Green, *Holyoke, Massachusetts* (New Haven, CT: Yale University Press, 1939), 223–224.

13. See discussion in Dubofsky, *Industrialism and the American Worker*, 97, 100.

14. Daniel R. Fusfeld, *The Rise and Repression of Radical Labor, USA, 1877–1918* (Chicago: Charles H. Kerr, 1980), 3–5. See also Selig Perlman, *A Theory of the Labor Movement* (New York: Macmillan, 1928).

15. See, for example, Rosenstone et al., *Third Parties in America: Citizen Response to Major Party Failure* (Princeton, NJ: Princeton University Press, 1984).

APPENDIX I: BIOGRAPHIES OF FEATURED MAYORS

1. Quoted in Howe, "Milwaukee—A Socialist City."

2. Seidel, *Sketches from My Life*, 1916, 1938–1944, Part 2, 122, 123, Emil Seidel Papers, University of Wisconsin at Milwaukee.

3. Miller, "Seidel, George Lukas Emil," American National Biography Online, February 2000. http://www.anb.org.ezproxy1.1ib.asu.edu/articles/06/06-00588.html.

4. Debs to Carl D. Thompson, December 16, 1914, in *Letters of Eugene V. Debs*, vol. 2, ed. J. Robert Constantine (Urbana: University of Illinois Press, 1990), 116–117.

5. Fulda, "Daniel Hoan and the Golden Age of Socialist Government in Milwaukee."

6. See Griffin, "The Rising Tide of Socialism"; and "The Reds Raise Hell," *Labor Argus* (Charleston, WV), November 9, 1911, 1.

7. "Schenectady's Experiment in City Socialism," *Sun* (New York, NY), October 13, 1912, 45.

8. "Former Butte Mayor Dies," *Montana Standard* (Butte, MT), January 28, 1936, 3.

9. "In the Calcium Glow," *Western Comrade* (Los Angeles, CA), April 1913, 11.

10. "Duncan Now Mucker in Copper Mines of Butte," *American Socialist* (Chicago, IL), February 19, 1917, 2.

11. Barton, "Berkeley Mayor J. Stitt Wilson: Mayor Christian Socialist, Georgist, Feminist"; and Barton, "J. Stitt Wilson, Berkeley's Socialist Mayor."

12. J. Stitt Wilson, *How I Became a Socialist, and Other Papers* (Berkeley, CA: author, 1912), 2.

13. Kipnis, *The American Socialist Movement*.

14. "Socialist Raps Socialist Head," *LAT*, August 23, 1911, 1–3.

15. See, for example, the account of his distinguished career in Holli, *The American Mayor*.

16. Dan Hoan, "Socialists Made City What It Is—In 1910 Milwaukee Graft-Ridden," *Socialist Campaigner*, March 1, 1936, found in SPP.

17. Nathanson, "Thomas Van Lear."

18. Nathanson, "Thomas Van Lear"; and, generally, Nord, "Minneapolis and the Pragmatic Socialism of Thomas Van Lear."

BIBLIOGRAPHY

NEWSPAPERS, MAGAZINES, AND ARCHIVES

Aberdeen Herald (Aberdeen, WA)
Abilene Weekly Reflector (Abilene, KS)
Advocate (Meriden, KS)
American City (New York, NY)
American Socialist (Chicago, IL)
Appeal to Reason (Girard, KS)
Arizona Democrat (Phoenix, AZ)
Arizona Republican (Phoenix, AZ)
Arizona Sentinel (Yuma, AZ)
Arizona Socialist Bulletin (Phoenix, AZ)
Atlanta Constitution (Atlanta, GA)
Baraboo Weekly News (Baraboo, WI)
Barre Daily Times (Barre, VT)
Barton County Democrat (Great Bend, KS)
Bemidji Daily Pioneer (Bemidji, MN)
Bennington Evening Banner (Bennington, VT)
Billings Gazette (Billings, MT)
Birmingham News (Birmingham, AL)
Bisbee Daily Review (Bisbee, AZ)
Bismarck Daily Tribune (Bismarck, ND)
Bottineau Courant (Bottineau, ND)
Bowbells Tribune (Bowbells, ND)
Bridgeport Evening Farmer (Bridgeport, CT)
Butte Daily Bulletin (Butte, MT)
Butte Socialist (Butte, MT)
Cairo Bulletin (Cairo, IL)
California Social Democrat (Los Angeles, CA)
Camas Prairie Chronicle (Cottonwood, ID)
Carson City Daily and/or *Carson City Daily Appeal* (Carson City, NV)
Catholic Bulletin (St. Paul, MN)
Chattanooga News (Chattanooga, TN)
Chicago Daily Socialist (Chicago, IL)
Chico Record (Chico, CA)
Citizen (Honesdale, PA)
Clarksburg Telegram (Clarksburg, WV)
Coeur D'Alene Evening Press (Coeur D'Alene, ID)

Colorado Socialist Bulletin (Unknown, CO)
Commoner (Lincoln, NE)
Commonwealth (Everett, WA)
Cook County Herald (Grand Marais, MN)
Cresco Plain Dealer (Cresco, IA)
Cut Bank Pioneer Press (Cut Bank, MT)
Daily Adamston (Clarksburg, WV)
Daily Arizona Silver Belt (Globe, AZ)
Daily Capital Journal (Salem, OR)
Daily Missoulian (Missoula, MT)
Daily Sentinel (Grand Junction, CO)
Daily Star-Mirror (Moscow, ID)
Daily Tribune (Terre Haute, IN)
Day Book (Chicago, IL)
Democratic Banner (Mt. Vernon, OH)
Detroit Times (Detroit, MI)
Dickinson Press (Dickinson, ND)
Durango Democrat (Durango, CO)
El Paso Herald (El Paso, TX)
Ellensburg Dawn (Ellensburg, WA)
Evening Capital News (Boise, ID)
Evening Times (Grand Forks, ND)
Fairmont West Virginian (Fairmont, WV)
Fargo Forum and Daily Republican (Fargo, ND)
Fergus County Democrat (Lewistown, MT)
Fort Scott Daily Tribune (Fort Scott, KS)
Freeland Tribune (Freeland, PA)
Free Trader-Journal (Ottawa, IL)
Fulton County News (McConnellsburg, PA)
Fulton County Tribune (Wauseon, OH)
Galena Weekly Republican (Galena, KS)
Goodwin's Weekly (Salt Lake City, UT)
Grand Forks Daily Herald (Grand Forks, ND)
Grant County Socialist (Medford, OK)
Greeley Tribune (Greeley, CO)
Greenville Journal (Greenville, OH)
Harrisburg Telegraph (Harrisburg, PA)
Hartford Courant (Hartford, CT)
Hawaiian Star (Honolulu, HI)
Herald (Los Angeles, CA)
Herald-Advance (Milbank, SD)
Herald Democrat (Leadville, CO)
Idaho Republican (Blackfoot, ID)

Indianapolis Journal (Indianapolis, IN)
Indianapolis News (Indianapolis, IN)
Inter-Mountain Republican (Salt Lake City, UT)
Inter-Mountain Worker (Salt Lake City, UT)
International Socialist Review (Chicago, IL)
Iowa County Democrat (Mineral Point, WI)
Irish Standard (Minneapolis, MN)
Iron County Record (Cedar City, UT)
Kalispell Bee (Kalispell, MT)
Labor Argus (Charleston, WV)
Labor Journal (Everett, WA)
Labor World (Duluth, MN)
Ladysmith News (Ladysmith, WI)
Las Vegas Optic (East Las Vegas, NM)
Leavenworth Echo (Leavenworth, WA)
Leavenworth Times (Leavenworth, KS)
Little Falls Herald (Little Falls, MN)
Literary Digest (New York, NY)
Los Angeles Herald (Los Angeles, CA)
Los Angeles Times (Los Angeles, CA)
Lower Coast Gazette (Pointe-a-la-Hache, LA)
Madison Daily Leader (Madison, SD)
Mahoning Dispatch (Canfield, OH)
Manitowoc Pilot (Manitowoc, WI)
Marion Daily Mirror (Marion, OH)
Medford Mail Tribune (Medford, OR)
Meridian Sun (Meridian, OK)
Miners Magazine (London, EN)
Minneapolis Morning Tribune (Minneapolis, MN)
Mitchell Capital (Mitchell, SD)
Montana News (Helena and Lewistown, MT)
Montana Standard (Butte, MT)
Montana State Archives and Historical Society (Helena, MT)
Montrose Daily Press (Montrose, CO)
Morrow County Republican (Mt. Gilead, OH)
Municipal Journal (New York, NY)
Museum of North Idaho Quarterly Newsletter
National Municipal Review (various locations)
Nevada Forum (Sparks, NV)
New Nation (The) (Boston, MA)
New York Call (New York, NY)
New York Times (New York, NY)
New York Tribune (New York, NY)

Newark Evening Star and Newark Advertiser (Newark, NJ)
News-Democrat (Canton, OH)
Norfolk Weekly News-Journal (Norfolk, NE)
Northwest Worker (Everett, WA)
Norwich Bulletin (Norwich, CT)
Ogden Standard (Ogden City, UT)
Ogden Standard-Examiner (Ogden, UT)
Ohio Socialist (Cleveland, OH)
Omaha Daily Bee (Omaha, NE)
Oregon Union (Corvallis, Benton County, OR)
Orleans County Monitor (Barton, VT)
Oskaloosa Independent (Okaloosa, KS)
Ouray Herald (Ouray, CO)
Outlook (New York, NY)
Owosso Times (Owosso, MI)
Palatka News and Advertiser (Palatka, FL)
Parsons Daily Sun (Parsons, KS)
Party Builder (Official National Bulletin, Socialist Party, Chicago, IL)
Pennsylvania Socialist (Reading, PA)
Pensacola Journal (Pensacola, FL)
Perth Amboy Evening News (Perth Amboy, NJ)
Philip Weekly Review (Philip, SD)
Pierre Weekly Free Press (Pierre, SD)
Pittsburg Daily Headlight (Pittsburg, KS)
Pittsburg Dispatch (Pittsburg, PA)
Red Cloud Chief (Red Cloud, NE)
Republican-Atlas (Monmouth, IL)
Richmond Palladium and Sun-Telegram (Richmond, IN)
River Press (Fort Benton, MT)
Rock Island Argus and Daily Union (Rock Island, IL)
Rocky Mountain News (Denver, CO)
Rogue River Courier (Grants Pass, OR)
Ronan Pioneer (Ronan, MT)
Roundup Record (Roundup, MO)
Salida Mail (Salida, CO)
Salida Record (Salida, CO)
Salt Lake Telegram (Salt Lake City, UT)
Salt Lake Tribune (Salt Lake City, UT)
San Francisco Call (San Francisco, CA)
Santa Fe New Mexican (Santa Fe, NM)
Scott County Kicker (Benton, MO)
Searchlight (Culbertson, MT)
Seattle Post-Intelligencer (Seattle, WA)

Seattle Star (Seattle, WA)
Sequachee Valley News (Sequachee, TN)
Sisseton Weekly Standard (Sisseton, SD)
Sistersville Daily Oil Review (Sistersville, WV)
Social Democratic Herald (Chicago, IL)
Socialist (The) (New York, NY)
Socialist and Labor Star (Huntington, WV)
Socialist Campaigner (location not known)
Socialist Party of America Papers (Duke University, Durham, NC)
Stark County Democrat (Canton, OH)
Star Press (Muncie, IN)
Stillwater Gazette (Stillwater, OK)
St. Johns Review (St. Johns, OR)
Sun (The) (New York, NY)
Tacoma Times (Tacoma, WA)
Texarkana Socialist (Texarkana, AR)
Times (Richmond, VA)
Topeka State Journal (Topeka, KS)
Twin City Star (Minneapolis, MN)
Urbana Daily Courier (Urbana, IL)
Valdez Daily Prospector (Valdez, AK)
Valentine Democrat (Valentine, NE)
Virginia Enterprise (Virginia, MN)
Ward County Independent (Minot, ND)
Washburn Times (Washburn, WI)
Washington Herald (Washington, DC)
Washington Socialist (Everett, WA)
Washington Standard (Olympia, WA)
Washington Times (Washington, DC)
Watertown Leader (Watertown, WI)
Weekly Chieftain (Vinita, OK)
Western Comrade (Los Angeles, CA)
Wheeling Intelligencer (Wheeling, WV)
Wibaux Pioneer (Wibaux, MT)
Willmar Tribune (Willmar, MN)
Will Maupin's Weekly (Lincoln, NE)
Winfield Daily Press (Winfield, KS)
Wray Gazette (Wray, CO)
Zion City Independent (Zion, IL)

BOOKS, ARTICLES, AND OTHER SOURCES

Abbreviations Used in This Section

ATR   *Appeal to Reason* (Girard, KS)
ISR   *International Socialist Review* (Chicago, IL)
LAT   *Los Angeles Times*
NMR   *National Municipal Review* (various locations)
NYT   *New York Times*
SDH   *Social Democratic Herald* (Chicago, IL)
SPP   Socialist Party Papers (Duke University, Durham, NC)

Abbott, Leonard D. "The Socialist Movement in Massachusetts." *Outlook* (New York, NY), February 17, 1900, 410–412.

Anderson, David D. *Brand Whitlock*. New York: Twayne, 1968.

Barkey, Frederick A. *Working-Class Radicals: The Socialist Party in West Virginia, 1898–1920*. Morgantown: West Virginia University Press, 2012.

Barnard, Harry. *Eagle Forgotten: The Life of John Peter Altgeld*. New York: Duell, Sloan & Pearce, 1938.

Barton, Stephen E. "Berkeley Mayor J. Stitt Wilson: Christian Socialist, Georgist, Feminist," *American Journal of Economics and Sociology* 75, no. 1 (January 2016): 193–216.

———. "J. Stitt Wilson, Berkeley's Socialist Mayor." *Newsletter of the Berkeley Historical Society* 29 (Summer 2011): 4.

Beard, Charles A. *American City Government: A Survey of Newer Tendencies*. New York: Century, 1912.

Bedford, Henry. *Socialism and the Workers in Massachusetts, 1886–1912*. Amherst, MA: University of Massachusetts Press, 1966.

Berman, David R. *Radicalism in the Mountain West*. Boulder: University Press of Colorado, 2007.

Blassingame, Lurton W. "Frank J. Goodnow: Progressive Urban Reformer." *North Dakota Quarterly* 40 (1972): 23–30.

Bohn, Frank. "The Socialist Party and the Government of Cities," *ISR* 12 (November 1911): 275–278.

Boyle, James. "The Increase of Municipal Socialism in England." *Barton County Democrat*, September 5, 1902, 6.

Browne, Waldo R. *Altgeld of Illinois*. New York: B. W. Huebsch, 1924.

Bushnell, Mark. "Then Again: A 'Hotbed of Radicalism,' Barre Was First in Vermont to Elect Socialist Mayor." VTDigger. March 29, 2020. vtdigger.org/2020/03/29/then-again-a-hotbed-of-radicalism-barre-was-first-in-vermont-to-elect-socialist-mayor/.

Calvert, James W. *The Gibraltar Socialism and Labor in Butte, Montana, 1895–1920*. Helena: Montana Historical Society Press, 1988.

Chaplin, Ralph. *Wobbly: The Rough-and-Tumble Story of an American Radical.* Chicago: University of Chicago Press, 1948.
Chase, John C. "What Socialists Can Do in Office." *Chicago Daily Socialist*, March 26, 1910, 8. Available at www.marxisthistory.org/history/usa/parties/spusa/1910/0326-chase.
Chester, Eric Thomas. *True Mission: Socialists and the Labor Party Question in the U.S.* London: Pluto, 2004.
Childs, Richard S. *Civic Victories: The Story of an Unfinished Revolution.* New York: Harper & Brothers, 1952.
Clark, Norman H. *Mill Town: Social History of Everett, Washington.* Seattle: University of Washington Press, 1970.
Constantine, J. Robert, ed. *Letters of Eugene V. Debs.* Vols. 1 and 2. Urbana: University of Illinois Press, 1990.
Cornford, Daniel Allardyce. "Lumber, Labor, and Community in Humboldt County, California, 1850–1920." PhD diss., University of California, Santa Barbara, 1983.
Cresswell, Stephen. "When the Socialists Ran Star City." *West Virginia History* 52 (1993): 59–72.
Cross, Ira Brown. "Socialism in California Municipalities." *NMR* 1 (1912): 611–619.
Cumberland, William H. "The Davenport Socialists of 1920." *Annals of Iowa* 47 (Summer 1984): 451–474.
Dahl, Robert A. "The Analysis of Influence on Local Communities." In *Social Science and Community Action*, edited by Charles R. Adrian. East Lansing: Michigan State University, 1960.
———. *Who Governs?* New Haven, CT: Yale University Press, 1961.
Davis, George D. "Comrade Davis Discusses S.E.C." *Commonwealth* (Everett, WA), March 7, 1913, 2.
Dawson, Frank. "St. Mary's Fighting Mayor," *ISR* 13 (June 1913): 874–876.
Debs, Eugene V. "Danger Ahead," *ISR* 11 (January 1911): 413–415.
DeMatteo, Arthur E. "Socialist Municipal Administrations in the Progressive Era Midwest. A Comparative Case Study of Four Ohio Cities, 1911–1915." www.ohioacademyofhistory.org/wp-content/uploads/2013/04/DeMatteo.pdf.
De Witt, Benjamin Parke. *The Progressive Movement.* Seattle: University of Washington Press, 1915.
Douglas, Paul H. "The Socialist Vote in Municipal Elections of 1917." *NMR* 7 (March 1918): 131–139.
———. *The Coming of a New Party.* New York: McGraw-Hill, 1932.
Drew, Donald, and Stow Persons, eds. *Socialism and American Life*, vol. 1. Princeton, NJ: Princeton University Press, 1952.
Dubofsky, Melvin. *Industrialism and the American Worker, 1865–1920.* Arlington Heights, IL: Harlan Davidson, 1975.
Duncan, Lewis J. "The Butte Municipal Administration." In *The American Labor Yearbook 1916*, 116–117. New York: Rand School of Social Science, 1916.

———. "Socialist Administration: Butte, Montana." Socialist Party of America, Information Bureau Press Release (May 1, 1911–April 30, 1912), SPP.

———. "Socialist Politics in Butte, Montana." *ISR* 12 (November 1911): 287–291.

———. "The Trouble in Butte: Mayor Duncan's Statement to the Socialist Party and Press of America." July 21, 1913, SPP.

Duverger, Maurice. *Political Parties: Their Organization and Activity in the Modern State.* London: Methuen, 1954.

Ebner, Michael H. "Redefining the Success Ethic or Urban Reform Mayors." In *The Age of Urban Reform*, edited by Michael H. Ebner and Eugene M. Tobin, 86–101. Port Washington, NY: Kennikat, 1977.

———. "Socialism and Progressive Political Reform: The 1911 Change-of-Government in Passaic." In *Socialism and the Cities*, edited by Bruce M. Stave, 116–140. Port Washington, NY: Kennikat, 1975.

Edler, A. B. "A Reply to Opportunists." *Utah Labor Journal*, April 17, 1902, 1.

Edmunds, A. G. "Butte Socialists Hand Smashing Blow to Capitalistic Ring Rulers." *California Social Democrat*, August 26, 1911, 2.

Emmons, David M. *The Butte Irish.* Urbana: University of Illinois Press, 1989.

Fenton, John H. *Midwest Politics.* New York: Holt, Rinehart & Winston, 1966.

Flynn, Elizabeth Gurley. "Industrial Workers of the World (IWW)." Address, Northern Illinois University, November 8, 1961. Occasional Papers Series No. 24 (1977), American Institute for Marxist Studies.

Folk, Richard A. "The Golden Age of Ohio Socialism." *Northwest Ohio Quarterly* 41, no. 3 (1969): 91–112.

Fones-Wolf, Ken. *Glass Towns: Industry, Labor and Political Economy in Appalachia, 1890–1930s.* Champaign-Urbana: University of Illinois Press, 2007.

Fox, Kenneth. *Better City Government: Innovation in American Urban Politics, 1850–1937.* Philadelphia: Temple University Press, 1977.

Fulda, Todd J. "Daniel Hoan and the Golden Age of Socialist Government in Milwaukee." *American Journal of Economics and Sociology* 75, no. 1 (January 2016): 246–260.

Fusfeld, Daniel R. *The Rise and Repression of Radical Labor, USA, 1877–1918.* Chicago: Charles H. Kerr, 1980.

Gay, J. B. "The Poll-Tax Evil." *Texarkana* (AR) *Socialist*, January 9, 1913, SPP.

George, Henry. *The Menace of Privilege.* New York: Macmillan, 1905.

———. *Progress and Poverty.* New York: Robert Schalkenbach Foundation, 1955. Originally published 1879.

Graham, James D. "Corporate Corruption in the Socialist Party. *Montana News* (Helena and Lewiston, MT), October 21, 1909, 2–3.

Green, Constance McLaughlin. *History of Naugatuck, Connecticut.* New Haven, CT: Yale University Press, 1948.

———. *Holyoke, Massachusetts.* New Haven, CT: Yale University Press, 1939.

Green, James R. "The 'Salesmen-Soldiers' of the 'Appeal Army': A Profile of Rank-

and-File Socialist Agitators." In *Socialism and the Cities*, edited by Bruce M. Stave, 13–40. Port Washington, NY: Kennikat, 1975.

Griffin, Henry Farrand. "The Rising Tide of Socialism." *Outlook* (New York, NY), February 24, 1912, 438–448.

Griffith, Ernest S. *A History of American City Government: The Progressive Years and Their Aftermath, 1900–1920.* New York: Praeger, 1974.

Gutman, Herman G. "The Worker's Search for Power." In *The Gilded Age*, edited by H. Wayne Morgan, 31–53. Syracuse, NY: Syracuse University Press, 1970.

Hagensick, Clarke A. "Influences of Partisanship and Incumbency on a Nonpartisan Election System." *Western Political Quarterly* 17 (March 1964).

Hall, Covington. "With the Southern Timber Workers." *ISR* 13 (May 1913): 805–806.

Hamilton, John J. *The Dethronement of the City Boss.* Freeport, NY: Books for Libraries Press, 1971. Originally published 1910.

Hasson, Yossi, Maya Tamir, Kea S. Brahms, J. C. Cohrs, and E. Halperin. "Are Liberals and Conservatives Equally Motivated to Feel Empathy Toward Others?" *Personality and Social Psychology Bulletin* (October 2018): 1449–1459.

Hays, Samuel P. "The Politics of Reform in Municipal Government in the Progressive Era." *Pacific Northwest Quarterly* 55, no. 4 (October 1964): 157–169.

Heberle, Rudolf. *Social Movements.* New York: Appleton-Century-Crofts, 1951.

Hendrickson, Kenneth E., Jr. "Tribune of the People: George R. Lunn and the Rise and Fall of Christian Socialism in Schenectady." In *Socialism and the Cities*, edited by Bruce M. Stave, 72–115. Port Washington, NY: Kennikat, 1975.

Henry, W. G. "News and Views: Grand Junction's Socialist Mayor." *ISR* 10 (June 1910): 1139–1141.

Hicks, Granville. *Small Town.* New York: Fordham University Press, 2004. Originally published 1946.

Hodges, George. "A Mighty Influence." *Pittsburg* (PA) *Dispatch*, June 30, 1889, 15.

Hofstadter, Richard. *The Paranoid Style in American Politics and Other Essays.* New York: Vintage, 1967.

Holli, Melvin G. *The American Mayor.* University Park: Pennsylvania State University Press, 1999.

———. *Reform in Detroit: Hazen S. Pingree and Urban Politics.* New York: Oxford University Press, 1969.

Howe, Frederic C. "Milwaukee—A Socialist City." *Outlook* (New York, NY), June 25, 1910, 411–421.

Hoxie, Robert F. "The Rising Tide of Socialism." *Journal of Political Economy* 19 (October 1911): 609–631.

———. "The Socialist Party in the November Elections." *Journal of Political Economy* 20, no. 3 (March 1912): 205–223.

Johnson, Tom, and Elizabeth J. Hauser, eds. *My Story.* New York: B. W. Huebsch, 1911.

Jones, Marnie. *Holy Toledo: Religion and Politics in the Life of "Golden Rule" Jones.* Lexington: University Press of Kentucky, 1998.

Jorsch, Thomas F. "Modernized Republicanism: The Radical Agenda of Socialists in Manitowoc, Wisconsin, 1905–1917." *Historian* 70 (Winter 2008): 716–731.

———. "Radical Municipal Socialism in Madrid, Iowa, 1903–1920." *Socialist History* 56 (2019): 66–88.

Judd, Richard W. *Socialist Cities*. Albany: State University of New York Press, 1989.

Kaltinick, Arnold. "Socialist Municipal Administration in Four American Cities (Milwaukee, Schenectady, New Castle, Pennsylvania and Conneaut, Ohio), 1910–1915." PhD diss., New York University, 1982.

Karnig, Albert K., and B. Oliver Walter. "Joint Electoral Fate of Local Incumbents." *Journal of Politics* 43 (August 1981): 889–898.

Keister, Jack. "Why the Socialist Won in Butte." *ISR* 11 (June 1911): 731–733.

Key, V. O. *Politics, Parties, and Pressure Groups*, 5th ed. New York: Thomas Y. Crowell, 1964.

Kipnis, Ira. *The American Socialist Movement, 1897–1912*. New York: Columbia University Press, 1952.

Kiser, Gregory G. "The Socialist Party in Arkansas, 1900–1912." *Arkansas Historical Quarterly* 40 (Summer 1981): 119–153.

Kolehmainen, John I., and George W. Hill. *Haven in the Woods: The Story of the Finns in Wisconsin*. Madison: State Historical Society of Wisconsin, 1951.

Liazos, Ariane. "Ministering to the Social Needs of the People: Samuel Jones, Strong Mayor Government, and Municipal Ownership, 1897–1904." *American Journal of Economics and Sociology* 75, no. 1 (January 2016): 86–115.

Lippmann, Walter. "On Municipal Socialism." In *Socialism and the Cities*, edited by Bruce M. Stave, 184–196. Port Washington, NY: Kennikat, 1975.

Lipset, Seymour Martin, and Gary Marks. *It Didn't Happen Here: Why Socialism Failed in the United States*. New York: W. W. Norton, 2000.

Livermore, H. A. "In Skagit County." *Commonwealth* (Everett, WA), October 4, 1912, 7.

Lockard, Duane. *The Politics of State and Local Government*, 2nd ed. New York: Macmillan, 1969.

Lough, Alexandra W. "Hazen S. Pingree and the Detroit Model of Urban Reform." *American Journal of Economics and Sociology* 75, no. 1 (January 2016): 58–85.

———. "Tom L. Johnson and Cleveland Traction Wars, 1901–1909." *American Journal of Economics and Sociology* 75, no. 1 (January 2016): 149–192.

Lunn, George R. *Testimony to the Special Investigative Committee of the New York State Assembly, January 28, 1920*. Albany, NY: J. N. Lyon, 1920.

Lynd, Robert Staughton, and Helen Merrell Lynd. *Middletown: A Study in Modern American Culture*. New York: Harcourt, Brace, 1929.

Macdonald, Austin F. *American City Government and Administration*. New York: Thomas Y. Crowell, 1956.

Madison, R. W. "Millionaire Thum, Elected Mayor of Pasadena, Is Also Strong Exponent of Municipal Ownership." *Detroit* (MI) *Times*, April 19, 1911, 1.

Maxwell, Robert. *La Follette and the Rise of the Progressives in Wisconsin*. New York: Russell & Russell, 1956.

McClennen, Molly Ann, and Stephen Edward Cresswell. *Socialists in a Small Town: The Socialist Victory in Adamston, West Virginia*. Buckhannon, WV: Ralston, 1992.

McCormick, John S., and John R. Sillito. *A History of Utah Radicalism*. Logan: Utah State University Press, 2011.

McDonald, Neil A. *The Study of Political Parties: Short Studies in Political Science*. Garden City, NY: Doubleday, 1955.

Miller, Sally M. "Milwaukee: Of Ethnicity and Labor." In *Socialism and the Cities*, edited by Bruce M. Stave, 41–65. Port Washington, NY: Kennikat, 1975.

———. "Seidel, George Lukas Emil." American National Biography Online, February 2000. http://www.anb.org.ezproxy1.1ib.asu.edu/articles/06/06-00588.html.

———. *Victor Berger and the Promise of Constructive Socialism, 1910–1920*. Westport, CT: Greenwood, 1973.

Morrissey, John. "Some Suggestions." *ATR*, December 13, 1902, 5.

Morton, Richard Allen. *Justice and Humanity: Edward F. Dunne, Illinois Progressive*. Carbondale: Southern Illinois University Press, 1997.

Nathanson, Iric. "Thomas Van Lear, City Hall's Working-Class Champion." *Minnesota History* 64 (July 1, 2015): 224–233.

Nevins, Allan, ed. *The Letters and Journal of Brand Whitlock*. New York: D. Appleton-Century, 1936.

Noble, David W. *The Progressive Mind, 1890–1917*. Minneapolis, MN: Burgess, 1981.

Noble, Ransom E. *New Jersey before Wilson*. Princeton, NJ: Princeton University Press, 1946.

Nord, David Paul. "Minneapolis and the Pragmatic Socialism of Thomas Van Lear." *Minnesota History* 45, no. 1 (Spring 1976): 2–10.

Nye, Russel B. *Midwestern Progressive Politics*. Lansing: Michigan State University Press, 1959.

O'Hare, F. P. "The Red Card Organization and State Election Laws." *ISR* (April 1912): 668–669.

Overacker, Louise. *Money in Elections*. New York: Arno, 1974. Originally published 1932.

Parker, Frank. "On an 8,000 Mile Swing." *Winfield (KS) Daily Press*, July 26, 1911, 2.

Patek, Allan. "The 1911 Election of Socialist Mayor Henry Stolze, Jr., of Manitowoc." Manitowoc County Historical Society, monograph 74 (1996): 1–16.

Patton, Clifford W. *The Battle for Municipal Reform, Mobilization and Attack, 1875 to 1900*. College Park, MD: McGrath, 1969.

Paul, Brad Alan. "Rebels of the New South: The Socialist Party in Dixie, 1892–1920." PhD diss., University of Massachusetts Amherst, 1999.

Perlman, Selig. *A Theory of the Labor Movement*. New York: Macmillan, 1928.

Phipps, Stanley S. "Building Socialism in One City: Coeur d'Alene, Idaho's, 1911 Municipal Government." *Museum of North Idaho Quarterly Newsletter* 7 (Winter 1986): 1–5.

Pittenger, Mark. *American Socialist and Evolutionary Thought, 1870–1920*. Madison: University of Wisconsin Press, 1993.

Polsby, Nelson W. *Community Power and Political Theory.* New Haven, CT: Yale University Press, 1963.

Putnam, Jackson. "The Socialist Party of North Dakota, 1902–1918," MA thesis, University of North Dakota, 1956.

Quint, Howard H. *The Forging of American Socialism.* Columbia: University of South Carolina Press, 1953.

Radford, Gail. "From Municipal Socialism to Public Authorities: Institutional Factors in the Shaping of American Public Enterprise." *Journal of American History* 90 (December 2003): 863–890.

Randolph, Carman F. *Opinion on Municipal Ownership of Public Utilities.* New York: De Vinne, 1907.

Rice, Bradley Robert. *Progressive Cities: The Commission Government Movement in America, 1901–1920.* Austin: University of Texas Press, 1977.

Ricker, A. W. "The Coming Battle at Flint." *ATR*, February 3, 1912, 2.

———. "Socialists at Work." *ATR*, September 2, 1911, 3.

Riordan, William L. *Plunkitt of Tammany Hall.* New York: E. P. Dutton, 1963.

Rodgers, Bruce. "Political Socialists vs. Socialist Politicians." *Washington Socialist* (Everett, WA), April 15, 1915, 4.

Rosenstone, Steven J., Roy L. Behr, and Edward H. Lazarus. *Third Parties in America: Citizen Response to Major Party Failure.* Princeton, NJ: Princeton University Press, 1984.

Ross, Jack. *The Socialist Party of America: A Complete History.* Lincoln, NE: Potomac, 2015.

Sandburg, Carl. "Otis Fakes About Milwaukee." *Labor Argus* (Charleston, WV), December 28, 1911, 4.

Scheuerman, William. "The Politics of Protest: The Great Steel Strike of 1919–20 in Lackawanna, New York." *International Review of Social History* 31 (August 1986): 121–146.

Schiesl, Martin J. *The Politics of Efficiency: Municipal Administration and Reform in America, 1800–1920.* Berkeley: University of California Press, 1977.

Schultze, William A. *Urban and Community Politics.* North Scituate, MA: Duxbury, 1974.

Seidel, Emil. *Sketches from My Life,* 1916, 1938–1944, Part 2. Emil Seidel Papers, University of Wisconsin at Milwaukee.

———. *Thy Kingdom Come: Some Sketches from My Life.* Part 3. Microfilm, State Historical Society of Wisconsin.

Shannon, David A. *The Socialist Party of America.* New York: MacMillan, 1955.

Shea, George William. *Spoiled Silk: The Red Mayor and the Great Paterson Textile Strike.* New York: Fordham University Press, 2000.

Sitton, Tom. "John Randolph Haynes and the Left-wing of California Progressivism." In *California Progressivism Revisited*, edited by William Deverell and Tom Sutton, 15–33. Berkeley: University of California Press, 1994.

———. *John Randolph Haynes: California Progressive.* Stanford, CA: Stanford University Press, 1992.

Smith, Clarence A. "Miners' Union Day in Butte." *ISR* 12 (July 1911): 5–6.
Smith, Duane A. *Rocky Mountain West: Colorado, Wyoming, and Montana, 1859–1915.* Albuquerque: University of New Mexico Press, 1992.
Smith, Jeanette. "Walter Walker and His Fight against Socialism." *Journal of the Western Slope* 12 (Fall 1997): 1–18.
Sokolow, Alvin D. "Small Local Governments as Community Builders." *National Civic Review* 78 (September-October 1989): 362–370.
Starr, Kevin. *Inventing the Dream: California through the Progressive Era.* New York: Oxford University Press, 1985.
Stevens, Errol Wayne. "Heartland Socialism: The Socialist Party of America in Four Midwestern Communities, 1898–1920." PhD diss., Indiana University, 1978.
Stewart, Frank. *A Half Century of Municipal Reform.* Berkeley: University of California Press, 1950.
Thierry, Edward. "Socialist Mayor May Lead Party Campaign." *Ogden Standard-Examiner,* May 9, 1920, 12.
Thompson, Carl D. "Have the Socialists Made Good in Office?" *Washington Socialist* (Everett, WA), June 18, 1914, 1, 4.
———. "Middleman Eliminated." *Labor Journal* (Everett, WA), October 7, 1910, 1.
———. "The Socialist Argument against Non-Partisan Elections." April 16, 1913. SPP.
———. "Socialist Try Hand at Regulation." *Labor Argus* (Charleston, WV), August 10, 1911, 6.
———. "The Vital Points in Charter Making from a Socialist Point of View." *NMR* (July 1913): 416–426.
Timberlake, James H. *Prohibition and the Progressive Movement, 1900–1920.* Cambridge, MA: Harvard University Press, 1963.
Velicer, Lloyd. *Municipal Ownership and the Manitowoc Wisconsin Socialists.* Manitowoc County Historical Society, occupational monograph 35, 1978.
Wachman, Marvin. *History of the Social-Democratic Party of Milwaukee, 1897–1910.* Urbana: University of Illinois Press, 1945.
Warner, Hoyt Landon. *Progressivism in Ohio, 1897–1917.* Columbus: Ohio State University Press, 1964.
Webster, Christopher. "Growth of Socialism as Observed in this County." *Hopkinsville Kentuckian,* April 14, 1906, 6.
Weinstein, James. "Anti-war Sentiment and the Socialist Party, 1917–1918." *Political Science Quarterly* 74 (June 1959): 215–239.
———. *The Decline of Socialism in America, 1912–1925.* New York: Monthly Review Press, 1967.
———. "Organized Business and the City Commission and Manager Movements." *Journal of Southern History* 28, no. 2 (May 1962): 166–182.
Weir, Robert E. "Solid Men in the Granite City: Municipal Socialism in Barre, Vermont, 1916–1931." *Vermont History* 83, no. 1 (Winter/Spring 2015): 43–57.
Wells, Hulet M. "The State Convention Echoes." *Commonwealth* (Everett, WA), April 11, 1913, 1.

White, W. J. "Our Elected Servants." *ISR* 13 (June 1913): 868–869.

Wiegand, Wayne A. *Main Street Public Library: Community Places and Reading Spaces in the Rural Heartland, 1876–1956.* Iowa City: University of Iowa Press, 2011.

Wilson, J. Stitt. "The Berkeley Municipal Administration." In *The American Labor Yearbook.* New York: Rand School of Social Science, 1916.

———. *How I Became a Socialist, and Other Papers.* Berkeley, CA: author, 1912.

———. "Letter to Berkeley Socialists, Declining the Nomination for the Mayoralty of Berkeley, February 19, 1913." Found in collection of articles on Hathi Trust Digital Library: 33, 36.

———. "The Story of a Socialist Mayor." *Western Comrade* (Los Angeles, CA) 1 (September 1913): 186–187, 196.

Wolfson, Daniel Frederick. "A History of the Socialist Party of Los Angeles from 1900 to 1912." PhD diss., University of Southern California, 1964.

Wood, J. W. *Pasadena, California, Historical and Personal.* N.p.: author, 1917.

Wood, Robert C. "A Re-examination of Local Democracy." In *Democracy in Urban America: Readings on Government and Politics,* edited By Oliver P. Williams and Charles Press, 109–125. Chicago: Rand McNally, 1961.

Woodruff, Clifton Rodgers. "American Municipal Tendencies." *NMR* 1 (1912): 3–20.

Wright, Chester M. "The Socialist Spirit in the City." *Western Comrade* (Los Angeles, CA) (June 1913): 92–93.

Zueblin, Charles. *American Municipal Progress.* New York: Arno, 1974. Originally published 1916.

INDEX

absentee ownership, 74
advanced resignation (recall) system, 15–16, 99
Aker, Ferdinand, 76
Alliance, Ohio, 76
Amalgamated Copper Company, 127, 132, 133
American Alliance for Labor and Democracy, 69
American Federation of Labor (AFL), 4, 25
American Locomotive Company, 196
American Railway Union, 166–167n25
American Socialist, 123
Anaconda, Montana, 27, 57, 84, 132, 133, 159
Anaconda Copper Mining Company, 27, 132
Anderson, J. L., Socialist mayor, Hillsboro, North Dakota, 33, 160
annexation, used against Socialists, 27
anthracite coal strike (Pennsylvania, 1902), 73
Appeal to Reason, 20, 21, 58, 61, 83, 94, 111
Arma, Kansas, 129, 157
Austin, Ray, Socialist mayor, Red Lodge, Montana
    and city council battle over eight-hour day for police, 129
    election of, 57, 58
    general information on, 58, 159

Bading, Dr. Gerhard, 65, 79
Bakeman, Robert A., 34, 174n25
Barewald, Dr. Charles, Socialist mayor, Davenport, Iowa
    conservative platform of, 70
    election of, 70
    general information on, 70, 156
    resignation from party, 96
Barre, Vermont, 20, 67, 121, 163
Beatrice, Nebraska, 52, 61, 94, 97, 116, 159
Belgium, 113
Bellamy, Edward, 32, 34, 71, 168n13, 172n15
Bemidji, Minnesota, 125, 158
Bennington, Vermont, 19, 48
Berger, Victor
    and Daniel Hoan, 152
    Henry George's influence on, 32
    as a party boss, 15, 180n19

and revisionist movement in the United States, 2
Robert La Follette and Wisconsin Progressives, relations with, 39
and the Social Democratic Party (SDP), 167n25
Socialist Party in Milwaukee, leader of, 59, 128
Socialists engaging in local politics, advocate of, 5
Socialists' outlook, similar to, 16, 45, 56, 58, 92
and trade unionists, 2
Berkeley, California, 14, 33, 62, 63, 87, 91, 95, 97, 109, 112, 118, 144, 152, 154
Bernstein, Edward, 1
Bicknell, Indiana, 20, 21, 66, 80, 123, 156
Biloxi, Mississippi, 50
Bitterly, J. B., Socialist mayor, Victor, Colorado
    election of, 61
    and financial management, 117, 119
    general information on, 155
    municipal scales and, 134
    public health and, 121
blacklisting (blacklisted), 21, 23, 78, 132, 149
Black people, 116, 117, 194n18
Bohn, Frank, 29, 76
Boot and Shoe Workers' Union, 149
Born, Charles A., Socialist mayor, Sheboygan, Wisconsin
    appointments of, 115, 116
    election of, 58
    general information on, 164
    platform of, 58
Brace, Duff, Socialist mayor, Conneaut, Ohio
    appointment power, use of, 115
    constituency of, 66
    as a crisis manager, 113
    election of, 66, 67
    general information on, 66, 160
    and new municipal recreational enterprise, 137
    people around, 107
    and police court fines, 192n18
    war, reaction to, 183n65

219

Brainerd, Minnesota, 58, 135, 158
Bridgeport, Connecticut, 52
Brockton, Massachusetts, 57, 77, 131, 157
Brookneal, Virginia, 27, 67, 163
Brueckmann, William, Socialist mayor, Haledon, New Jersey
   city council, battle with, 94
   election of, 66, 67, 68
   general information on, 159
   information request to national office seeking help, 108
   local party organization, commitment to, 99
   silk workers strike in Paterson, New Jersey, involvement in, 130
   voters appeal to, 82–83
   war-time hysteria directed against, 68
Bryan, William Jennings, 36
Bundle Brigade, 60
Bureau of Economy and Efficiency (Milwaukee), 115
Burnquist, John, 130
business leaders
   and business socialism, 78
   Christian Socialists, view of, 32–33
   and IWW, 131
   and municipal reform movement, 9, 29 30, 31, 40, 41, 171n3
   as Progressive reformers, 34, 35, 36
   in small towns, 74
   opposing Socialist candidates, 27, 78, 93, 102, 104, 107, 145
   and Socialist mayors, 88, 89, 91, 92, 93, 102, 104, 107, 132–139, 145
   as Socialists, 20, 21, 58, 73
Business Men's Association, 93
Butte, Montana, 9, 19, 25, 27, 33, 62, 63, 66, 77, 88, 90, 101, 111, 112, 113, 116, 117, 118, 121, 125, 128, 130, 133, 150, 151, 159
Butte Miners' Union, 111
Butte Socialist, 63

Cameron, West Virginia, 134, 164
Canton, Illinois, 67, 79, 88, 124, 155
Canton, Ohio, 61, 84, 87, 123, 160
Carriers' Association aligned with United States Steel, 66
Catholic, 33, 37, 82, 117
Chaplin, Ralph, 17
Chase, John, Socialist mayor, Haverhill, Massachusetts
   coming into office, 86–87
   co-option of, 78
   general information on, 56, 149
   labor, and, 128
   mayoral elections of, 56–57, 73, 149
   and municipal ownership, 135
   platform of, 57
   predictions of success of, 6, 90
   private bidders, view of, 50
   and public utilities, 134
   Sam Jones, compared to, 35
Chester, Eric Thomas, 12
Christian Socialists, 32, 33, 175n62. *See also* Social Gospelers
Cincinnati, Ohio, 38
Citizen, 159
city manager plan, 11, 31, 41, 171–172n3
civil service, 31, 114, 194–95n18
Clark, Norman, 21
class conflict, 1, 37, 38, 43, 44, 74, 75
class consciousness, 44, 62, 75, 124, 147
   versus job consciousness, 147
Cleveland, Ohio, 34, 36, 38, 46, 52
coal town, 66, 67
coal vote, 73
Coeur d'Alene City, Idaho, 61, 79, 96, 112, 137, 155
Columbus, Ohio, 35, 38
commission plan
   in New Castle, Pennsylvania, 95
   Socialist attitudes toward, 51, 52
Congregationalists, 33, 150
Conneaut, Ohio, 66, 67, 107, 113, 115, 116, 137, 160
Constructive Socialists, 3, 82
contracting out with private companies, 49–50, 58, 93, 139
Cook, W. H., Socialist mayor, Edmonds, Washington
   election of, 60
   general information on, 88, 163
   goals of, as mayor, 88
cooperative commonwealth, 9, 37, 101, 143, 165n2
cost of living, 49, 72, 137
Coulter, Charles H., Socialist mayor, Brockton, Massachusetts
   co-option of, 78
   election of, 57
   general information on, 57, 157
   and municipal ownership, 135
Crank, George W., Socialist mayor, Madrid, Iowa
   elections of, 58, 65, 68
   general information on, 58 156
   newspaper coverage of, 103
   and war, 82
   winning ability of, 82

Cross, A. Barton, Jr., Socialist warden, Naugatuck, Connecticut
  election of, 66
  general information on, 155
  and spending, 118

Dale, Hin, Socialist mayor, Rugby, North Dakota
  general information on, 160
  newspaper coverage of, 104
Daly City, California, 46, 65, 119, 154
Debs, Eugene, 2, 6, 35, 62, 64, 66, 72, 75, 81, 89, 150, 167n25
De Leon, Daniel, 166n25
Democracy, 28, 29, 40, 41, 43, 50, 51, 61, 69, 110, 145
Democratic Party, 38, 151, 153
Democrats, 4, 53, 54, 60, 64, 65, 77, 88, 103, 115, 116, 118, 140
Des Moines, Iowa, 51
Des Plaines, Illinois, 80, 156
Detroit, Michigan, 34
Detroit Socialist Party, 34
direct primary, 19, 51
drinking (drunks), 46, 83, 101, 124, 125, 126, 137, 141
Duncan, Lewis, Socialist mayor, Butte, Montana
  and Amalgamated Copper, 133
  aspirations as mayor, 88, 89, 92, 202n1
  and Black police officer, 117
  Butte finances, under leadership of, 118
  Butte riot and removal from office of, 27, 113, 130–131
  and Catholic vote, 77
  and city workers, 128
  conference in Milwaukee, attending, 112
  council rejection of police officers appointed by, 116, 117
  elections for mayor, 62–63, 66, 150
  enforcement liquor laws and in red light districts, 125
  general information on, 151–152, 159
  as a gubernatorial nominee, 19
  and Los Angeles Times building dynamiting, 25
  as a minister, 33, 151
  and police, 116, 117
  and President Taft, 112
  and Socialist Party, 19–20, 98–99, 111
  stabbed, 101
  statement after election, 88
Dunne, Edward, mayor of Chicago, 174n26, 176n15

elections at large, 40, 102, 145, 146
England, 1, 31
Episcopal clergy, 32
espionage law, 80
Eureka, Utah, 58, 68, 94, 123, 132, 162
Europe (European), 1, 31, 32, 70, 80
Everett, Washington, 17, 21, 52
"evolutionary" Socialists. *See* Constructive Socialists

Fabian Socialists, in England, 1
Fagin, Mark, mayor of Jersey City, New Jersey, 173n14, 174n26
Fairhope, Alabama, 66, 120, 154
Federated Trades Council of Milwaukee, 25, 59
Ferguson, Reverend Harry, 131, 167n27
Finns, 16, 58, 66, 94, 103
Fitchburg, Massachusetts, 46, 51
Flanders, Parkman B., Socialist mayor, Haverhill, Massachusetts
  elected mayor, 57
  general information on, 157
  hiring and firing personnel, 114
Flint, Michigan, 23, 61, 65, 77, 88, 94, 111, 112, 116, 124, 158
Flynn, Elizabeth Gurley, 17
Foe, Sam, Socialist mayor, Red Cloud, Nebraska
  general information on, 159
  predictions of success of, 91
  time of service, limited, 105
  touring Red Cloud, 105
Frinke, John, Socialist mayor, Anaconda, Montana
  election of, 57, 132
  challenge of holding office, 27, 84
  departure from Anaconda, 132–133
  general information on, 132–133, 159
  and mining company, 132
Frontenac, Kansas, 23, 80, 157
Fulda, Todd, 82
fusion tickets, 65, 66, 67, 77–78, 81, 109, 185n29

Galveston, Texas, 51
gambling, 46, 91, 101, 105, 123, 126, 141
General Electric, 63, 89, 127, 130
General Motors, 65
George, Henry, 32, 36, 120, 152, 172 n13, 173n14
Getchell, Andrew, Socialist mayor, Missoula, Montana
  general information on, 159
  and local Socialist Party, 97, 98

Gibbons, John H., Socialist mayor, Lackawanna, New York
  coalition behind, 69–70
  election of, 69–70
  general information on, 159
Gilham, Harry, Socialist mayor, Oswego, Kansas
  election of, 58
  general information on, 157
  gubernatorial nomination of, 19
  and municipal takeovers, 135, 136
Girard, Alabama, 65, 111, 154
Girard, Kansas, 25, 61, 65, 111, 112, 154
Gladden, Washington, 35
glassblowers, 20
Globe, Arizona, 51
Goldman, Emma, 151
Goldstein, David, 78
Gompers, Samuel, 4, 69
Good Government forces ("goo-goos"), 7, 9, 11, 29, 30–31, 34, 35, 39–42, 41, 51–56, 61, 71, 73–74, 115, 119, 145–146
Gordon, Robert, Socialist mayor, Barre, Vermont
  accident of, 121–122
  election of, 67
  general information on, 67, 121, 163
  priorities of, 121
Grafton, Illinois, 50
Grand Junction, Colorado, 49, 58, 73, 99, 100, 112, 122, 131, 138, 155
Granite City, Illinois, 23, 66, 67, 80, 108, 118, 124, 129, 132, 134, 156
Grants Pass, Oregon, 26, 71, 122
Green, Constance McLaughlin, 147
Griffin, W. E., Socialist mayor, Beatrice, Nebraska
  and city council, 94, 116
  election of, 61
  general information on, 61, 159
  and local Socialist Party, 97
Gronlund, Laurence, 165n1
Gulfport, Florida, 65, 120, 155
Gutman, Herman, 74

Haledon, New Jersey, 66, 67, 68, 82, 94, 99, 108, 130, 159
Halliday, Alexander, Socialist mayor, Two Harbors, Minnesota
  election of, 61
  general information on, 158
  as speaker at rally, 111

Hamilton, Ohio, 66, 67, 76, 108, 114, 117, 118, 132, 160
Hanna, Mark, 37
Harbor Springs, Michigan, 125, 158
Harriman, Job, 111
Harthill, Lewis, 122
Haverhill, Massachusetts, 6, 35, 56, 57, 73, 75, 77, 78, 90, 114, 128, 134, 146, 149, 157
Haywood, William D. ("Big Bill"), 61, 75, 111, 152
Henning, R. A., Socialist mayor, Brainerd, Minnesota
  election of, 58
  franchise agreements, opposed to, 135
  general information on, 158
Herron, George D., 3
Hicks, Granville, 106, 192n25
Higgins, John F., Socialist mayor-elect, Star City, West Virginia
  election of, report on, 20
  general information on, 164
  ineligible to serve, 84
Hillquit, Morris, 112
Hillsboro, North Dakota, 33, 160
Hinkle, Frederick, Socialist mayor, Hamilton, Ohio
  and appointments, 114
  campaigning, 76
  and city council, 117
  election of, 66, 67, 108
  general information on, 67, 160
  machinist strike and, 132
  and national Socialist Party, 108
Hoan, Daniel, Socialist mayor, Milwaukee, Wisconsin
  as advisor to Socialist mayors, 108
  and Belgium royalty visit, 113
  and Berger, 180n19
  and Catholic vote, 77
  constituency of, 82
  electoral success of, reasons for, 82
  general information on, 152–153, 164
  and municipal ownership, 136–137
  and non-partisan elections, 54
  and public marketing system, 137
  Seidel compared to, 150
  "small doses of socialism" quote by, 8
  and streetcar companies, 134
  and World War I, 68
Hodges, George, 32–33
Hodghead, Beverly, 63
Hodson, Dale, 97–98
Holi, Melvin, 31, 60

honesty and efficiency in government, 9, 29, 30, 31, 34, 37, 40, 43, 46, 72, 114, 126, 141, 145, 146
Hoquiam, Washington, 131, 167
Houghton, H. P., Socialist mayor, Girard, Kansas
  conference in Milwaukee, attending, 112
  election of, 61
  fusion, and bid for re-election of, 189n29
  general information on, 61, 157
  and Los Angeles Times building dynamiting, 25
Hoxie, Robert F., 16, 75, 181n46
Huscher, George A., Socialist mayor, Murray, Utah
  election of, 66
  general information on, 162
  and municipal takeovers, 135, 136
Hutchinson, S. B., 122, 131

impeachment, 80, 151
impossibilists, 3
Industrial Workers of the World (IWW)
  Bill Haywood, as leader of, 61, 75
  Butte riot, involvement in, 130–131
  and Grand Junction, Colorado, 131
  and mayor of Hoquiam, Washington, 131
  and Mayor Scott Wilkins, 109
  and Mayor Willam Brueckmann, 130
  members (IWWs or Wobblies), 17, 131
  political action view of, 3
  and revisionist, right-wing Socialists, 3, 17, 131
  strike in Paterson, New Jersey, 130
Information Department of the national Socialist Party, 93, 105, 135
initiative and referendum, 36, 50, 51, 57, 87
inspections (foods, factories, safety), 45, 121
International Association of Machinists, Minneapolis, 25
International Socialist Review, 111

Jasper, Tennessee, 27
Johnson, John Franklin, Socialist mayor, Fairhope, Alabama
  boosterism of, 120
  election of, 66
  general information on, 66, 174
Johnson, Tom, mayor of Cleveland, Ohio, 34, 36–37, 38, 171n3, 173n14
Jones, M. M., Socialist mayor, Liberal, Kansas
  general information on, 157
  statement of, coming into office, 88

Jones, Sam M., mayor of Toledo, Ohio, 34, 35–36, 38, 39, 46, 126, 171n3, 173n14
Judd, Richard, 89, 103, 181n33

Kaltinick, Arnold, 72, 94, 184n4
Kipnis, Ira, 146
Kirkpatrick, Marshall E., Socialist mayor, Granite City, Illinois
  electoral success of, 83
  financial sacrifice of, to become mayor, 23
  general information on, 156
  jailing of drunks, views on, 124
  and national office assistance, 108
  strikes, opinion on, 129
  and taxing and spending increases, 118
  and utility franchise, 134
  and war-time conditions, 80
Knapp, John, Socialist mayor, Sisseton, South Dakota
  general information on, 162
  newspaper editor's assessment of, 90
  quasi-municipal saloon experiment, 137
  war issue, broke with party, 183n6
Knights of Columbus, 78
Knights of Labor, 21, 153

labor unions, 2, 4, 24–26, 56, 59, 72, 96, 127, 130, 132 153. *See also* strike activity; *and specific unions*
Lackawanna, New York, 69, 114, 159, 193–194n2
La Follette, Robert, 38, 39
laissez-faire capitalism, 1, 37
Lautner, Edward, Socialist mayor, Traverse City, Michigan, 55, 158
law enforcement, 104, 112, 122–126. *See also* Mayor's Court; police
Lawrence, Henry, 167n27
Lawson, W. M., Socialist mayor, Des Plaines, Illinois
  anti-solider comments, 80
  general information on, 156
Lawton, Tyler, Socialist mayor, Bicknell, Indiana
  election of, 21, 66
  general information on, 20, 21, 156
  and law enforcement, 123
  resignation from party, 183n65
  war-time pressure on, 80
left-wing Progressives, 32, 37, 38, 39, 40, 48, 140
Le Sueur, Arthur, Socialist mayor, Minot, North Dakota
  and city council problems, 95
  David Goldstein, debate with, 78

Le Sueur, Arthur, Socialist mayor, Minot, North Dakota, *continued*
  election of, 58
  general information on, 160
  and law enforcement, 123
  nonpartisan elections, view of, 54
  resignation from office, 95
Lewis, John, Socialist mayor, Elwood, Indiana
  appointments of, 114
  general information on, 156
  war-time problems, 81
Liberal, Kansas, 88, 157
Lima, Ohio, 23, 62, 98, 116, 123, 180
Lindsay, Estelle Lawton, 167n27
Lippmann, Walter, 7, 119
liquor, 80, 122, 123, 124, 125, 137
literacy ("understanding") tests, 31
Liverpool, 31
Looking Backward, 32
Los Angeles Times building, dynamiting of, 25
Love, David, Socialist mayor, West Alliance, Wisconsin
  general information on, 164
  war, rejected party's position on, 183n65
Lunn, George, Socialist mayor, Schenectady, New York
  anti-war rally speaker, 80
  appointments to office by, 115
  budget-making by, 119
  campaign spending of, 23
  and corporate taxation, 89–90, 196n37
  demands on, 82
  general information on, 63, 150–151, 159
  inaugural address of, 89
  mayoral campaigns and elections of, 63–64, 65, 67, 77
  mayoral goals and aspirations of, 92
  Milwaukee visit by, 108
  as a minister, 33, 150, 151
  and municipal commercial enterprises, 138–139
  Socialist Party, expulsion from, 99
  Socialist Party bosses, views of, 15
  statements after election in 1911, 89
  strike involvement, 129–130
  Walter Lippman on, 7, 119

Madrid, Iowa, 58, 65, 67, 68, 82, 103, 156
Maley, Anna, 96
Malzhan, Fred, Socialist mayor, Bemidji, Minnesota
  general information on, 158
  and liquor fees, 125

Manitowoc, Wisconsin, 57, 58, 77, 82, 94, 116, 132, 135
Marchant, J. P., Socialist mayor, Girard, Alabama
  election of, 66
  general information on, 66, 154
  socialist literature distribution of, 11
  white supremist views of, 194n18
Martins Ferry, Ohio, 62, 66, 67, 81, 92, 119, 122, 123, 134, 160
Marxist (revolutionary) Socialists, 2, 33
Marxist theory, 1, 2
Massillon, Ohio, 69, 160
Matthews, William H., Socialist mayor, Rockaway, New Jersey
  general information on, 159
  speech coming to power, 86
Mayor council form of municipal government, 10–11
Mayor's Court, 104, 192n15, 192n18
mayor's office
  as a bully pulpit, 110
  plans for, 10–11
  in small towns, 102–108
McCormick, John, 101
McKay, John S., Socialist mayor, Village of Salem, Ohio
  election of, 103
  general information on, 103, 161
  judicial work of, in the police court, 104–105
  minister, occupation of, 33
  newspaper coverage of, 103–104
  and utility franchise, 134
Medford, Oregon, 20, 167n27
Menton, John, Socialist mayor, Flint, Michigan
  appointment of Black police officer, 116–117
  conference in Milwaukee, attending, 112
  council opposition to, 94
  election of, 61, 65, 77
  general information on, 61, 88, 158
  jailing of drunks, views on, 124
  losing money by becoming mayor, 23
  and party building, 111
  statement after election, 88–89
Methodists, 33
Mill and Smelter Union, 83
Millar, George H., 20, 167n27, 192n15
Miller, Guy, 25
Miller, Salley, 25
Milwaukee, Wisconsin, 1, 2, 7, 8, 9, 15, 18, 22, 25, 38, 39, 49, 50, 54, 58, 59, 60, 64, 65, 68, 72, 75, 77, 79, 80, 82, 87, 90, 96, 102, 108, 112,

113, 115, 116, 117, 119, 120, 121, 128, 134, 136, 137, 138, 145, 146, 147, 149, 150, 151, 152, 153, 164
Milwaukee Electric Railway and Light Company, 136
Milwaukee Pattern Manufacturing Company, 59
Milwaukee Voters' League, 79
Miners Magazine, 99
Miners' Union Hall (Butte), 51, 131
mining towns/areas, 16, 58, 61, 117
ministers and the Socialist Party, 17, 20, 33, 34, 63, 74, 89, 150, 152
Minneapolis, Minnesota, 25, 26, 68, 69, 80, 122, 123, 130, 152, 153, 158
Minneapolis Liberty Society, 69
Minneapolis Machinist Union, 122
Minnesota Daily Star, 153
Minot, North Dakota, 54, 58, 78, 95, 123, 160
Missoula, Montana, 97, 159
Mitchell, Andrew, Socialist mayor, Eureka, Utah
    city council battle with, 94
    election of, 58, 68
    general information on, 58, 162
    and saloons and gamblers, 123
    and strikes, 132
Montana Lookout, 62
Morgan, Evan, Socialist mayor, Arma, Kansas
    legal trouble of, 129
    general information on, 157
Mormon Church (The Church of Jesus Christ of Latter-day Saints), 33
Mott, Charles, 65
Mount Vernon, Ohio, 23, 62, 98, 119, 123, 160
municipal corruption, 9, 47
municipal employees, 32, 45, 49, 61, 81, 93, 112, 114, 118, 128, 144,
municipal employment/labor bureaus, 45, 128, 138
municipal franchises, 32, 34, 35, 36, 46, 48, 59, 68, 83, 87, 95, 127, 134, 135
municipal government structure, 10–11, 39, 40, 51, 50–55
municipal home rule, 10, 35, 40–41, 87, 90, 102
Municipal Nonpartisan League, 153
municipal ownership, 9, 18, 31, 35, 36, 38, 47, 48, 57, 58, 59, 61, 87, 95, 114, 135, 136, 140, 143, 146
municipal reform movement in the United States, 8, 9, 12, 29, 145, 146
municipal scales, 134
Municipal Socialism, 7, 8, 9, 29, 31–34, 35, 37, 39, 43, 140, 146

Murray, Robert, Socialist mayor, Toronto, Ohio
    election of, 66
    general information on, 161
    minister, status as, 33
    speech coming into office, 92
Murray, Utah, 66, 119, 135, 161

Naugatuck, Connecticut, 66, 188, 155
New Nation, 34
nonpartisan elections, 11, 40, 51, 52, 53, 54, 55, 145
Nonpartisan League, 152
Northport, Washington, 57, 83–84, 163

Oswego, Kansas, 19, 57, 58, 135, 157

Pape, Thomas, Socialist mayor, Lorain, Ohio
    campaign spending of, 23
    election of, 61
    general information on, 61, 160
    and law enforcement, 123
    and local party attempted ouster, 98
parlor Socialist, 89, 202n1
Pasadena, California, 20, 23, 61, 73, 135, 136, 154
patronage, 31, 99
Patterson, Joseph Medill, 47, 76n15
Perrine, Alfred, Socialist mayor, Mount Vernon, Ohio
    campaign spending of, 23
    and city cleanup, 123
    and city financial problems, 119
    election of, 62
    general information on, 62, 160
    and local party recall effort, 98
Perth Amboy, New Jersey, 44, 45, 125
Pingree, Hazen, mayor, Detroit, Michigan, 34–35, 36, 38, 87, 126
Pinkerton detectives, 132
Plunkitt, George Washington, 30
Pocatello, Idaho, 52
police, 36, 45, 97, 104, 109, 112, 116, 117, 118, 120, 122, 124, 125, 128, 129, 130, 131, 132, 138
police court. *See* Mayor's Court
political action, 1, 4, 5, 6, 8, 17, 18, 45, 62, 66, 99, 109, 146, 166–167n25
political machines, 31, 171n3, 190n61
political science, 30
poll tax, socialists opposed to, 51
Populists, 56, 73, 147
Potato Patch, 35, 86

Progressives
  left-wing, 7, 9, 29, 32, 34–39, 40, 47, 48, 65, 140
  right-wing, 48
prohibition, 77, 124, 125, 138, 197n62
prostitution, 46, 91, 105, 116, 123, 125, 126, 137, 141
public education, 2, 18, 33, 45, 46, 57, 61, 128, 144
public health and safety, 18, 45, 46, 61, 62, 121, 144
Public Ownership League, 39
public utilities, 31, 47, 48, 57, 63, 77, 87, 90, 135, 137. *See also* municipal ownership; utility regulation

Quinlan, Patrick, 130
Quint, Howard, 36

railway brotherhoods, 58
Ralston, W. M., Socialist mayor, Fostoria, Ohio
  general information on, 160
  progress report, 93
recall process established by law, 16, 50, 87, 131
Red Cloud, Nebraska, 91, 105, 159
red-light districts, 88, 124, 125
red scare, 80
Republican Party, 35
Republicans, 38, 41, 53, 54, 57, 65, 77, 90, 94, 116, 128, 140
"revisionist" Socialists. *See* Constructive Socialists
revolutionary socialists, 2, 4, 7
Richardson, N. A., 21
Richmond, Indiana, 45
right-wing Socialists, 3, 4, 5, 8, 17, 29, 31, 37, 38, 39, 43, 45, 57
Robinson, E. E., Socialist mayor, Mineral Ridge, Ohio
  council opposition to, 93
  general information on, 160
Rockaway, New Jersey, 86, 159
Roosevelt, Theodore, 63, 112

Salem, Ohio, 33, 103, 104, 134, 161
saloons, 91, 123, 125, 137
sanitary conditions, 46, 116, 125
Santa Fe Railroad, 23
Schenectady, New York, 7, 9, 15, 23, 33, 34, 48, 62, 63, 64, 65, 67, 77, 82, 89, 99, 119, 134, 138, 150, 151, 159
Schildknecht, John, Socialist mayor, Frontenac, Kansas
  general information on, 157
  German name misquote, 80
  job lost, 23

Schilling, Harry, Socialist mayor, Canton, Ohio
  constituency of, 84
  election of, 61
  expulsion from the party, 84
  general information on, 61, 160
  getting into office and staying in office, trouble, 84–85
  and law enforcement, 123
  and police officers firing, 116
  statement after election, 87–88
Schumacher, William, 76
Seidel, Emil, Socialist mayor, Milwaukee, Wisconsin
  calming fears, 1
  as chief administrator, 112, 115
  and cost of living, 49
  criticism and pressures of the office, reacting to, 101, 191n2
  evaluation of, 145
  female police officer appointment, 116
  financial problems, dealing with, 117
  general information on, 59, 149–150, 164
  George Lunn, visit from, 108
  German connections, 60, 149, 150
  inaugural speech, 87
  and local party organization, 99
  mayoral election of 1910, 59, 60
  mayoral election of 1912, 65, 79–80
  and municipal employee benefits, 128
  and nonpartisan coalition opposition, 68, 77
  planning, need for, 120
  and public utilities, 134
  and Theodore Roosevelt, 112
Sheboygan, Wisconsin, 52, 57, 58, 75, 115, 116, 164
Shook, Corbin, Socialist mayor, Lima, Ohio
  campaign spending of, 22–23
  election of, 62
  expelled from party, 98
  general information on, 62, 160
  and party organization trouble, 98
  and police chief, firing, 116
  and vice campaign, 123
Sillito, John, 101
single tax, 32, 95, 152, 173n14
single tax candidate, 66
single taxers, 73
Sisseston, South Dakota, 90, 96, 134, 137, 138, 162
slot machines, 122, 123
slums, 33, 59, 121, 124
Small town government and politics
  business leaders in, 27, 74
  community atmosphere, 103

conditions regarding authority, finance, professional help, 10, 102–108
distribution of power in, 9–10
election success of Socialists in, 9, 38, 72–75, 77, 101, 140–141
expectations of performance of officials, 103, 106
mayor's office in, 102–108
newspaper coverage of Socialist mayors, 11, 104
parochial environment of, 107
personal government of, 106
reform agenda in, 93, 103, 114
Socialist campaigns in, 74–75, 141
Socialist mayors in, 9, 10, 38, 72, 74–75, 93, 102–108, 114, 140–141
tyranny of the majority in, 10
voting in, 103
See also specific small towns
Social Crusade, 152
Social Democrat(s), 25, 57, 58, 59, 115, 149
Social Democratic Party (SDP), 11, 22, 25, 26, 31, 33, 36, 59, 87, 149, 167n25
Social Gospel, 32, 33, 150
Socialist campaigns
and business opposition, 27, 78, 93, 102, 104, 107, 145
coalition-building, 70, 77
common charges against Socialist candidates, 78–81
common themes, 9, 73, 146
finance of, 21–22
nature of, 75–77, 84, 127
newspaper and literature distribution in, 15, 24, 58, 61, 63, 75
party control, issue of, 143
party control of, 15, 22
party leaders and workers, leading role of, 22
small jurisdictions in, 74–75, 141
Socialist Labor Party (SLP), 15, 36, 73, 150, 166n25
Socialist mayors
appointments, disputes over, 15, 23, 84, 94, 95, 96, 97, 98, 99, 114, 115, 116, 117, 144
attitudes of, coming to office, 49, 86–92
attitudes of, toward the job, 109–113
authority, limits on, 90, 101, 102
and budgeting, taxing, and spending, 119–120, 144
and business leaders, 88, 89, 91, 92, 93, 102, 104, 107, 132–139, 145
city councils, relations with, 93–96, 107, 129, 135

constituency of, 7, 66, 82, 84
and corporations, utilities, and municipal ownership, 132–139
decision rule regarding the working class, 107
and development and planning, 120–122
distinctive qualities of, 13, 113, 142–143
and educational and social programs, 144–146
election of, 16, 72–75, 77–81, 140–141
expectations as to performance, 10, 91, 103, 106, 143
and expulsion from the party, 16, 69, 81, 84, 97, 98, 99, 153, 182n54
financial losses incurred by successful candidates, 23
and fiscal management, 117–120
and Good Government reformers, 146
and health and safety programs, 116, 121, 125, 144
and hiring and firing duties, 114–117
and honesty and efficiency, 144, 145–146
and labor protection, 127–132
and law enforcement, 104, 112, 122–126
ministerial backgrounds of, 33
and morality issues, 125
and municipal employment, 144
and municipal reform movement, 145–146
and municipal takeovers and enterprises, 135–139
newspaper coverage of, 11, 104
obstacles to serving, 27, 83–84
as opportunists, 92, 142
and party-building, 111–112
party organization relations with, 96–100
predictions as to behavior of, 5–6
and protecting labor, 107, 127–132
public engagements of, 103
qualifications for the job, 107
role-playing of, 112–113
routine matters on their agenda, 101
in small towns, 9, 10, 38, 72, 74–75, 93, 102–108, 114, 140–141
source of new ideas, as a, 145
and state officials, 101
technical services available to, 108
tenure and re-election of, 81–82
union members being supportive of, 96, 128
and utility and other business regulations, 134–135, 144
and working class focus and benefits, 107, 119–120, 121, 127–128, 142–143, 145
See also specific mayors

Socialist municipal program and platform, 43–55
  Bellamy, influence of, on, 32
  common themes of, 13, 18–19, 43–44, 61
  compared to leftist Progressives, 37–38
  co-optation of, 77–78, 140
  core message of, 43
  local focus of, 19, 141, 144
  national party influence on, 18, 19
  variations in, 19
  watered-down nature of, 5, 13, 142
  See also specific policies
Socialist Party of America (SPA)
  advanced resignation (recall) system, 15–16, 19
  bosses of, 15, 59, 128, 180n19
  challenges to candidate victories, 26–27, 84
  control of candidates and office holders, 15–16, 22, 96–100, 143
  discriminated against, 27
  divisions within, 16–17
  divisions within over political action, 1–8, 17
  expulsion from, 16, 81, 99
  information services provided by the national party, 18–19, 93, 108, 135
  IWW's or Wobblies as members and critics of the right wing, 17, 131
  literature and the press of, 23–24
  membership, vii, 8, 14–15, 16
  municipal candidates, characteristics of, 20–21, 25
  municipal ownership as an issue, 146
  and nominations for office, 19–21
  organization of, 8
  other parties, compared to, viii, 22, 26
  resiliency of, 147
  third-party status of, 8, 14, 27, 52, 140, 145, 147
  and unions, 2, 24–26, 56, 59, 96, 127, 153
  voting, party rules on, 14, 36
  working class focus of, 2, 13, 21, 31, 38, 40, 44–46, 47, 48, 52, 64, 77, 95, 99, 107, 119–120 121, 127–128, 142–143, 145, 146, 147
  working class support for, 72–74, 77, 140–141, 146–147
Socialists
  annexation, used against, 27
  business leaders as, 20, 21, 58, 73
  labor union members as, 25
  left-wingers and right-wingers, 3, 4, 7, 8, 17, 19
  legal challenges to election of, 26–27, 84
  and the municipal reform movement
  candidates for municipal office, characteristics of, 20–22; general involvement, 8, 9, 145–146; home rule, position on, 40–41; relations with Good Government types, 39–42, 51–56, 145–146; relations with Progressive left, 7, 9, 29, 37–39, 40, 47, 48, 65, 140, 146; relations with unions, 24–26; and structural reforms of the Good Government reformers, 39, 40, 41, 50–55. *See also* Socialist mayors; Socialist municipal program
  organized labor, relations with, 2, 4, 24–26, 56, 59, 72, 96, 127, 130, 132, 153
  parlor types, 89, 202n1
  perceptions of, 26–28, 145
  political skills of, 26
  reds and yellows, 16
  revisionists, 2, 3, 56, 59. *See also* Constructive Socialists
  revolutionary types, 2, 4, 7
  right-wing types, 3, 4, 5, 8, 17, 29, 31, 37, 38, 39, 43, 45, 57
  and religion, 33, 78
  as targets, 14, 28
  and World War I
    anti-war activity and reaction to, 80–81; municipal campaigns and elections, effects on, 68–70, 82–83, 146, 152; national party stance on, 68; party's status change in war-time, 12, 28, 55, 56; resignations from the party, 68; pressure on those with German names, 68; Socialist mayors opposed to party's stand, 183n65
Sombart, Werner, 202n2
Spanish-American War, 150, 153
Standard Oil Company, 61
Star City, West Virginia, 20, 27, 49, 55, 84, 103, 117, 119, 139, 164
Stedman, Seymour, 18
Stewart, Peter, Socialist mayor, Hartford, Arkansas, 66, 154
St. John, Vincent, 3
St. Johns, Oregon, 67
St. Marys, Ohio, 23, 61, 109, 128, 129, 133, 161
St. Marys Machine Company, 133
Stolze, Henry, Socialist mayor, Manitowoc, Wisconsin
  efficiency and economy approach of, 82
  election of, 58, 82
  general information on, 58, 164
  and municipal ownership, 82, 135, 136

and police chief firing, 116
reform program of, 58, 82
streetcar companies, 34, 36, 38, 47, 59, 70, 93, 134, 144
Strickland, Frederick, 76
strike activity, 62, 66, 68, 69, 72, 73, 95, 129–132
Swain, Fred, Socialist mayor, Minden, Missouri
election of, 93
general information on, 159
progress report from, 93–94

Tammany Hall, 30
term limitations, 143
third parties, 8, 14, 27, 52, 140, 145, 147
Thompson, Carl D., 92, 93, 95, 108, 188n30
Thum, William, Socialist mayor, Pasadena, California
campaign spending of, 23
election of, 20, 61
general information on, 20–21
and municipal ownership, 135, 136, 154
refusal to run for re-election, 81
Todd, Thomas M., Socialist mayor, Grand Junction, Colorado
conference in Milwaukee, attending, 112
election of, 58
general information on, 155
and IWW, 131
and municipal ownership, 49, 138
and police chief, 122
and Socialist Party workers, 99–100
Toledo, Ohio, 24, 34, 35, 36, 38, 39
Toomey, John A., 69
Topeka, Kansas, 55
Toronto, Ohio, 33, 66, 92, 161
Traverse City, Michigan, 54, 158
Trumbull, Arthur, 84
Two Harbors, Minnesota, 57, 58, 61, 66, 67, 111, 122, 134, 139, 158
Tyler, Walter V., Socialist mayor, New Castle, Pennsylvania
council trouble, 94–95
general information on, 156
power company, trouble with, 134–135
Typographical Union, 84

understanding tests, 31
union label, 45, 128, 146
union members
lobbying on behalf of Socialists, 96
as non-Socialists on the city council voting with Socialists, 128

as Socialist candidates, 20
Socialist mayors, assisted by, 127–132
as Socialist Party members, 25
United Mine Workers, 66, 67
United People's Church, 190, 174n25
United States Army, 80, 150, 153
United States Steel, 62, 66, 72, 73, 126
Untermann, Ernest, 18
utility regulation, 24, 46, 81, 145, 146

Van Leer, Thomas, Socialist mayor, Minneapolis, Minnesota
Black citizens, endorsed by, 194n18
election of, 68
expulsion from the Socialist Party, 69, 153
general information on, 68, 153, 158
and law enforcement, 122, 123
Morris Hillquit, campaigning for, 112
on practical politics training for Socialists, 26
and Socialist party building in Minneapolis, 25
speech, congressional campaign , 127
and strike of newsboys in Minneapolis, 130
on World War I entry, 69, 80
Victor, Colorado, 61, 117, 119, 121, 134, 155
village(s), 9, 10, 48, 58, 61, 65, 71, 72, 93, 102, 105, 120
Vogt, Henry H., Socialist mayor, Massillon, Ohio
election of, 69
general information on, 69, 160
voting
of "better people," 40
and blacklisting, 78
by city council, 95, 128
fraud, 27
legal regulations regarding, 27
rights, 43
in small towns, 103
Socialist Party rules on, 14, 36
turnout for, 78
by workers, 146
See also specific requirements

Wachman, Marvin, 22
wage slavery, 9, 43
Walling, William English, 2
Walsh, John, 18
Warnock, Joseph, Socialist mayor, Harbor Springs, Michigan
general information on, 158
prostitution, view of, 125

West Alliance, Wisconsin, 164, 183n65
Western Federation of Miners (WFM), 61, 130
Whalen, Homer, Socialist mayor, Canton, Illinois
  campaign attack on, 79
  election of, 67
  general information on, 67, 155
  law enforcement against vice, 123
  prohibition ordinance, 124
  statement on coming into office, 88
Wheeling, West Virginia, 72
Whitlock, Brad, mayor of Toledo, Ohio, 36, 39, 174n26
Wilkins, Scott, Socialist mayor, St. Marys, Ohio
  and attack on large employer, 133
  blacklisted, 23
  driven out of office, 133–134
  election of, 61
  encouraging strike activity, 129
  general information on, 61, 161
  income reduced after becoming mayor, 23
  as revolutionary mayor, 109
  and workers' pay boost, 128
Wilson, J. Stitt, Socialist mayor, Berkely, California
  accomplishments of, 95, 144–145
  and budgeting matters, 118–119
  and bully pulpit use of his office, 110
  conference in Milwaukee, attending, 112
  election of, 63
  as executive, 109–110
  general information on, 152, 154
  Henry George, influence of, 172n13
  idea of success one of moving in the right direction, 144–145
  Job Harriman, endorsement of, 111
  job of mayor, attitude toward, 110
  as minister, 33, 152
  as party-builder, 111
  and party nomination for mayor of Berkeley, 14
  predictions of success in office of, 91
  Progressives, ties to, 38–39
  reelection refusal, 81, 109–110
  and resignation demands from the party, 97
  statement after election, 87
  war issue, broke with party over, 183n65
Wilson, Woodrow, 68, 69, 71
Wintersgill, E. E., Socialist mayor, Gulfport, Florida
  election of, 65
  general information on, 155
  growth, views on, 120
Wisconsin Social Democratic Party, 25
Wobblies, 17, 131
woman suffrage, 51, 110
Wood, John T., Socialist mayor, Coeur d'Alene City, Idaho
  election of, 61, 112
  conference in Milwaukee, attending, 112
  general information on, 61, 155
  and local Socialist party, 96–97
  on municipality going into the saloon business, 137
  perception of, 79
worker support, 147
working class, 13, 21, 31, 35, 38, 40, 44–46, 47, 48, 52, 64, 77, 95, 99 107, 119–120, 121, 127–128, 140–141, 142, 143, 145, 146, 147
Wycoff, Newton, Socialist mayor, Martins Ferry, Ohio
  election of, 61–62, 66, 67, 81
  electric rates for local companies, 134
  financial problems, dealing with, 119
  general information on, 61–62, 160
  hopes for his administration, 92
  law and order expectations, 123

yard stick regulation, 49
Young People's Socialist League, 103
Yuma, Arizona, 45

www.ingramcontent.com/pod-product-compliance
Lightning Source LLC
Chambersburg PA
CBHW030647230426
43665CB00011B/989